THE EMPIRE OF THE TEXT

THE EMPIRE OF THE TEXT

Writing and Authority in Early Imperial China

Christopher Leigh Connery

ROWMAN & LITTLEFIELD PUBLISHERS, INC.
Lanham • Boulder • New York • Oxford

ROWMAN & LITTLEFIELD PUBLISHERS, INC.

Published in the United States of America
by Rowman & Littlefield Publishers, Inc.
4720 Boston Way, Lanham, Maryland 20706

12 Hid's Copse Road
Cumnor Hill, Oxford OX2 9JJ, England

British Library Cataloging in Publication Information Available

Library of Congress Cataloging-in-Publication Data

Connery, Christopher Leigh.
　　The empire of the text : writing and authority in early imperial
China / Christopher Leigh Connery.
　　　　p.　cm.
　　Includes bibliographical references and index.
　　ISBN 0-8476-8738-4 (alk. paper). — ISBN 0-8476-8739-2 (pbk. :
alk. paper)
　　　　1. Chinese literature—History and criticism—theory, etc.
2. Literature and society—China.　3. Intertextuality.　I. Title.
PL2262.C75　1998
895.1′09—dc21　　　　　　　　　　　　　　　　98-22604
　　　　　　　　　　　　　　　　　　　　　　　　　　CIP

Printed in the United States of America

♾ ™ The paper used in this publication meets the minimum requirements of
American National Standard for Information Sciences—Permanence of Paper for
Printed Library Materials, ANSI Z39.48–1984.

Contents

Abbreviations

Full citations appear in the bibliography.

CHC   Michael Loewe and Denis Twitchett, eds. *The Cambridge History of China*. Vol. 1, *The Ch'in and Han Empires 221 B.C.–A.D. 220*.

DHHY   Xu Tianlin (12th century), comp. *Donghan huiyao* (Essential Eastern Han Miscellany). Shanghai: Shanghai guji chubonshe, 1978 rpt.

HS   Ban Gu (39 C.E.–92 C.E.). *Han shu* (History of the Former Han Dynasty).

HHS   Fan Ye (398–445). *Hou Han shu* (History of the Latter Han dynasty). Beijing: Zhonghua shuju, 1963 rpt.

QHW   Yan Kejun (1762–1843), comp. *Quan Shang gu Sandai Qin Han San guo Liu chao wen*. (Complete Writings of prehistory, the Three Dynasties, Qin, Han, Three Kingdoms, and the Six Dynasties). QHW is used for the Former Han, QHHW is used for the Latter Han, and QSGW is used for the Three Kingdoms.

SGZ   Chen Shou (233–297). *San guo zhi*. (Record of the Three Kingdoms). Beijing: Zhonghua shuju, 1959 rpt.

WXDL   Liu Xie (c. 465–c. 520). *Wenxin diaolong* (The Literary Mind and the Carving of Dragons). Annot. Fan Wenlan, *Wenxin diaolong zhu*. Beijing: Renmin wenxue chubanshe, 1978 rpt.

YFSJ   Guo Maoqian (12th century), comp. *Yuefu shi ji* (Collected yuefu poems).

Preface

This book is intended primarily as an interpretive and theoretical work, and it deviates, therefore, from common sinological practice. Sinological convention holds that the scholar should provide, in footnotes or in the text, complete bibliographic and philological detail on the history of an important text or phenomenon each time it is mentioned. There are several assumptions behind this practice. One of them is communitarian and laudatory: Since scholarship is cumulative, the efforts of generations of scholars will exhaust the evidence on a particular topic or set of topics, and the fullest possible understanding will thereby be reached. I have benefited from this scholarship, and I am glad that it continues to be practiced. This book, however, is not one of those works, but is conceived as an analytical experiment, and the scholarly apparatus that supports that particular kind of cumulative, communitarian project will not be found in it. The introduction describes my analytical position at greater length. I think that there is room in early Chinese studies for a wide variety of work, and I hope that this book's benefit to students and scholars will be in its analytical terms, in its juxtaposition of materials, in the kinds of questions it asks, and in the conceptual framework it provides. I hope that my approach will allow certain assumptions to be questioned and certain hitherto unexplored questions to be asked and investigated. Most translations, from all languages, are my own unless specified. I have not done this because I feel that mine are superior to previous translations but for stylistic consistency or emphasis.

Acknowledgments

There are many scholars, readers, and collaborators whose thanks I have expressed privately, and I underscore my gratitude here. I would like to single out a few for special mention. Professor Kao Yu-kung, my first teacher of Chinese literature, conveyed the intellectual excitement that theoretical engagement with texts in Literary Sinitic could produce. Professor Ferenc Tőkei, Hungarian sinologist and student of Lukács, showed me in his writing, and in generous conversation in Budapest, the continuing vitality of Marxist analysis of early imperial China. John X. Keenan, whose insights into linguistics and textual practice have shaped this work in many ways, read and commented on it at every stage of its conception and writing. Sharon Kinoshita gave careful readings and made suggestions on drafts of several parts of the book; her perspective as a French medievalist taught me much about strategies for historicizing engagement with textual work. John Christopher Hamm was an effective, judicious, and dependable research assistant during an early stage of the project. Keith McMahon served as an attentive and encouraging reader at several important stages of the writing. Arif Dirlik gave an early version a helpful and critical reading, and encouraged me to publish with Rowman and Littlefield, and I am grateful to him on all counts. Rowman and Littlefield's editors and production staff have been patient, supportive, thorough, and timely. Mary Scott gave the text several close interrogations and edits; her comments and suggestions were thorough, insightful, and inspiring. Research for this book was supported by grants from the American Council of Learned Societies–Chiang Ching-kuo Foundation, the University of California Academic Senate Research grants, and the University of California Santa Cruz Junior Faculty Fellowships.

The writing of this book was of particular importance to four people— Maurice Connery and Mary Frances Haifleigh Connery, my parents; Mary Scott, my wife; and Sandy Connery, my son. This book is dedicated to them.

Names and Chronology

Note: Names that appear in italics are mentioned prominently in the text.

B.C.E.

17th–11th centuries	Shang dynasty.
1025–771	(Western) Zhou Dynasty.
722–453	Spring and Autumn period (Eastern Zhou). Many of the classic *Confucian* texts were claimed to be composed or compiled in this period.
453–221	Warring States period. Legalist texts, Mozi, Zhuangzi, *Mencius*.
221–206	Qin dynasty. Unification; burning of the books; banning of private teaching; writing reform.
202 B.C.E.–9 C.E.	Former Han dynasty (also known as Western Han).
141–87	Reign of *Emperor Wu*.
124	Classical canon established.
c. 145–c. 86.	Life of *Sima Qian*, principal author of the *Shi ji* (*Records of the Grand Historian*).
6 B.C.E.	Death of bibliographer/compiler *Liu Xiang*.

C.E.

9–23	Wang Mang interregnum (Xin dynasty).
23	Death of bibliographer/compiler *Liu Xin*.
25–220	Latter Han dynasty (also known as Eastern Han).
79	White Tiger Hall Discussions (on the classics).
92	Death of *Ban Gu*, principal author/compiler of the *Han shu*, which includes the *Yiwen zhi* bibliography.

100	*Xu Shen* presents his dictionary, the *Shuo wen jie zi.*
146–168	Emperor Huan.
168–189	Emperor Ling.
169–184	Affair of the Proscribed Factions.
175	Stone Classics engraved under supervision of *Cai Yong.*
184	Yellow Turban Revolt.
189–190	Open warfare between eunuchs, shi factions, and various armies. Dong Zhuo destroys the capital.
196–220	Jian'an era. *Cao Cao* in control. Hostile regional powers in southwest (Liu Biao) and southeast (Sun Quan) for part of this period. *Cao Zhi, Cao Pi,* and the *Seven Masters of the Jian'an* era are acclaimed literary figures.
200	Death of teacher and classicist *Zheng Xuan.*
220	Han dynasty ends. Cao Cao's son *Cao Pi* becomes first emperor of *Wei* dynasty. Beginning of Period of Division.
220–581	Period of Division (Northern and Southern Dynasties; Six [southern] dynasties: Wu, Jin, Song, Qi, Liang, Chen).
581–618	Sui dynasty.
618–917	Tang dynasty.
960–1127	Northern Song and Liao dynasties.
1127–1279	Southern Song and Jin dynasties.
1271–1368	Yuan (Mongol) dynasty.
1368–1644	Ming dynasty.
1644–1911	Qing (Manchu) dynasty.
1911–1949	Republican period.
1919 ff	May Fourth era (*Lu Xun*).
1949–	People's Republic of China.

Introduction

In recent years, U.S. scholarship in the area of Classical Chinese literature and culture has seen a new emphasis in studies of textual practice, including commentary, anthologizing, book production, writing groups (Pauline Yu 1987 and 1990, Saussy 1993, Henderson 1991, Cherniack 1994), topics less frequently addressed during the earlier heyday of individual author study, genre survey, and scholarly translation. This is due to the theoretical milieu in which we all work, but it is also a sign of the new intellectual possibilities that have arisen since the end of the Cold War. The figuration of China's imperial past has been negotiated and renegotiated throughout the twentieth century according to the political and ideological needs of the moment in China, Japan, Taiwan, and the West. As a consequence, the literary and textual medium through which the empire was lived and by which it operated has been subject to greater or lesser degrees of scrutiny. During the May Fourth period in China, significant intellectual energy was devoted to issues of media and language; most reformist intellectuals regarded Literary Sinitic[1] (*wenyanwen*) as a medium whose institutionalization was part of an ideological apparatus that demanded and created a certain kind of imperial political subject. It was this subject, as well as the system, that was foremost on the reformist agenda. The modern Chinese intellectual, the new kind of subject that was emerging around the turn of the twentieth century, became a coherent social formation in significant part through oppositional *linguistic* politics, i.e., use and advocacy of writing in a vernacular. Chiang Kai-shek's New Life Movement in 1934 included in its project a "return" to Literary Sinitic. Although this counterreform was taken seriously by reformers, rapid changes in media and intellectual social life had made this effort more symbolic than practical. If advocates of writing in non-Hanographic script (Latin letters, phonetic symbols, etc.) or in regional vernaculars (rather than the national vernacular) had triumphed, Literary Sinitic would not have been displaced to the extent that it was. Before long, it became a "dead" language. Although it lived on in corners of the bureaucracy and belles lettres, it has since become, like all dead languages,

1

the domain of scholars and specialists. After writing in Literary Sinitic ceased to be an immediate object of polemic, as it had been in the writings of Lu Xun and his provernacular and pro-Latinization allies, discussion of the political and ideological character of the imperial writing medium naturally waned. With the decoupling of the imperial past from its work in the Literary Sinitic medium, the Chinese imperial past, as with all new nations' creations of their histories, was itself later able to be figuralized, textualized, and suffused with ideological functionalism in the various narratives of nationalism and modernization.

The figuration of China's imperial past had a global dimension as well. The dawn of the Cold War and the concomitant global rise of the U.S. national security state brought a redefinition of the world in cultural-essentialist terms. This of course raised the political stakes in the popular and scholarly representation of China's imperial past. In the Cold War dispensation, civilization, and by extension modernization itself depended on the capacity for rationality, abstraction, and other markers of Western high textual culture. Thinkers in U.S. higher education influenced the coalescence of a particular Cold War consensus, one whose hypostasized ideal figure was the transcendent liberal intellectual, the man (gender-specified) of great influence who, formed and shaped through "conversation" with his counterparts over the long course of post-Homeric history, would be the guarantor of conscience alongside technological and administrative modernization. These thinkers included prewar advocates of the "Great Books," the "Great Ideas," or the "Great Conversation"—Mark Van Doren, Mortimer Adler, John Erskine, Maynard Hutchins, Jacques Barzun, and others concentrated mainly at Columbia or the University of Chicago—and Karl Jaspers, who in 1949 popularized the idea of "axial age civilizations"(Jaspers 1953). Although these thinkers were true to their Hegelian origins in locating the telos of history in the West, the global reach of Cold War U.S. liberalism—and its program of ideological and economic hegemony without the formal trappings of empire—required a strengthened and literalized universalism that admitted other axialities, variations in the modernizing trajectories. The birth of the People's Republic of China, Cold War enemy and, not coincidentally, repudiator of China's own "axial age" origins, had a great effect on the scholarship of China's imperial period. In the United States, scholars of imperial China found themselves occupied not only with the philological work that guild sinology had done for generations but also in teaching to wider audiences in the newly established "Great Civilizations" programs and core curricula that were springing up all over the country in the immediate postwar years. The faith in civilizational essence that gave rise to the Great Civilizations courses, coupled with the immense Cold War expansion of area studies programs, resulted in a huge growth in the number of U.S. scholars who worked on the East Asian imperial period. These scholars, for the most part, carried on the guild tradition of sinology, and their scholarly work, though unprecedented in quantity, was little read beyond the guild's confines. Still, the Cold War rhetoric of heroic, defensive custodianship of tradition, implicit in most studies of imperial China in Taiwan and in the United States, had shaped sinology's intellectual project in profound ways. China's great tradition was foundationalized: The greatness of its content was self-evident. And as one would expect with all such foundationalisms, the material and ideological character of the tradition's means of transmission received relatively little attention, until recently.

The end of the Cold War has had, not surprisingly, a substantial effect on studies of premodern China in the United States. Judging from course enrollments, faculty hiring, and publication patterns, there are indications as of 1998 that the Cold-War era hegemony of premodern studies in departments of Chinese (or East Asian) literature, language, and cultures[2] has given way to a modernist or postmodernist ascendancy. Within the Cold War ideology of custodianship, those who conserved the imperial past were implicitly combating the communist present. Now that the Cold War has ended, perhaps there is no need for figurations of the imperial era to have any content outside the arena of specialized study. China's earlier "greatness" can now be deployed solely in fleeting tropes of monumentality or in generalizations like "Confucianism," and left at that. The world is now supposedly on the verge of an "Asian century," when China will be a world power, great again.

Tropes of "rebirth" are always strongest when the prior occurrence is itself dehistoricized and rendered into some set of general or essential qualities. The West was also written as a rebirth, a Renaissance that only recently has begun to be understood as a rewriting, with all its attendant exclusions and omissions.[3] In "the West," Rome could decay and then be reborn as the West; individual nations or "cultures" could "rise again." But like the West itself, which has always known and defined itself through its others (among which "China" has been prominent), the history of rebirth has also required a supporting cast of others. For most of the history of the West's othering, with the exception of the Maoist interlude, when China was part of the United States' Cold War big other that served the ideological needs of the national security state, the singular feature of the other that was "China" was its zombielike status of being neither alive nor dead. Neither within history in the Hegelian, telic sense, nor wholly out of it, China was, like an antiquarian volume, the antiquity that persisted.[4] When European and U.S. imperialism in China was at its height, China was figured as a weak, diseased land. But its diseases were those of old age visited on a lifespan without phase or content: China had

had a wrong history, a history without temporality. Western history's othering needed an other history, and that other history was, as Said has reminded us, the unchanging, self-identical Orient. In the other history, history as rebirth does not find its mirror opposite in the realm of the dead, but in the zombie realm of the undead, the living dead. The great portions of Hegel's *Lectures on the Philosophy of World History* spent on the non-West were not devoted to "dead" civilizations like Babylon or Assyria but to undead China.[5]

The difference between the other history that is Babylon and the other history that is China is the difference between the ruin and the book. It is certainly the pronounced character of China's textuality that has kept it circulating in the world of representation and makes for its particular role as undead civilization. A ruin speaks a concrete nonpresence in a way that a text never can, and textual saturation is central to China's particular other history. The popular image of imperial China foregrounds this: "The oldest continuous writing tradition in the world" is the stock phrase deployed in so many articulations of the imperial sublime. I propose in this book that one way to write of China's history without writing within the ideological legacy of the other history is through a direct confrontation with textuality itself. The critique of Eurocentric knowledge formation that became prominent with Edward Said's publication of *Orientalism* has since gained force in postcolonial studies, cultural studies, and Marxist scholarship throughout the world. This body of work reinforces our conviction that foundations are never innocent and that the very categories and media through which knowledge is constructed reflect some kind of prior settlement. The function of the settlement changes in its historical moment: Even over the course of the twentieth century, foundational categories like "Confucianism," "intellectuals," or "aesthetics" have served a wide variety of positions. Subjecting textuality itself to question should allow some reflection on the ideologically determined foundationalisms that arise when the texts—with their immanent authority— are considered transparent records of the social real.

"Han bureaucracy, as I have reconstructed it from the sources, existed." This, the penultimate sentence of Hans Bielenstein's authoritative *The Bureaucracy of Han Times*, speaks perhaps to the anxiety of the early Chinese institutional historian. Given China's location as central undead civilization, could the Han bureaucracy itself have been confined to "the sources" rather than to "China"? Sinology has the virtue of being a field of study defined simultaneously by methodology—a philological approach to texts written in Literary Sinitic—and by object of study—imperial China. The boundaries between object and medium are often indistinct. A strong impression received by any student of imperial China is that of a will toward textual totalization, the grand system of the *Book of*

Changes, or in the text-conjured phantasms of the bureaucracy in heaven (Levi 1989; Kalinowski 1982: 187–92), or in the wholly administered world of the *Rites of Zhou (Zhou li)*. The *Rites of Zhou* delineates a textual empire par excellence: a ritualized, oversaturated bureaucracy of pure structure that is stripped of traces of temporality or narratability, rendering it not an organ of rulership or decision making but something like a dance in tune with the equally textualizable working of the cosmos. Every scholar of early imperial China must grapple with the systematicity of the empire's textuality; for nowhere in the premodern world, perhaps, do the textual sources appear to have a greater capacity to exceed their referent. Before the critique of orientalism injected a degree of self-consciousness into broad cross-cultural comparisons, it was common to ask questions about the lack of existence of a Chinese Homer or a Chinese Bible. But compared with Homer-centered paideia or biblical exegeses, the world of the Han and pre-Han Chinese texts appears far broader in its referential scope. Although "the sources" might not be complete in many of the ways that the modern scholar would like them to be, the primary sources, in their totality, certainly produce the effect of completeness.

A fundamental assumption of this book is that the Han is the era of consolidation. There is nothing controversial in this; most sinologists would agree. A story I will not tell in this book, but a story that could indeed be told, is that any history of systemic consolidation—Han China, imperial Rome, the British Empire, late twentieth-century capitalism, for example—is also a story of that consolidation's failure and incompleteness: No system ever wholly totalizes itself. But it is in the nature of a system to represent itself as a totality. My argument, then, is that this represented consolidation was deep and widespread, and it occurred on a number of fronts. First, I hold that Literary Sinitic itself is a Han creation. This judgment could be supported not only in the work of Victor Mair (cited earlier) but in much recent work on the history of Chinese script. William Boltz compares the normative script in Xu Shen's (fl. 100–121) dictionary, the *Shuo wen jie zi* (referered to hereafter as the *Shuo wen*) with variant versions in early Han or pre-Han archaeological finds and concludes that the Chinese script as we now know it became fixed during the course of the Han dynasty. Boltz convincingly advances the hypothesis that the Han normativization checked an incipient tendency toward desemanticization in writing, which could have led to a syllabary or even an alphabet (Boltz 1994: 129–77). In a formation that I find convincing and useful, Boltz suggests that Xu Shen's dictionary was prescriptive rather than descriptive. The Han also saw the consolidation of the referential capacity of texts: Earlier "classical" texts became, with their Han commentaries, foundational texts that could explain the workings of the cosmos and the human world. This scope was also the aim of early Former Han compendia such as the *Luxuriant Dew of the Spring and Autumn Annals*, Yang Xiong's rewriting of the *Yi jing*—the *Taixuan jing*, and in the first large-scale historiographical works of Sima Qian and Ban Gu. It is equally evident in the bibliographic work of Liu Xiang and Liu Xin at the end of the Former Han, when, I argue, the classical canon as we know it today took definitive shape. Xu Shen's dictionary follows Emperor Wu's reign by about two hundred years, and the bibliographic work of the Liu family by about one hundred years. Following Xu Shen, the consolidation process continues apace. The late Han appearance of encyclopedic compendia like the *Fengsu tongyi* (*Comprehensive Discussion of Customs*) and the *Dian lun* (*Authoritative Discourses,* now in fragments), continuing the scope of inquiry that was established with works like the *Luxuriant Dew of the Spring and Autumn Annals*, are further indications of the coterminous character of political and textual empire. Surviving evidence suggests that the totalizing scope of textual possibility—the capacity of a textual scene to figure and represent the sociohistorical-cosmological whole—had become naturalized by the Han's end. Not only did the Han witness the production of works like the above but bibliographic and anthological practice also accelerated in scope toward the latter part of the dynasty. Still, in spite of a wealth of sources, the contemporary scholar of the Han has nothing approaching the physical immediacy delivered by the epigraphic and manuscript record available to the scholar of the classical and medieval period in Europe and the Mediterranean region. New philological studies in Western medieval and Renaissance texts are drawing important conclusions from the materiality of the texts—their layout, format, orthography, errors, stains, overwrites—that are not possible with the Han materials. With few exceptions, "the sources" are always already recombined, annotated, canonized, worked on, anthologized: Those sources now available to the modern scholar's hand were not physically extant objects until many hundreds of years after their composition. The sources the sinologists use have, with few exceptions, no auratic value; nothing adheres to their individuatable instantiation. They remain vehicles of transmission, media for a message whose content is the power and range of the medium itself.

The assiduity of modern sinology's self-insertion into the mediatorial tradition of textual transmission and annotation can lend an almost ritualistic character to its own scholarly production, one that might naturally admit the occasional anxiety over the "it existed." My sources for this book are the same textual sources available to all scholars of the early imperial period, with some reference to recent archaeological finds. My experiment—and naming it an experiment is one way in which my work differs from the sinological tradition of transmission and annotation—is to treat the sources and their contents not simply as transparent or semi-transparent records of the social existant but also as constitutive elements in the consolidation of an early imperial textual regime. My hypothesis is that textual authority existed, with a logic and ordering principles not wholly commensurate with political authority. Official texts certainly served certain political ends, but my hypothesis is that textual production must also be read as autonomous—as serving to constitute and strengthen its own authority. I am not referring here to the idea, popular now in studies of late Han literati in particular, of an independent intelligentsia with interests distinct from imperial authority, who use texts to express the interests of their social formation. That would assume the model of texts as communicative media, a model I wish to contest. To contest the communicative function of media has consequences in the discipline. Much of the sinological work of translation and annotation implies a postponement of other sorts of analysis. In literary scholarship, the scholar's explicit or implicit position is often that of "establishing the foundations"—dates, authorship, textual variants, biographical and historical background—with the assumption that theorization can occur only after a literary text's circumstances of composition have become transparent. The impulse to rely on these foundations is itself symptomatic of an undertheorization. To see a text simply as, for example, a product of "a scholar's frustration" is to make a host of assumptions about mentalities, ideologies, and the relation between text and psyche that are at bottom unprovable, all the while adhering to a basic structure of empirically minded common sense. My experiment is to treat the social construction of the textual in a provisional way: not to deny it but not to assume too much. The political empire expresses and records itself through texts, of course, but the workings of the textual empire exceed the requirements of the social and the political. A straightforward index of textual excess is that the texts survive, whereas the empire of which they were a part is no more. Another way of writing this book would be to figure the political and the textual in contestation, to view Han textual politics as an attempt at control that never wholly succeeded. Proof could be found in the numerous slander laws, the political consequences for intemperate writing, and the heterodox character of writings, not all of which fit into a programmatic straitjacket. Yet such a perspective would require numerous suppositions of intentionalities, mental states, and individual dispositions. My experiment here is, first, to view textual production not as expressive of mentalities, but as constitutive of an explicitly textual logic and, second, to find a space for inquiry between the Han bureaucracy's "existence" and the description of it in "the sources."

Even on the level of administrative content and function, the textual character of Han government was pronounced; memorials, interpretation of portents, orders, diplomacy, record keeping, and other textual productions constituted much of what government and its officials did. Administrative conduct, ritual, and other activities were recorded in the texts as having been performed according to prescriptions detailed in texts. The content of knowledge was also textually based, in contrast, for example, to Athens in Plato's period and earlier. In Han China, knowledge and the transmission of knowledge derived authority from reference to a set of officially designated "classical" texts through clearly delineated lines of commentary. There was a fundamental presumption of textual competence among national elites, officeholders, and local elites; this meant familiarity with the classical canon and its official commentary, as well as other texts, and compositional facility in a variety of genres and forms. When I claim that textual authority existed, I mean to denaturalize it, to underscore the fact that its formation is historicizable and particular. Societies of great social and administrative complexity have existed without relying on texts to a degree even approaching the textual saturation of the imperial Chinese bureaucracy, a bureaucracy that is knowable in some detail thanks to the assiduity of the textual record itself. How did textual authority operate? How did it order and maintain itself? What kinds of subjects and subjectivities did it create? These are some of the questions that this book seeks to answer.

The medium of Han textual authority was a highly codified system of signification, and the consolidation of the medium itself was a Han achievement. Texts were composed in a purely written language that did not base its communicative authority on its capacity to represent or reproduce a prior orality. I refer to this language, following Victor Mair, as Literary Sinitic.[6] Use of Literary Sinitic in the Han was dependent on lexical, syntactic, generic, and subgeneric conventions. These conventions included, for certain textual practices, an intertextual deployment of elements from a body of source texts that became progressively more codified over the course of the Han. Intertextuality—the linkage of texts, contemporaneous or not, through direct and indirect quotation, allusion, and other markings—is better understood as a defining feature of Literary Sinitic than as a literary technique or a stylistic device to be applied according to an author's skill or whim. "Empire" is also a significant qualifier of the scope of this study. The Qin and Han dynasties administered a huge land area containing a diversity of local traditions, spoken languages, and dialects. There is no evidence, though, that any written language other than Literary Sinitic was used, officially or semiofficially, within the boundaries of this empire. In the Roman republican and imperial periods, by contrast, not only was Latin-Greek bilingual literacy widespread among the literate minority, but other written languages were in official use as well.[7] Even the Christian God—as evidenced by the Hebrew, Greek, and Latin inscriptions nailed to Christ's cross—gave a foundational validation to multilingualism. The codification and hegemonic use of Literary Sinitic were coterminous with the political administration of imperial China; the two projects are inseparable. We could add, to Hans Bielenstein's remarks quoted above, that the Han bureaucracy existed *because* the sources existed; its existence and the sources' existence were mutually dependent.

To read, to write, to recite: The verbs we choose in describing the human scene of textuality reveal much of our scholarship's conceptual framework. Reading, writing, and recitation are actions that subjects perform on texts. Although Literary Sinitic has many equivalents to these words, they are unsatisfactory determinators for this experiment, which aims to consider the textual scene and the social scene together, without subjectivity being considered the anterior condition for expressive textual production. A history of *writing* in Literary Sinitic, for example, in contrast to a history of textual authority, would be predicated on successive generations of authors who use the medium for expression. Familiar teleologies follow: In a history of belletristic literature, for example, one would expect the birth, maturation, and decline of a genre, or lines of influence between one author and another. There is of course nothing wrong with such an approach, since its foundational assumptions, whether articulated or not, are quite clear. A history of *reading* would be more difficult to reconstruct for the Han dynasty: The sources and material evidence are too limited for the kind of history of reading that is possible in periods with more complete data on production, circulation, use, and distribution of written materials, and on the physical and material properties of the material to be read.[8] There is one word, though, that expresses the interrelationship of text and subjectivity in a way more illustrative of the terms of this experiment. Since Confucius's time at least, a common expression for working with texts is found in the graph *xue*, commonly translated as "to study." In the *Analects* Confucius is quoted as saying to his son, "*bu xue shi, wu yi yan*" ("If you have not studied the *Poetry Classic*, then you will have nothing to say").[9] "Study" of the master texts is here figured as ontologically prior to communication. A commonsense translation of this passage would be along the lines of "without a classical education you will have nothing worthwhile to say." A literal interpretation might suggest that since there is evidence that lines from the *Poetry Classic* found heterogeneous use as coded units of communication in diplomacy and other formal situations, "without learning the lines of the *Poetry Classic* you will not be able to speak in those situations where speech consists of quotations from the *Classic*." By the time of the composition of the *Analects*, a preimperial version of textual authority and text-centered education had likely become normativized in certain sectors of the literate elite. Indeed, this must have been a precondi-

tion for the reception and transmission of a body of written political philosophy like that attributed to Confucius. It is possible that texts were
not always the primary content of education. Ritual, whether considered
as action in accord with the state-sanctioned version of the sacred or simply as repetition, is the originary content of study. *Xue* can also mean
something like "to model after"; the acts of modeling and repetition show
the common character of study and ritual. Zheng Xuan's commentary to
the *Rites of Zhou* stresses the indivisibility of ritual and education in the
early Zhou kingdom: Ritual is the content of education. The Palace of the
Semicircular Moat (*bi yong*) was the scene of Zhou ritual instruction, the
only kind of "public" instruction then extant. The first university (*tai
xue*), which referred either to the same or an adjacent building, was for
educating young royalty not in textual learning, as the greatly expanded
Han dynasty institution of the same name would do, but in ritual archery
and other physical activities.[10] Leon Vandermeersch has suggested that
xue, the graph for "university" or "study," originally refers to an archery
hall.[11]

From bow and arrow to text is the foundational phase in the consolidation of textual authority, a process that once was called "civilization."
Bielenstein's anxiety, if that is what his language betrays, is the anxiety
of textual overconsolidation—another term for "civilization" perhaps—
illustrated in the *Rites of the Zhou* (itself probably a Han text, though
reputed to be much earlier), where nothing is *hors texte*, and where, as in
a Borgesian map, the ritualized representation of the functioning of the
state is coterminous with that functioning itself.

> *Ai gong wen zheng. Zi yue, wen wu zhi zheng bu zai fang ce.* Duke Ai asked
> of government. The master said, "The government of Kings Wen and Wu
> [of the Zhou] is laid out on the wood and bamboo tablets.[12]

The historicity of the move from bow and arrow to text, suggested in
Vandermeersch, is also a feature of Mark Edward Lewis's study, *Sanctioned Violence in Early China* (1990). Lewis characterizes the Warring
States transition (fifth century to 221 B.C.E.) as centering on new forms
and relationships of authority, especially as manifested in warfare and
other forms of sanctioned violence, and culminating in "a single cosmic-
ally potent ruler"(Lewis: 54), the precursor of the emperor. Although
Lewis does not specifically deploy the category of the textual, the textual-
izing process is an insistent feature of his book. His discussion of the
evolution from lineage-based blood covenant to bond (*yue*) to law (pp.
67ff) is an account first of the textualization of body ritual, leading to the
establishment of legal authority that lay in a definitive and invariant body
of texts. Warfare itself, the focal activity of the new central authority that

characterized the Warring States transition in Lewis's analysis, is given a distinctly textual context:

> One of the primary features of this new pattern of violence was the belief that warfare was an intellectual discipline based on textual mastery, so the sage-king who had created proper warfare was also the first recipient of a military treatise and hence the originator of warfare rooted in text-based skills. (Lewis: 99)

Such accounts of the Warring States transition are common in Lewis's book. He is able to form his analysis without the analytical category of textuality because he sees textuality, correctly, as a primary indicator of centralized authority; it is this change in the nature of authority that is the focus of his study. The increasingly centralized form of authority that emerged in the Warring States did not require this textual character, although that was in fact the form it took. Lewis's book provides evidence against the assumption that textual authority was somehow "natural." There is a possible temptation in Lewis's narrative that my experiment here seeks to resist. The move from blood covenant to law, from raw, primitive violence to ritualized warfare, from clan to state, fits too easily into the telic narrative of "progress" from brute physicality to abstraction, from the material to the mental, from coercion to ideology. Although the sources allow limited elaboration on this point, it is important to keep in mind that the operation of textual authority is itself also a material practice. Scholarship itself is a textual practice that reflects on its own material conditions of possibility only in violation of professional decorum or with the risk of monotonous solipsism that meta-meta-critique provides; but resistance to overhomologization with the object of study needs to be registered. Let me remind the reader that this experiment seeks to position textuality as one form of authority among many possible ones, and as a distinct set of practices.

Central political authority and textual authority gather momentum throughout the Warring States transition. The Qin-Han period (Qin 221–206 B.C.E.; Han 206 B.C.E.–221 C.E.) establishes imperial rule over much of what thereafter would be referred to as geographic "China" and consolidates textual authority as we know it from the sources. The imperial system exists and functions coterminously with the logic of textual authority. By the end of the Han, signs of textual saturation are everywhere: in administration, human relations, bureaucratic recruitment, and elite social life. The dynastic transition from Han to Wei in 221 C.E. was itself wholly a textual affair, carried out under the aegis of Cao Pi, the Wei dynasty "Textual" Emperor (Wei Wendi), and his allies.[13] A series of texts— portents and prognostications— were proclaimed and interpreted in such a way as to render the dynastic transition from Han to Wei a "natural" and logical thing. This particular dynastic transition was castigated throughout most of the historical record as one of the great sunderings in Chinese history and thus is an oblique sign of the far more important consolidation of textual authority. Although debate over legitimate and illegitimate succession (*zhengtong* vs. *batong*) would begin not long after the fall of the Wei dynasty and continue into this century, this should not obscure the fact that the legitimacy of dynastic succession itself had been established and that legitimacy was predicated on a textual logic.

Centering my analysis on textual authority produces a narrative that differs in certain ways from the standard version of early imperial and early medieval elite cultural history. The most common version has the period from the end of the Han through the Jin marked by the transition from public to "private," from imperial authority to lineage alliance, from an ethos of elite participation in government to eremetic withdrawal; and, in philosophy, from a public-spirited Confucianism[14] to a quietistic and initially extrastatist Taoism and Buddhism. This version also has the late second and third centuries witness a rise of a tradition of belletristic writing and criticism that signals, to most literary historians, the birth of lyricism, literary subjectivity, and self-consciousness—of independent "literature" itself.[15] The coincidence of "aesthetic" flourishing in a period of perceived political, social, and moral disintegration is viewed as either symptomatic (devotion to frivolous aesthetic pursuit is a sign of disregard of government duties) or melodramatic (tragic times stir the hearts of men in ways that produce profound reflections thereon). In an analysis centered on textual authority, the late second and third centuries can be seen as a period of expansion of the textual sphere.[16] Textualization becomes the medium for increasingly diverse aspects of social and nonofficial life, and one consequence of this is the rise of textual genres and subgenres creating what I would call the "subjectivity effect." My analysis diverges from standard literary history analyses in a clear-cut way. I see the subjectivity effect as conditioned by texts and the institutions that produced the texts. Other literary historians would see the "inward turn" psychohistorically: The scholar-official despairs of life at court and devotes himself to private pursuits. The Kyoto school of Japanese scholars (Tanigawa Michio being the representative figure) describes a new mentality, which in one formation is called *ningenshugi* (interpersonalism or humanism) (Utsunomiya 1954: 508–12). This humanism, they argue, is reflected in new directions in thought and writing that are produced when lateral and nonhierarchical ties displace official, hierarchical ties. Where the Kyoto scholars would see *ningenshugi* in an obverse relationship with the official sphere, I argue that we could also consider the new subjectivities presenced through the expanded textual sphere as coterminous with the more long-term consolidation of textual authority, which was in process before the period of the Han dynasty's decline, and was formed and shaped very much *within* the official sphere.

There are several reasons why my study of the rise of textual authority in the early imperial era centers on the late Han. The late Han is commonly figured as a period of "crisis" or "transformation," those temporalities beloved of modernist historiography. My shift of focus away from crisis and toward consolidation is an experiment in reading against the historiographical grain, an experiment that I think will shed some light on certain problems, among them the character of the Han scholar-official "class," its relation to the Wei-Jin-Southern dynasties lineage aristocracy, and the nature of its power, as well as the ideological character of interpersonal relations and their representation in the sources. Second, since the late Han and immediate post-Han period are responsible for what has been called a new autonomy for the category "literature," it seemed to me that the focus on textual authority as a whole might allow for a questioning of this autonomy and, indeed, of the category "literature" itself. Haun Saussy writes in the preface to *The Problem of a Chinese Aesthetic*:

> In Chapters Three and Four I push the idea of "construction" a little harder and find reasons for believing that the invention of China and the invention of Chinese poetic language are not only roughly contemporary but also related events. (Saussy 1993: 4)

With "the invention of Chinese poetic language," Saussy is referring to the authority accorded to the Mao "Old Text" commentary to the *Poetry Classic*, an authority that ebbed and flowed through the early Latter Han but was consolidated by the dynasty's end. The ascendancy of the Mao commentary was a sign of the expansion of the referential scope of the classics. In the Mao transmission the *Poetry Classic* embodied the principles of "princely transformation" itself; rulership was textualized. Saussy, in my view, emphasizes the "poetry" of the *Poetry Classic* to the detriment of its status as a "classic" in a manner that might be unwarranted for the Han. I would not grant the autonomy to "poetic language" that he does here, but I agree with him that "China" was invented in the texts as much as it was on the ramparts and the battlefields.

An experiment like this one entails certain risks. By calling it an experiment, I am attempting to ward off the claims for interpretive authority and conclusiveness that are central to the sinological genre. We scholars of the other—the temporal, spatial, or "ethnic" other—can no longer innocently ignore the question that Edward Said poses *Orientalism*: Is it possible to "divide human reality, as indeed human reality seems to be genuinely divided, into clearly different cultures, histories, traditions, societies, even races, and survive the consequences humanly" (Said 1978: 45)? As I suggested in the first part of this introduction, the figure of China as monolithic, continuous, and heavy with "tradition" is a primary means of China's particular othering in the West. Even scholars who profess love and reverence for their imperial Chinese object of study—such professions of affection are common in sinological refutations of Said's applicability to Chinese studies—contribute to orientalist discourse to the extent that they reinforce the project of a monolithic cultural essence. The basic thesis of this book—in Han China there was such a thing as textual authority and it structured representation in specific ways—is clearly not an attempt to counter the claims of cultural essence by championing the discrepant particular. For the particular too carries its ideological weight and is in fact the primary object of the guild version of sinology.

The title of this book, *The Empire of the Text*, deliberately risks association with Roland Barthes's *L'empire des signes*, which has been criticized along with those other totalizing abstractions of the non-West—Wittfogel and Kristeva come immediately to mind—who deploy Asia to serve and buttress a Western Big Idea, and thus recapitulate Western imperial expansion itself. My version of the textual empire might seem to have affinities with Barthes's *"système symbolique inouï,"* but my claim is ultimately closer to Bielenstein's *"it existed."* Clearly, some form of textual authority has existed everywhere that writing itself has existed. I claim no particularity for imperial China on that count; I do claim that the imperial political system created roles for textual authority that were to a great extent specific to that system in its various historical phases. I hope to avoid the functionalism of "textual culture served the interest of the elites" in my suggestion that the elites, as we know them today, are a *product* of textual culture, that in early imperial China, "elite" is a coherent concept only in sociotextual terms. Textuality, then, was not a means of representing the social. It is representational authority that was a primary content of elite political and social life. When I first began work on this topic, I conceived it as a more standard Marxist study of the ideological work performed through the textual production of the dominant culture, elite literati culture, the small "class" that served and was served by the regime. But I grew unsatisfied with the various ways of defining this category in social terms (about which more below), and so I began to think of the relationship between textuality and authority in the ways described here. There was of course an *hors texte*, which by its nature has had little means of entry into the historical record; the work that has been done on women's history, early Buddhist and Taoist communities, vernacular literature, and other "unofficial" spheres serves to remind us that the construction of hegemonic authority is always simultaneously a process of exclusion. In my focus on textual authority as a denaturalized and historicizable *process*, though, I hope to stress that this authority is not analyzable as simply an airy regime of pure representation but functioned socially, as hegemony has always functioned, with winners, losers, and consequences.

Chapter 1 introduces the concepts of textuality and textual authority in the context of Han China, with reference to textuality, literacy, reading, and writing as theorized and historicized in the classical Mediterranean, Europe, and the early postconquest Americas. Textual authority in the Han can be understood in several ways: The practice of empire was dependent on the circulation of texts, and authority itself was invested in a set of texts with established lines of transmission: the canonical classics, known in the West as the Confucian canon. My primary focus in this chapter is on the canonical classics in their written forms and the particular ideologies and practices of textuality behind the history of canonical formation and transmission from the Former to the Latter Han. My comparative discussion is indebted to a number of contemporary classicists and medievalists, including William Harris, Rosalind Thomas, Eric Havelock, Kevin Robb, Henri Martin, Roger Chartier, and Brian Stock, as well as to contemporary theorists of literacy, cultural authority, and textuality. A discussion of textuality's "others" shows significant differences between China, on the one hand, and the classical Mediterranean and Europe on the other. In both of these periods in the West, textuality and orality had a complex interrelationship, with the oral often being expressly figured as authoritatively anterior to the written. Until printing became widespread in the West, most writing was experienced as texts read aloud. It is striking to find so little evidence in China of orality being accorded the authority of the anterior, or of any kind of authority at all. While the historian can reconstruct through written texts evidence of an oral elite culture in the early Zhou period, as Mark Lewis did in the book discussed above, the sources do not acknowledge any system of oral authority "before the letter." In the sources, textual culture was always the only culture; writing and civilization were coterminous. If there is an "other" to textuality, it is the "human," or the "humane," which was the bulwark of the "genuine" against the possible formalism of the textual-institutional. In this chapter I also make comparisons between my notion of the empire of the text and two ideas from the West: the medieval textual community[17] and the "imagined community" of "print capitalism."[18] I argue that the Empire of the Text figured a textual totality that was far more comprehensive than the class or single-text based communities in the other cases, even though the ratio of extant texts to population was probably greater in both the late medieval West and the early modern period. The totality of the textual also provides a context for a discussion of the material dimension of textual culture: modes of circulation, writing materials, personal collections, and libraries. I also offer a theory of writing and reading in the Empire of the Text, again with reference to the West. Authorship and readership, as understood in the West, both implied particular kinds and stages of subjectivity (my references are to Barthes, Bourdieu, Foucault, and de Certeau, among others) that simply did not exist in Han China. A different relationship to texts and textuality, and to subjectivity, was figured among what have been variously called the scholar-officials, the *shi*, or the literati.

Chapter 2 centers on the analysis of this class, or social formation, or elite, the name of which, following several contemporary historians, I will hereafter leave untranslated. This group, along with the hereditary aristocracy that ruled China between the Han dynasty and the Song dynasty (221–960), has been a notoriously difficult group to categorize using the tools and terminology of contemporary social history. I hold that theirs is a statist identity that derives from the textual-bureaucratic regime, the ultimately determining structuration of elite identity that I characterize as follows: The late Han shi maintained, operated, and expanded the scope of textual authority, in which all other forms of authority— military, economic, legal—were implicated. I would add the important caveat that beginning in the late second century, imperial political authority and textual authority coincided to a lesser and lesser degree. I agree with the Kyoto school, whose arguments I engage critically, that the *shi* were a distinct social formation whose activities are not wholly reducible to the operation of the imperial bureaucracy. But I would add that they can also be viewed as *effects* of the textual regime. In my analysis I choose to deemphasize the ideological difference between the *shi* and the imperial court, a difference that has been exaggerated by twentieth-century social, literary, and art historians. I concentrate on the practices of identification, affiliation, and evaluation among the shi, practices that I argue are analyzable only given the external referent of the imperial court. These practices constitute the field of the "social" within a group whose primary role is the maintenance and practice of textual authority.

Chapter 3 examines *shi* discourse on "homosociality," a term borrowed from Eve Sedgwick. I use this term instead of the more common "friendship" in order to sidestep issues of affection while retaining the term's gendered and extrafamilial specificity. The previous chapter delineated the proliferation and importance of nonfamilial, nonofficial, and semiofficial social relations in the late Han. I argue that these relationships, which I subsume under the general category of homosociality, were central problematics of Han state ideology. Toward the end of the Han there was a proliferation of discourse on homosocial relations. On the one hand, there were manuals of character analysis and categorization, and a great increase in the quantity and public importance accorded to the homosocial-centered textual genres of epistles, epistolary verse, encomia, and eulogies. On the other hand there appeared many essays critical of extant forms of social, nonofficial intercourse. The message of these essays was that in the golden age, people devoted all of their time to their jobs (service) and had no leisure for social life or anything else, whereas in the decadent present, people neglect their official duties for "empty" social intercourse, much of which is conducted with the aim of securing personal enrichment. This discourse was critical of "factionalism," even in texts authored by shi who have been identified as important factional partisans. This chapter contains close analyses of a number of the antihomosocial texts—texts that have been largely unstudied to date—and argues that they represent the staging of official Confucianism's inadequate ability to theorize and prescribe the homosocial, and a coterminous extension and deepening of the scope of textual authority by rendering the homosocial a primary content of *shi* textual activity. Social relations are not purely "leisure" when they can be textualized.

Chapter 4 discusses the place of "literature" within the Empire of the Text. As an operating premise in this chapter, I take seriously the low esteem assigned to belletristic writing by its late Han practitioners, a judgment that has been disregarded in this century as typical literati self-effacement. By "belletristic" writing I refer primarily to *shi* poetry, *yuefu* poetry, and *fu* (translated, variously, as rhyme-prose or rhapsodies), though I emphasize that the generic division along lines of belletristic/nonbelletristic was a product of later critics and was not central to the Han. I treat the low esteem accorded to belletristic writing not within a discourse of critical judgment but within the context of an exploration of shi temporality. If the shi ideal life is a life of work, and if belletristic production is an activity of "leisure," what is the content of "leisure" and what does that say about the temporal representation of an individual life? This chapter, more than others, is an intervention into the consensus view of the birth of "lyric" writing. By specifying belletristic writing as a group compositional or intertextual practice within the temporal context of shi "leisure," I hope to provide an alternative to the claims for the birth of individualist literature in the late Latter Han.

Chapter 1 is divided fairly evenly between the Former and the Latter Han. Canon formation, the main subject of this chapter, occurred across the two halves of the dynasty. Chapters 2, 3, and 4, however, are largely concerned with the Latter Han. There are several reasons for this. The main subject of these chapters is the shi and their textual practices. The historical record is far more complete for the Latter Han, which makes my job easier and gives my conclusions a more solid base in the primary and secondary sources. This period, particularly the late Latter Han, is generally viewed as witnessing a rise in shi autonomy: an intellectual or literati class. The figuration of shi identity in this period has been a dominant concern in historiography for hundreds of years: in the work of Gu Yanwu and other participants in the "feudalism" debate from the Ming dynasty onward; in the historical scholarship of Lu Xun in the early part of this century; in the figuration of an Asiatic "community" in postwar anticommunist Japanese academic circles; in the work of diasporic Chinese intellectuals searching for a reconstruction of an antistatist transhistorical moral authority for an intellectual subclass; and in statistical and textual work of social historians in Japan, Taiwan, and the West. I do not claim that my focus on textuality and textual authority will solve these long-debated issues, but it is a discussion to which I feel my perspective makes a contribution.

I come to this work as a critic whose approaches to authority, politics, history, and literature have been shaped by Marxism. I believe, with Adorno, Marcuse, and Jameson, in the utopian character of the "aesthetic dimension" and in the idea that artistic expression is always already capitalist society's negation, whether intended as such or not. I also believe that this view of the "aesthetic," like "cultural capital" and other analyses of cultural production that are based in political economy, is not applicable to China before the Song dynasty, and perhaps not before the advent of capitalist social relations in China. My approach to early imperial Chinese textual culture is an experiment, one that I think uses the sources as honestly as other versions have used them. What I see is a system that does not simply foreclose the distance between the "social" and the "aesthetic," but a regime of textuality—the hyperaesthetic, some might say—within which the social itself was constituted. I am aware that my suggestion of this totalizing textual power risks association with orientalist figurations of Asian absolutism, and I have resisted suggestions to subtitle this book *The Asiatic Mode of Cultural Production*. Like Stefan Balazs, the midcentury Hungarian sinologist whose work remains enormously influential on all who work on the early imperial and early medieval period, I am conscious of and sympathetic with those whom the empire excluded even as I write of the Empire's power. I support and admire scholars who have done research on excluded and marginalized groups, but I feel that it is equally important to continue to analyze and theorize the structure and workings of hegemonic authority, which I have tried to do in this book.

Notes

1. I use this term, following Victor Mair (1994), instead of "Classical Chinese." Mair describes Literary Sinitic's relationship to the vernacular as analogous

to "the relationship between a code or a cipher and the natural language upon which it was based" (p. 708).

2. The best analysis of this situation is in the work of Rey Chow, in particular, "The Politics and Pedagogy of Asian Literatures in American Universities," in Rey Chow (1993), 120–43. Chow also makes the important and related point that the social science dominance of Area Studies programs also had a clear ideological character.

3. Edward Said, *Orientalism*, and Samir Amin, *Eurocentrism*, are two accounts, one more Foucaultian, one more Marxist, of this othering process.

4. For analyses of Hegel's and Hegelianism's China, see Saussy (1993), 151–88, and Hulin (1979).

5. Eduard Gans, quoted in Saussy (1993), 152.

6. I would like to emphasize that in my view the textual authority of Literary Sinitic derives in no way from its base in any spoken "real" language, but that its linguistic authority is constructed internally, by the interrelationships of its constituent elements. See the next chapter for more on this.

7. Many classicists have described this situation. For a useful summary see Harris (1989), especially chapter 7, 175–284.

8. For examples of this kind of work, see the special issue on the new philology in *Speculum: A Journal of Medieval Studies* 65, no. 1 (January 1990).

9. In one instance in the *Analects* where mastery of the *Poetry Classic* is insufficient (13.5), the verb is *song*, to recite or chant the text.

10. Levi (1990), 150–151, following Vandermeersch (1980), 389.

11. Vandermeersch (1980), 415, following Shirakawa Shizuka.

12. *Doctrine of the Mean*, chapt. 20. Sibu beiyao ed.

13. No intentionality is suggested in my use of the word "textual," which could be better translated as "civil." The events are recounted in SGZ (Wei), 62 ff. The textual character of this selection is apparent in Carl Leban (1978), 315–42.

14. In this book, I use the term "Confucianism" as a translation for *Rujia sixiang*, which some scholars translate "Ru-ism." I approve of the translation Ruism, but until it becomes common practice I will continue to use "Confucianism," the parameters of which are generally well understood.

15. A recent study of Han-Jin poetry according to these very principles is in Cai Zongqi (1996).

16. This is not necessarily the same as increased literacy. There is a well-known passage from the *Wei lue*, appended as a commentary to the biography of Wang Su in the SGZ (Wei) 13, 420–421, which suggests a great decline in textual competence by the mid-third century. I would suggest that the real import of the passage is that the capital was not at this time the epicenter of textual activity that it had earlier been. Textual activity was certainly altered by the destruction of the Imperial University, but I would argue that it was decentralized more than decimated.

17. See, for example, Brian Stock (1990).

18. The terms are of course from Benedict Anderson (1991). Anderson's idea of the imagined community has been applied to medieval China, incorrectly, in my view, in Charles Holcombe (1994).

1

Textual Authority and Textual Practice

In response to Duke Ai's question about government in the *Doctrine of the Mean*, Confucius begins by saying that "the government of Kings Wen and Wu [of the Zhou] is laid out on the wood and bamboo tablets."[1] A short homily follows on the need for the right kind of ruler to ensure a well-functioning government. The primary claim is the more important one for our purposes: The tablets are not simply "about" government in the referential sense; they are not vehicles for explanatory or instructional content.[2] Content is not the issue; entextualization, rather, is how government is done.

Texts, Textual Authority, Literacy, Ideology

The capacity of "government" to be present, "laid out" in the tablets, is at the heart of what I mean by "textual authority." A study of textual authority in early imperial China raises certain questions: How did it operate? What did it do? What was within its purview? Certain other questions cannot be answered. Since the early imperial textual regime did not posit its own outside, or defer in any overt way to nontextual modes of authority (oratory, spectacle, conversation, etc.), it is difficult to answer questions about earlier or concurrent modalities. Since commentary on and transmission of the regime's canonical texts was a primary activity among the *shi*,[3] as I discuss in greater detail in chapter 2, scholarship itself becomes implicated in the regime's operation. Even contemporary scholarship's particular relationship to the early imperial past, mediated as it is by the very textual authority that is concurrently our object of study, should complicate our ability to occupy a critical space over and "about" the texts. As Paul Ricoeur writes,

> The eclipse of the circumstantial world by the quasi-world of texts can be so complete that, in a civilisation of writing, the world itself is no longer what

can be shown in speaking but is reduced to a kind of 'aura' which written
works unfold. Thus we speak of the Greek world or the Byzantine world.
This world can be called 'imaginary', in the sense that it is represented by
writing in lieu of the world presented by speech, but this imaginary world is
itself a creation of literature. (Ricoeur 1981: 149)

It is useful to keep as our starting point the idea that early imperial China
is as imaginary as the "worlds" of the Greeks or the Byzantines, and that
the "quasi-world of texts" is in fact our object of study.

But I want to make a claim for particularity in the imaginary that is
"China," and its relation to the textual. The quotation above from the
Doctrine of the Mean suggests that the texts do not just constitute but
also *perform* textuality's authority. Just as every classical Chinese poem
can be read as a poem of praise to the emperor, so every text in early
Literary Sinitic works to bolster the authority of the textual regime. The
question for present-day scholars is: From what standpoint can an analysis of the workings of textual authority proceed? As the Ricoeur passage
suggests, hermeneutics claims for its object a wider field than that af-
forded by the "quasi-world" of the wholly textualized. In Ricoeur's
model, although the textual scene is differentiated phenomenologically
from the world of speech, there remains in his hermeneutics an anchor to
spoken language that is not present in what he calls, referring obliquely
to Derrida and his fellow-travelers, "the ideology of the absolute text"
(Ricoeur 1981: 148). Ricoeur's hermeneutic project cannot proceed with
the "absolute text" as object; it depends on a distancing from textuality
that precludes that very absoluteness. Although it shows awareness of the
very different metaphysics of text and of speech, his hermeneutic none-
theless demands a reader whose function is at minimum analogous to that
of the listener in a speech situation. And such is indeed the common strategy of most "interpretations" or "readings" of early imperial writing.

If we choose to take seriously the "quasi-world" of the textual imaginary, it would be reckless to conjure up the transhistorical phantasms
of subjectivity and intentionality that the communicative model would
produce. The antihermeneutics of Derrida's *Of Grammatology*, which
Fredric Jameson has called "the last text of Derrida in which the possibility for philosophy to produce new and Utopian concepts is raised" (Jameson 1995: 80) suggests a scene of writing disconnected from the a priori
nature of speech and the attendant metaphysics of presence. The priority
assigned to writing itself has made *Of Grammatology* important to all of
us who write on textuality and the writing scene. But its strategic location
within and against the tradition of the Enlightenment makes it other than
a "method" that could be "applied" to a radically different historical situation. If, as Alfred Sohn-Rethel has suggested, the particular form of ab-

straction in the Enlightenment West, with all of its metaphysical and sub-jective-idealist consequences, is impossible outside of the system of commodity exchange,[4] then carrying a post-Enlightenment antimeta-physics into an analysis of precommodity writing might result in decep-tive homologization of the pre- and the post-.

Derrida's critique of logocentrism made important if indirect contribu-tions to the analysis of premodern textualities by clarifying the stakes involved in positing binaries such as written/oral, writing/reading, or lit-erate/illiterate. The word "textual" in this book is one equivalent of the Chinese word *wen*. The most common binaries of which *wen* is one part—*wen/wu* (civil/military) and *wen/zhi* (adorned/unadorned)—refer not to an antonymic outside, but to a *degree* of refinement or "civiliza-tion." The positions "outside" textuality articulated in the words "oral" or "illiterate" are not significant binarizing categories within the regime of Literary Sinitic. In the following note on *wen* by F. W. Mote, the vary-ing senses of the word give a sense of the nature and scope of textuality:

> The word that Legge here translates as "regulations" is *wen*, the same word that throughout this chapter has been most frequently translated "refine-ment," as in the expression . . . "to esteem, or over-emphasize refinement." Both meanings are included, and are obviously related. "Refinement" is prior; "regulations" are an expression of Chou [Zhou dynasty] emphasis on refinement. "Literature" *wen* is an extension of "regulations," which were written, and which represented the increasingly important literary aspect of Chou "culture"—also *wen* (Hsiao 1979: 124).

Refined behavior—regulation—literature: Although I am aware of the pit-falls of reading too much into comparative lexical categories, Mote's ety-mology suggests both the diachronic process from body to textualization discussed in the introduction and the totalizing, absolute quality that characterized the textual regime synchronically.

Even after the textual scene becomes much more complex and far less monological than it was in the Han dynasty, the very totality of the early textual regime gives it, like the word *wen* itself, a seemingly unapproacha-ble authority. To write at all is to seem too close to textual authority's power, obeying its rules. There are a variety of strategies for coping with this situation. The most common solution, and one that is useful for many sorts of questions, is the empirical compromise: viewing the texts as semi-transparent records of the real world—records whose veracity or reliabil-ity it is up to the scholar to gauge. Philological sinology is primarily of this kind. In some recent scholarly work on writing in Literary Sinitic that has availed itself of various Western critical practices—which one could call both more international in scope and more literary in orientation—the sinological urge to face down the power of textuality by mastering one small instantiation is replaced by a desire to express more directly the special ontological status accorded to imperial textuality. In recent Western studies of poetic genres such as the Tang or pre-Tang *shi* poem, or the *ci* lyric of the Tang and Song, for example, one can sense a telic individuation of generic identity: A particular literary genre is alleged to reach, at a certain historical period or in the hands of a select group of masters, a stage of full development of its immanent potentiality; it will be capable of nearly infinite expressiveness. In work on Tang poetry especially—James J.Y. Liu, Francois Cheng, Yu-kung Kao, and Tsu-lin Mei are examples—the reader gets the sense that what the greatest Tang poetry has achieved is a distillation of the "world view" of Literary Sinitic itself. I will return at several points in this study to the question of the "Chinese world view" and the reasons for its recurrent invocation in so much of what is otherwise fairly empirically minded scholarly work. As I wrote in the previous chapter, the situation in scholarship is changing. Much of the new discussion of textual practice is centered on commentary, intertextuality, and anthology making—functions of the relationships of text to text. Still, even as scholarship begins to recognize that textual authority is constructed—a set of practices—it is difficult to denaturalize textuality's authority completely. This is understandable, for at its conceptual outer limit textual authority would be equivalent to Ideology in the Althusserian sense: the system of interpellation that is a productive precondition for subjectivity as such. Scholars such as Catherine Belsey, Terry Eagleton, and Slavoj Žižek have shown that the Althusserian category has great utility in the analysis of capitalist-era institutions of subject formation such as literature and education. In the precapitalist or noncapitalist world, though, when totality itself is not universalized, it is important to stress the specific locations of textual culture and its nonequivalence to society as a whole. Due to the nature of our sources, this is easier in some areas than it is with early imperial China.

In a recent study of ritual speech performance on the Indonesian island of Sumba, Joel Kuipers characterizes different genres of ritual speech along an axis of "entextualization," which he defines as

> a process in which a speech event (or series of speech events) is marked by increasing thoroughness of poetic and rhetorical patterning and growing levels of (apparent) detachment from the immediate pragmatic context . . . The end result is a relatively coherent text conceived "inter-textually" as an authoritative version of one that existed before, or elsewhere (Kuipers 1990: 4).

In a nonliterate society that is only marginally integrated into the capitalist world system, the ideological work by which a group's leaders exercise their authority is ritualized in oral performance but in a form that justifies the use of the term "entextualization." Like all careful anthropologists, Kuipers hastens to point out that "entextualization" does not have an inherent social character and that it could function differently in different societies. Still, the model from Weyewa society suggests that certain functions and modalities of authority are especially conducive to a "textual" form.

> The Weyewa entextualization process culminates in a narrative form known as the "path of the ancestors"—an authoritative style that exemplifies in a singular and consistent fashion the history of the "word" of a powerful forebear. (Kuipers 1990: 6)

The "authority" in Weyewa entextualization inheres in the performer's ability to create "the conviction that he is not speaking on his own, but on behalf of some distant person or spirit with a legitimate claim on the audience" (Kuipers 1990: 6). Here, in an orally determined scene of entextualization, we see in greater relief the capacities and possibilities of the wholly textualized scene. The entextualized oral performance must appear as a mediation of absent or abstract authority because of the potential interference of the physically present performer. A text holds presence and absence in tension, and it opens up the problematic of distanciation that hermeneutic activity requires.

The broader our sense of the text becomes, the more closely our notion of textuality approaches Ideology itself. I wish to maintain a distinction between textual authority and ideology for several reasons, not the least of which is that ideological analysis is more powerful and useful when confined to the capitalist era. For the contemporary period, the relation of ideology to textual authority has some similarities to the relationship between Althusser's Ideology and Ideological State Apparatuses (ISAs) (the army, the church, education, etc.), where the ISAs serve as the specific practice and concrete instances of operation of Ideology and where the specificity of the various ISAs implies the critical perspective from which noncontamination by Ideology can be maintained.[5] Althusser's dichotomy depends on there being multiple ISAs; otherwise the equivalence between ideology itself and a single ISA would disallow the dialectical effect. Our knowledge of early imperial China is structured differently. Since the consolidation of early imperial textual authority is the precondition for our knowledge of Han society, the very existence of any other ISAs in that period—military coercion or education, for example—is always already mediated through the primary structures of textual authority. In the case of early imperial China there is no remnant of non- or pretextualized ISAs. Nor does the kind of discursive continuum that

Kuipers describes exist: In the wholly textualized world of "the sources" there are no partial or pretextualities. It is very possible that early imperial textual authority was circumscribed to an extent greater than we can now know. But longevity inheres in the particular reproductive genius of the textual form. What might have once been a totalizing authority operative in particular situations has achieved absolute representational authority retroactively. And though it is useful and perhaps necessary for contemporary scholars to limn an "outside" to the early imperial textual regime, we must be aware of what presuppositions are involved in doing so. The greatest danger is to take as an outside of the textual a category—subjectivity, for example—that might just as easily be a pure product of the textual regime.

Textual authority's own historicity naturally determines its use in historical analysis. In a scene like the contemporary, where textual authority is circumscribed and coexists with various nontextual elements of authority (electronic media, police power, traffic regulations), it can appear as an object of contestation in a way that a totalized textual authority cannot. The term "textual authority," considered as an ideological practice if not an apparatus, occurs frequently in contemporary discussions of literacy and pedagogy; it was in the background of the canon debates that took place in U.S. universities in the late 1980s and early 1990s. The conservative position—that certain books or certain lessons contain truths whose transmission must be at the heart of education—is ideologically transparent to all but its defenders. The left or liberal position—that textual authority is socially and historically determined and needs to be apportioned by democratic means—is thus the denaturalizing strategy.

Common to both positions is the recognition of the stakes in mastery of what Pierre Bourdieu has called "symbolic capital,"[6] possession of which translates into real advantages in power, status, and income. The educational critic and theorist Henry Giroux has argued in a number of works that the goal of empowering students, a goal to which he believes all educators should aspire, is achievable by wresting control of the form and content of textual authority so that a wider variety of life experiences will be valued and new and varied masteries can be achieved (Giroux, 1988, 1990). Giroux's work comes out of an understanding of literacy most closely associated with historian and theorist of literacy Harvey Graff—the view that literacy is best understood not as an achieved capacity, like the ability to swim, but as an activity with a specific, politically and culturally determined object: Literacy is always literacy *of* something.[7] A discussion of literacy needs to take into account the specific texts which circulate within the bounds of what is called literacy; the nature of the authority that determines which texts those are and its goals in promoting those texts; and communities of readers, defined by their texts and their textual and extratextual activities. Graff's work shows us, for example, that contemporary Japan's official literacy rate, which approaches 100 percent, is a very different social phenomenon from the nearly universal literacy achieved in Sweden in the seventeenth century as a consequence of Lutheran Church–Swedish state joint enforcement of legally required literacy for all adults, with the stated goals of promoting "piety, civility, orderliness, and military preparedness" (Graff 1987: 9, 149–50). I avoid the category of literacy in this book in favor of "textuality." Brian Stock, one of the most important theorists of early textual culture in the medieval West, makes the important point that the position of textuality within medieval society following the great irruption of textual production was such that even the nonliterate were shaped by the interpellative character of textual culture. Literacy and the performance of textual authority must have coincided to a far greater extent in the early imperial Chinese case, since, unlike the medieval West, political authority was solely the province of the literate. But the evidence allows for few conclusions in this area.

Michel Foucault's work on productive power is behind Giroux's advocacy of power for the users of texts (students and readers), and it generally informs the more "liberatory," reader-oriented studies that seek to counter the hegemony of textual authority with a counterhegemony of the reader/user. In contrast to the *authority* of the textual regime, and the producers of texts, we find the *freedom* of the reader, which Michel de Certeau characterizes as follows:

> Far from being writers—founders of their own place, heirs of the peasants of earlier ages now working on the soil of language, diggers of wells and builders of houses—readers are travellers; they move across lands belonging to someone else, like nomads poaching their way across fields they did not write, despoiling the wealth of Egypt to enjoy it themselves. Writing accumulates, stocks up, resists time by the establishment of a place and multiplies its production through the expansionism of reproduction. Reading takes no measures against the erosion of time (one forgets oneself and also forgets), it does not keep what it acquires, or it does so poorly, and each of the places through which it passes is a repetition of the lost paradise. (de Certeau 1984: 174)

When I first read this passage, I wrote in my reading notes: "Han China = Writers // Nomadic Enemy (*xiongnu*) = Readers." This note led to some thoughts that I will develop later in this chapter, when I advance the proposition that in the early imperial Chinese textual regime there were no readers as such. As the de Certeau passage implies, an impediment to any historical study of textual practices is the immateriality of the reading process: Reading leaves no residue of its existence. What records we possess of the reading process have already crossed the boundary into writing. The sentence a few lines above that begins "[w]hen I first read this passage" is as pure a record of reading as one will find in this study, but the extent to which it too is marked by its entextualization illustrates the limited extent of our access to a pure scene of reading. Roger Chartier, an important and often dissenting voice in scholarship on reading, writing, authorship, and textuality in the medieval and post-medieval West, stresses the point that reading is a practice embedded in acts, spaces, and habits. "Readers and hearers, in point of fact, are never confronted with abstract or ideal texts detached from all materiality" (Chartier 1994: 3). Limited though our knowledge is, later in this chapter I will draw some tentative conclusions that are based on the material and social character of textual transmission in the early imperial period. But scholars of textuality in the medieval West have developed another category that has some affinities with readership and concerns the use of texts, but is also characterized by the activity of writing: the textual community. The idea of the textual community has some applicability to the social operation of the Empire of the Text, as I have conceived it. The differences are illuminating as well.

The term "textual community" is most closely associated with Brian Stock, who also uses the term with the greatest precision and with the broadest claims. What Stock and others have noted about the rise of textual culture in Europe in the Middle Ages is the sociohermeneutic consequences of the increased circulation of texts (Chartier 1994; Stock 1983 and 1990; Febvre and Martin 1976). In his collection of theoretical essays, *Listening for the Text*, Stock suggests several related approaches to the medieval textual community. First is the idea that meaning and significance became structured according to textual dictates:

> An invisible scripture seemed to lurk behind everything one said. Meaning gravitated to this written type of reference, rather than to the sense of the spoken alone; and what had been expressed in gestures, rituals, and physical symbols became imbedded in a set of interpretive structures involving grammars, notations, and lexica. (Stock 1990: 20)

In a more material sense, a textual community can refer to the group of people for whom a text is in some way socially operative. This would include readers and listeners, interpreters, and so on. This kind of textual community was "reborn" in the Middle Ages, in various heretical and reformist religious groups in medieval Europe. It is important for Stock to stress that the textual unifier of this community superseded "the differing economic and social backgrounds of the participants, welding them, for a time at least, into a unit" (Stock 1990: 150). The activities of these communities are analyzed under the category of ritual, which Stock deploys both to dispel the notion that ritual declined as textual circulation increased over the course of the Middle Ages and to claim the category's applicability to a textual instead of a purely oral scene.

Although Stock is careful to stress the nonuniversal character of early textual community—arguing, for example, that the notion of textual community has less applicability for those textual scenes that presume widespread literacy among those groups within which the texts circulate—the telic consequences of the rise of textual communities are substantial. The associated modes of thought and being are those that characterize the modern age itself:

> If there are ethically defensible principles for the activities of individuals and groups, they arise chiefly from the schemata of narratives that are heard or read. Action is an audience reaction within a largely literary experience. This means that the design of activity, which is shaped as a narrative, is derived from the same texts that medieval culture produces as part of its literate revolution. Interiorization, the first stage of understanding something written, is also the primary phase of rationalization. It requires only that communication take place, that it be formalized subsequently by norms or rules, and that eventually it regulate key sectors of experience. In other words, contrary to what Weber proposed, substantive rationalization takes place by its own means and obeys its own criteria of change. (Stock 1990: 134–5)
>
> In the later Middle Ages, people became just as convinced that an interior sense lurked behind every outer expression or behavioral pattern. It was this belief in the interior nature of meaning, as well as the formation of programs of action based on the linking up of individual cases of interiority that brought about change as often as real shifts in communication. There is no doubt that the rise of this idea paralleled the growth of a more literate society. For the written word was the symbol of the inner, often unconscious, and divinely or diabolically inspired network of sense. Out of this arose the desire for a grammar that could accommodate both literary and social relations. (Stock 1990: 146).

I quote Stock at some length partly because I support his advocacy of "large theses" to explain rationality, interiority, and other broad strokes of sociohistorical identification, against the prevailing scholarly tendency of the "cautious advance" (54). But as Stock advances further into his large theses, the "nostalgia for Gemeinschaft," his characterization of the utopian strain in Foucault's thought, begins to describe him as well. There is a circular seductiveness to the category of the textual: It serves perhaps too easily as a scene of pure explanation. In the end, it is perhaps the unavoidable nature of textuality as a category that it will always privilege itself, and there is nothing historically specifiable about that.

One's stance on the nature of textual self-privileging determines one's analytical categories. The use of the term "community" rather than "authority," for example, signals an orientation toward the productive power of the consumer, the reader, the user. When this productive power becomes aligned with rationality, interiority, and subjectivity itself, then we are squarely in the territory of Enlightenment liberalism. An example from late Han China—the relationship between Pure Criticism (*qingliu*) and the Affair of the Proscribed Factions (*danggu*)[8]—will illustrate two widely divergent analyses that proceed from two different positions on the textual. Briefly, this affair concerned a number of scholar-officials who were proscribed from officeholding between the years 159 and 184. These officials have been identified with a school of criticism termed "pure" criticism, in reference to their purportedly high and uncompromising principles. The general scholarly consensus is that the men who have been identified with the "pure" faction constituted something like a "textual community" with distinct normative codes of behavior and morality, and, like their heretical or reformist counterparts in medieval Europe, they could be loosely described as an "oppositional" community. Not coincidentally, this group is described as advocating a kind of transcendent text-based moral standard as opposed to the power politics of the supposed central authority. And as one would further suspect, it is among this group and their milieu that one finds the wellsprings of "individualism," aesthetics, subjectivity, and so on. All interpretive frames will impose their categories on the object of historical analysis, and I am not proposing that this narrative of the "pures" be rejected in favor of some phantasmatic framework that claims to derive more purely from the sources themselves. I will show in chapter 3 that, since the "pures" possibly did not even exist as a recognizable "community," any narrative that takes the existence of a self-recognized community of "pures" as its basis will follow a circumscribed range of trajectories. Call the "pures" an oppositional political community, and their social history practically writes itself. Take the position that there is no connection between the "pures" and the "proscribed faction," and a different discussion ensues. "Community" would seem to be a category by nature more flexible, productive, and liberatory than "authority," but the propensity of "community" to generate a recognizable and standardized set of narratives has led me to consider "authority" as more useful to the terms of this experiment.

This authority is not, however, the authority of "A Writing Lesson," a purported authority which Lévi-Strauss contests in *Tristes Tropiques* in a diatribe which was itself the subject of Derrida's critique in *Of Grammatology*.[9] Lévi-Strauss claims that his Nambikwara chief saw in the mimicry of writing a mimicry of the very authority wielded by Lévi-Strauss as colonial outsider, and the chief seized upon this authoritarian tool to increase his power over his fellow tribespeople. Derrida, in a fairly inconsequential part of a complex argument about the metaphysics of presence that leads to his critique of Rousseau, makes the obvious and important point that the chief's authority must have existed prior to the "writing" described by Lévi-Strauss. In the larger context of Derrida's reading of the Western philosophical tradition, "writing," as the chief deploys it in Lévi-Strauss's account, is one further instance of the foundational violence of communication itself, with its implicit othering of the addressee. If we are to consider the introduction of writing in terms of the binary literate/illiterate, then writing can only be understood, as Lévi-Strauss understands it, as another realm of differentiation for the functioning of authority: With writing, there are then writers and nonwriters, the literate and the illiterate. Those who deploy the idea of textual community seek to transcend this distinction, and I concur with that aim. The idea of the authority of the literate over the nonliterate is a fairly recent one worldwide, and my notion of textual authority certainly has nothing to do with that. But there is a kind of communitarian utopianism that surfaces in the discourse of textual community that does strike me as somewhat ahistorical, an ahistoricity that is revealed, for example, in the equation of the "pures" with a transhistorical, moral, "Confucian" intellectual. In one sense, textual authority, rather than textual community, poses a more primary question: How do texts acquire the authority that allows communities to be constituted by and within them?

Martin Irvine's *The Making of Textual Culture: 'Grammatica' and Literary Theory, 350–1100* illustrates the function of a specific kind of textual authority within a delimited social context. Grammatica, known in Rome and medieval Europe as "the art [or science] of interpreting the poets and other writers and the principles for speaking and writing correctly,"[10] emerges in Irvine's study not as one discipline among many but as the discipline that structures textual culture at the most foundational level. According to Irvine, it is within the discourse of *grammatica* that the canon itself is determined and that legitimate interpretations are sanctioned and transmitted: "With the institution of *grammatica*, a written work could become a text, that is, a work which takes its place in a larger cultural library, and which is interpreted as part of a system of other texts, genres, and discourses" (Irvine 1994: 15). In this framework there are no singular texts: Text, intertext, and interpretive text form an irreducible discursive system that allows a community's functions of "self-definition, authority, and authentification" (Irvine 1994: 15) to take place. There is no act of reading before the blank text: The reading process is always already structured by the textual culture of which it is a part. Irvine's work allows a corrective to the model of the humanistic textual community, wherein a text becomes the transcendent object for a new kind of cross-social community. When texts are understood as parts of a system, the kind of community constructed within and by that system can be seen as something that is neither a product nor a by-product of the texts. Like the textual scenes themselves, these communities share the underlying structure of authority.

Irvine is more circumspect than Stock in his inferences concerning the flesh-and-blood sociality that surrounded the texts. Unfortunately, theoretical tools for understanding the human outside to the various textual regimes are insufficient for the pre- or noncapitalist periods. Benedict Anderson's *Imagined Communities* has remained a powerful synthesis of the textual, ideological, and socioeconomic, within the rubric of emergent national identity formation. Slavoj Žižek and Etienne Balibar, in work on ideology and the nation, have explored the Lacanian psychoanalytic dimensions of the national "imaginary," a dimension overlooked in Anderson's book despite his use of the term (Balibar and Wallerstein 1991; Zizek 1989). Anderson's foundational work in articulating the systemic base for the national imagined community—"print capitalism"—suggests the difficulty in exporting his model. For print capitalism effectively ends the possibility of the regimes of reading and interpretation that characterized late classical and medieval *grammatica* as well as the varied kinds of textual communities discussed in Stock's work. Print capitalism means the production of texts under the regime of commodity exchange, and that has significant consequences. It is not coincident that in Anderson's analysis the authorization of the national imaginary does not inhere in the particular texts themselves but in the system of textual circulation, a subset of commodity circulation itself, that allows the formation of the imagined community of the nation. The mental forms by which this abstraction takes place could themselves be, recalling Sohn-Rethel, a dimension of commodity logic. That social formation defined by the consumption of the print-capital commodities newspapers, periodicals and books has as its primary subject formation the capitalist subject, defined, as are all capitalist subjectivities, by its constitutive lacks and absences. The compensatory production of the nation is the formal corollary to the capitalist subject itself. I bring up Anderson in order to suggest that although the level of theorization sketched above is not available to scholars of the pre- or noncapitalist world, we need to be aware of those points at which our theorizations derive from categories that should perhaps be limited to the capitalist subject. Irvine's analysis suggests, for example, that the "freedom of the reader" extolled in the quotation from de Certeau needs historical specificity. Perhaps the reader's freedom, as de Certeau conceives it, is only possible when another kind of bond has been made: to the nation, to subjectivity, to class. For eras before the nation, before the subject, before capitalism, eras in which our access to the details of material and social life is reduced, particularly when the questions we ask are about people whose lives were apparently structured more by the textual than by, say, crafts or agriculture, we must proceed with the understanding that we will be unable to posit a pure outside to textuality. The social and the textual are entwined in complicated ways.

The Origin of Writing

William Boltz begins his authoritative work on the origins and early history of the Chinese writing system (Boltz 1994) with a long quotation from a 1838 address to the American Philosophical Society by its president, Peter S. Du Ponceau, attacking the prevailing view in the West, probably originating with Leibniz, that Chinese writing could be considered an "ideographic" script that did not derive from a prior spoken language. The logical impossibility of an ideographic script—a writing system without reference to sounds, words, phrases, or any other element of a spoken language—has not prevented expressions such as the following, by an eminent sinologist, over 150 years after Du Ponceau's address:

> These inscriptions did not record language, but meanings—directly, and speechlessly: they transcended language . . . This Chinese emblematic meta-language developed independently from contemporary speech. For convenience, however, the written characters were progressively given conventional sounds; thus, eventually the inscriptions did not merely convey silent meanings, they could also be read aloud. In the end, they themselves generated a language—monosyllabic and non-inflected (features that remain as the special marks of its artificial origin)—and since this language carried all the prestige of magic and power, it gradually supplanted the vernacular originally spoken (Leys 1996: 29–30).

Pierre Ryckmans might defend this passage, the error of which he cannot be unaware of, by claiming that it better expresses something like the "poetry" of Chinese writing. The first chapter of Francois Cheng's *L'écriture poétique chinoise* is a development of a similar idea: The Chinese writing system *precedes* speech, and Chinese poetry derives much of its power through its unmediated access to the conceptual. A host of works on the Chinese writing system, Boltz's among them, makes adherence to the ideographic explanation untenable. But we should not expect its disappearance any time soon. The desire to believe in a universal language of pure concepts, a transparent language, has occupied Western philosophers and poets for centuries, and the figuration of Chinese as the scene of Pure Writing, the "European hallucination" in Derrida's words (Der-

rida 1976: 80), dates back to the first Western awareness of the existence
of the Chinese writing system. I would stress, as Derrida does not, the
links between the development of capitalist commodity abstraction,[11] European exploration and colonization of the non-European world, the origins of the theory of universal language, and comparative philology.

Just as a history of the ideographic myth is useful in ideological diagno-
sis, so are there lessons in all myths of graphogenesis. The tradition of the
ideographic explanation in China, in the form of the story of Cang Jie or
Fu Xi (variants: Pao Xi), goes back to at least the early Han dynasty. In
contrast to the graphogenesis myths that come from Babylon, Egypt, or
India, which at least mention the obvious temporal advantage of written
language over speech—writing's capacity to endure over time—the early
Chinese stories do not make it clear that writing and speech can even be
considered as two versions of the same phenomenon, namely, communication in language (Boltz 1994: 129–155). Ideographism is strengthened
by the direct connections drawn between the invention of writing and the
prior invention of the *Yi jing* trigrams, which clearly were and remain
abstractions of concepts with no direct reference to words as such. The
various stories on the origin of writing are concentrated in the *Xi ci* appendix to the *Yi jing* (c. third century B.C.E.), the *Huainanzi* (former Han
dynasty), and brief mentions in the the *Lu shi chun qiu* (Qin–Early Han
dynasty).[12] Xu Shen's postface to the *Shuo wen* dictionary, dated around
100 C.E., summarizes and synthesizes these various accounts and remains
the standard account for years to come. The relevant section is translated
in full below:[13]

> In ancient times, Bao Xi (variant forms: Fu Xi, Pao Xi) ruled the world.
> Looking upward he gazed on the images in heaven; looking downward he
> gazed on the patternings on earth. He saw the patterned markings (*wen*) on
> birds and animals, and their appropriateness to their terrain. Close at hand,
> he sought first on his own body; and sought afar from external things, and
> thus began to make the eight trigrams of the *Book of Changes*. This became
> known as the transmission of the heavenly and earthly patterns. Later, after
> Shen Nong [legendary emperor; inventor of agriculture] knotted the cords
> to establish order and to regularize affairs, various trades proliferated, and
> wasteful luxuries and artifice grew and thrived.
>
> Huang Di's clerk Cang Jie looked at the tracks of birds and animals, and
> knew then that their component structures were mutually distinguishable,
> so began to make Writing. The hundred crafts were thereby regulated, and
> the myriad groups were kept under surveillance. He probably took this idea
> from the hexagram *guai Guai*, glossed as "to make the matter known in the
> king's court,"[14] suggests that the patterns (*wen*) are themselves appropriate
> for instruction, illumination, and transformation at the king's court. "Thus
> the superior man dispenses riches downward and refrains from resting on

his virtue." When Cang Jie first created writing, he probably designed forms on the basis of general categories. So these were called simple graphs (*wen*).[15] Later, when the combination of pictographic components and sound components allowed for increased numbers of graphs, these were called compound graphs (*zi*).[16] Simple graphs (*wen*) are based on images and things.[17] Compound graphs (*zi*) develop in the manner of breeding offspring and gradual increase. When they are on bamboo and silk, they are called "texts" (*shu*). "Texts" means resemblance. (*Shuo wen jie zi gu lin*, 6709–10)

Socrates, inveighing against Thoth's invention of writing in Egypt, expresses fear of what writing would do to memory and mind, to thinking itself. In Plato, speech—human presence—is counterposed to writing. What strikes the reader about the *Shuo wen* account is that writing has no outside: The voice does not enter into the account. Fu Xi neither speaks nor listens. He sees. His body produces writing because it recognizes itself as being, like other bodies and their traces, a prior inscription, already a text. The writing system, then, was an analogical repetition of an ordering principle recognized as already present everywhere in the universe. This principle, centralized and codified in the writing system, allowed for the regulation and surveillance of human affairs. The subject of writing was the state. Calculation, facilitated by Shen Nong's knotted cords, had allowed for a preliminary "proliferation." Writing, then, was a second order of regularization that had the virtue of systematicity and centrality, rather than the dispersion and diffusion that characterized primitive calculation. A version in the *Huainanzi*, dating from the early Former Han dynasty, regrets Cang Jie's invention: "When Cang Jie created writing, Heaven rained millet and ghosts wailed in the night." This passage was widely quoted in texts throughout the Han. A Jin dynasty commentator adds that writing, like the other inventions mentioned in the *Huainanzi* passage, had had the negative consequences of all technological innovations: It took people away from "the basics" and allowed for a damaging indulgence in sophistication and artifice (Boltz 1994: 138–43). This accorded with the critique of proliferation that was leveled at Shen Nong's invention: a power of differentiation that escaped central control could only have bad consequences. The first phase of symbolization, Fu Xi's invention of the *Yi jing* trigrams, meets no criticism or comment in the *Shuo wen* passage. This would be unthinkable given the *Yi jing*'s status as a classic. Yet it is precisely its status as text, classic, representation, and singular resemblance that distinguishes Fu Xi's invention from Shen Nong's knotted cords: The knotted cords do not resemble or represent; they are pure technique. They are not reproducible as a total system, but they remain adaptable to a proliferating variety of situations. This proliferation was then brought under control by the texts: Representational power was again centralized and specified, and the foundation for the idea of a canon itself was in place.

Xu Shen's version of the origin of language, a synthesis of the sources that antedated his text, is the most elaborate that remains today. It accords, for the most part, with the ideographic myth as we know it in its contemporary form, as in the quotation from Ryckmans above: Writing is an analogical reproduction of cosmic signifying practices. In the myth's contemporary, romanticized version, there is at least an implicit potential for anarchy that is inconsistent with textual culture as we have known it throughout the history of imperial China. If writing provides immediate access to the conceptual, then there are no bounds at all to what ideographic writing can express. But surely, in the case of the Han purveyors of the ideographic myth, the cosmic signifying power of writing cannot be present in all instances of writing. A war declaration, for example, could be simply a war declaration and not a figuring of the cosmos. What is the writing system, then, for Xu Shen? His elaboration on the difference between simple and compound graphs—*wen* and *zi*—which appears to be a technical usage that dates from around Xu Shen's time, signifies what might have been a new view of writing and textuality. We move, in an explicit teleology that is cast in biological terms, from simple graph to compound graph: The writing system as a whole is "populated" in a manner reminiscent of the biological population of the world. But the population of the world is ordered within the structures of the imperial system; the warning against proliferation suggests that we should not use a purely biological metaphor for writing as a whole. I would question, in fact, whether there *is* a writing system as a whole, one that is abstractable from writing's instantiation in texts themselves. At the risk of reading too much into a single phrase, I would suggest that the concluding sentences translated in the passage above—"When they are on bamboo and silk, they are called 'texts' (*shu*); 'texts' means resemblance"—indicates that the ultimate horizon for graphs is not a "writing system" in toto but the canonical texts themselves. The canonical texts are not expressed by a preexistent writing system. Rather, the writing system is only conceivable as a system because of the existence of the canonical texts. To illustrate what I mean by this, consider the *Yi jing*. The trigrams of the *Yi jing* do not combine and recombine ad infinitum; they combine into the sixty-four hexagrams that are the content of a specific text: the *Yi jing*. Although the *Yi jing* has world-referential capability (recalling the phrase from the postface: " 'texts' means 'to resemble' "), this capability is finitized in physical form as a discrete text. The reference to texts in the *Shuo wen* passage quoted above, where "text" could also be translated as "writings," is somewhat ambiguous. Still, it is not unreasonable to infer that resemblance and representation, the functional capacities of a writing system, are themselves not fully activated on the level of the individual lexical item but finally acquire referential power only when words are combined in texts. The texts of reference are the canonical classics, of which all writing worthy of being so called is in some form a repetition.

Writing, Word, Lexicon

The ideographic myth and its critique leave out this element of textuality. Hegel's writings on Chinese fault the language precisely for its abstract, ideographic quality: The Chinese writing system's very derivation from the *Yi jing* trigrams (Hegel refers to the Fu Xi story) attests to its static, ideational character. Derrida points out in his discussion of Hegel on Chinese[18] that Hegel's criticism of Chinese, and his claims for the superiority of the alphabetic script, rested on Hegel's specifiable logocentrism:

> The linguistics implied by all these propositions is the linguistics of the word and singularly of the name. The word, and the name, which with its categories is the word par excellence, functions in this linguistics as the simple, irreducible and complete element that bears the unity of sound and sense in the voice. Thanks to the name, we may do without both the image and sensory existence . . . The irreducible privilege of the name is the keystone of the Hegelian philosophy of language. (Derrida 1992: 96)

Although Derrida's critique of logocentrism is commonly understood as a critique of the metaphysics of presence that inheres in any privileging of the originary oral, this passage reminds us that the individual and isolable word itself is also a centrally defining feature of logocentrism. In arguing for the *Shuo wen* as a register of textual authority, I am suggesting that there is little ontological weight attached to the individual word, a suggestion that might initially seem inappropriate for a lexicon that is, indeed, divided into single-word entries. But I think it is far more productive to consider the *Shuo wen* within the telos of an expanding textuality rather than associate it with a logocentric turn in linguistic or in philosophical thought generally. Let us consider the function of the lexicon itself, even though determinations of "original" functions will remain hypothetical at best. The earliest examples of dictionaries or lexicographies in nearly any culture serve more to regularize and standardize the lexicon than to list or inventory it, and as such would tend to take as their object textual rather than spoken language. In Xu Shen's dictionary, spoken language is rarely referred to,[19] which might initially seem somewhat odd considering the fact that a distinguishing feature of his new lexicon was the recognition of a "phonetic" element underlying the great majority of the entries.[20]

Boltz hypothesizes that the *Shuo wen* can be read prescriptively rather than simply as a description of the writing system of his age; it was part of a larger prescriptive effort of standardization and regularization of the written language over the course of the Han. The *Shuo wen* was almost certainly not the first lexicon; the *Han shu Yiwen zhi* lists several others, from the Qin and earlier, one of which, the *Cang jie*, is also mentioned in the *Shuo wen* postface. It is quite possible that these earlier lexicons also served prescriptive ends. The *Han shu Yiwen zhi* describes the history of lexicological work as follows:

> When the Han arose, the writing teachers of the lanes and neighborhoods assembled the *Cang Jie*, the *Yuanli*, the *Boxue* and made paragraph-units of 60 graphs each, with fifty-five graphs altogether, and called this the Cang jie fascicles. In the time of emperor Wu, Sima Xiangru composed the Fanjiang fascicles, without repeated characters. . . . In the *yuanshi* period, Wang Mang summoned several hundred experts in philology (*xiaoxue*) from throughout the empire, and ordered each to record words in the Palace Courts. Yang Xiong took those that were of use and compiled the Xunzuanpian. It followed the work of the Cang Jie, revising the duplicated words in the Cang Jie. It was in 89 zhang. I [Ban Gu] continued Yang Xiong's work and did 10 more zhang, for a total of 102 zhang, without duplication, and covered the corpus of the six classics and assorted other books. (HS: 1721)

Two features of lexicographical history stand out here: Lexicographic work was indeed done at imperial command, even though such was not the case for the *Shuo wen* itself, and it was based on written texts.

Broadly speaking, there were two periods of graphic standardization in Chinese history: the Shang, when the writing system was first developed, and the Qin-Han standardization and unification. The two periods are separated by over fifteen hundred years, and too little evidence survives to allow a reconstruction of the political or institutional character of the Shang standardization. Boltz demonstrates from variant versions of canonical texts, which have been unearthed in archaeological finds in China in the postrevolutionary period, that the Shang standardization had decayed and that by the early Han there was a pronounced tendency toward desemanticization and proto-phoneticization, in a logic similar to the history of writing in Egypt and the Near East. Boltz hypothesizes that had that development continued unchecked, Chinese could easily have evolved into a syllabary or even an alphabet, which was the course that writing took elsewhere (Boltz 1994: 156–177). That this development did not take place in China was a consequence of efforts toward graphical and lexical standardization of which, he argues, the *Shuo wen* was one representative part, perhaps a late and comprehensive entry in the cumulative efforts that began in those lost lexicons mentioned in the *Han shu* passage above. Although the *Shuo wen* itself was not produced by imperial command, an explicitly directed effort toward graphic standardization, it could certainly reflect a general tendency toward standardization, functioning in a manner akin to the late classical and early medieval European *grammatica*, albeit within a context in which canonization had a much clearer official character than in the medieval West.

All modern scholars of the *Shuo wen* recognize that the lexicon's stated purpose was the elucidation of the classical canon and other written texts rather than the explanation of "language" writ large, as with the commonsense understanding of dictionaries in modern times.[21] The postface, from which a large section was translated above, states that the *Shuo wen* was intended as an aid to the reading and the understanding of the canonical texts, and specifically as a countermeasure against heterodox and "private" teachings:

> The *Book of Documents* says, "I wish to contemplate the designs of the ancients." This means one must follow the old writings and not distort everything. Confucius said, "I can remember when a scribe left a blank in his text. Now this is no longer done, alas." It is not because men do not know and do not ask, but because if they all used their own private judgment, right and wrong would have had no standard, and clever opinions and heterodox pronouncements would have caused confusion among scholars. Now the written language is the foundation of classical learning, the source of kingly government. It is what the former generations relied on to transmit culture to later ages. Men of later times will rely on it to understand antiquity. (*Shuo wen jie zi gu lin*, 6712–13)

I want to pay particular attention to the invective in the passage above against private judgment and heterodox opinion, and the importance of textual standardization to "kingly government." Textual standardization—i.e., canonization—is here, as always, explicitly linked to the aims of the state. This is one indication of the great difference between the textual communities of the early Middle Ages in the West and the Empire of the Text as it was consolidating in China. The early imperial Chinese state aimed to regulate texts and interpretative traditions; private judgments and heterodox opinions, whatever their content, were ultimately the enemies of central authority.

The milieu of which the *Shuo wen* was a part had two components. First is the canonical. It is one part of a development that lasted nearly the whole of the Han dynasty: the consolidation of textual culture itself, as well as the determination of what kind of textual culture was being created, under whose auspices, and with what kind of authority it was invested. Second is the codification of writing practices and the determination of what, exactly, constituted grapho-literacy. The number of sinographs mastered was a measure of writing competency from an early date in the imperial examinations, however. Early in the Former Han, Xiao He achieved passage of a law stipulating that candidates for a number of offices be examined by the Grand Astrologer. This examination required knowledge of over nine thousand sinographs and mastery of six script styles (HS: 1720–21). This examination continued into the Latter Han. Xu Shen's lexicon consisted of about this same number of sinographs, and we have remarked above about the importance he placed on the form of the graphs. The lexicon could have been, like the examination itself, a simple measure of what writing competency meant.

Literacy, Canonicity, Transmission, and Text-systems

The "philology" section of the *Han shu Yiwen zhi*, which records the nine-thousand sinograph standard mentioned above, frames its discussion of orthoëpical standards as a defense against the entropic processes of memory loss and sloppy scholarship. Like the *Shuo wen* postface, it quotes Confucius's disapproval of the scribes who refuse to leave a blank in their text when they forget how to write a graph. This concern remained for some time, though the different ways in which it is deployed indicate the changing character of textual cultural norms. Yan Zhitui's (531–591) *Family Instructions for the Yan Clan* appeared during the period of division between North and South, over four hundred years after the *Shuo wen*. Substantial parts of the book are devoted to philological anecdotes. The author's professed philological expertise (the text contains high praise for the *Shuo wen*) and high orthoëpical standards are frequently mustered in admonitions against the laxity of his predecessors and contemporaries.[22] In decrying the lax standards of the recent past, he writes:

> In the most flourishing age of the Liang dynasty (502–556), the scions of royal stock were usually unlearned. . . . When seeking to pass the examination for the degree of "clearly understanding the classics," they hired others to answer the questions and compose essays. When attending public feasts for high state officials they used others' talents to compose poems for them. At that time such men were happy scholars. After the time of dispersion and disorder, when the court was overthrown and conditions changed, those in charge of civil service examinations were no longer their relatives as before . . . Forced to depend upon themselves, they could do nothing. . . . Tottering in the area trodden by military horses, they wandered here and there until they died in a ditch or a stream. At that time they had truly become worthless material. (Teng 1968: 54)

This passage illustrates the nature of the changes in textual culture over the centuries following the Han. By the Liang dynasty not only were essay compositions and group poetry compositions thoroughly naturalized as the formal content of literati social life, but the degree of formalization was such that it was possible to hire stand-ins to make up for one's own inability. It is only when the ideological underpinnings of textual culture are wholly consolidated that adherence to that culture can allow such an opportunistic or formal variant. The wasted scions of the Liang royalty were able, thanks to their riches and connections, to satisfy the formal textual requirements of royal life, even though they had failed, claims Yan Zhitui, to read adequately. Chapter 8 of the *Family Instructions*, "To Encourage Study," castigates deviation from the codes of the textual regime. Yan singles out for particular criticism those who rely solely on oral transmission, who mouth the words of their teachers but cannot write complicated graphs. His admonitions are saturated with the authoritative claims of the textual:

> Old literary allusions cited in speeches and writings should be personally checked and not based on hearsay. The so-called scholar-officials in the villages south of the Yangtze are usually not well educated, but as they are ashamed to appear mean and uncultured, they write what they know from hearsay evidence, using ill-fitted classical terms to embellish their statements. . . . Speaking of eating they say "to fill the mouth" [misunderstanding the expression *hu kou*, which means to look for a job with just enough pay to earn a living]; talking about marriage, they would say "to feast you" [an incomplete and therefore meaningless quotation from the Poetry Classic]. . . . All these faults are caused by learning by ear. Characters are the foundation of writings. Nowadays many students cannot recognize the characters. . . . they disregard Hsü Shen [Xu Shen]. (Teng 1968: 78–79)

The relationship implied here between the oral and the textual suggests a position not unlike Pierre Ryckmans's cited earlier in this chapter: that spoken language itself is generated by a prior textuality. Within the determinant logic of textual authority, as opposed to linguistic common sense, this is true: The only kind of speech worthy of recording in a text, worthy of being considered the speech of a person, is speech that adheres to the textual norms. The problem with orality—"hearsay"—is not merely that it constitutes a less worthy alternative culture, but that it is an inferior version of textual culture.

Yan Zhitui lived at a time when a standardization of the writing system's phonetic aspects was taking place in a manner reminiscent of the earlier standardization of graphic forms. The *Family Instructions*, in fact, is the earliest surviving text that notes historical changes in the pronunciation of certain words in texts, thus creating a discursive context for stan-

dardization. Yan Zhitui's life falls roughly in between the period marked
by Shen Yue, whose articulation of the phonetic rules and defects in
poetry composition prefigured the phonetic codification of Tang regulated verse and the compilation of the *Qie yun* rhyming dictionary, which
functioned as a prescriptive text for the composition of poetry that accorded with prosodic rules and categories. This kind of text-centered pronunciation regime is a far different matter, then, from modern practices
of national pronunciation regulation that have been pursued in Taiwan or
Great Britain. In the age of electronic media, speech can be disseminated
and reproduced without recourse to textuality at any point, and pronunciation without reference to texts is thus more available as an issue subject
to political control. The *Family Instructions* includes no admonition of
pronunciation defects in what we might call ordinary speech; it is only in
recitation or quotation of textual material that correct pronunciation is
an issue. The undereducated pedants in Yan Zhitui's example seek the
source of their speech in texts, but it is their faulty command of the texts
that leads to their errors in speech.

The *Family Instructions*, then, shows a strong impulse toward classical
textual foundationalism that we might call "conservative" in the standard
way. I begin this section with the *Family Instructions* because it illustrates
an important problematic that has its roots in the Han dynasty. To call it
an oral/textual dichotomy would be to use discursive categories that were
not operative at that time. But as we can see in the passage quoted above,
the oral as an inferior or negative *version* of the textual was very much an
operative category, and this gradation of textual culture does have its
roots in the Qin-Han period. One target of textual authority is the excess
that characterizes the oral, in contrast to the powers of control, limits,
and containment that inhere in the canonically textual. In the private
judgment and heterodox opinions that Xu Shen criticizes in the passage
quoted above (p. 39), it is the uncontrolled and excessive character of the
transmission that is the target. Speech is ultimately unbounded; a mouth
can produce sounds that range instantaneously from sense to nonsense;
from order to excess. In the most basic sense, speech at the moment of
production and reception cannot be regulated by outside human agency.[23]

A delimited canon exists, explicitly or not, to counter and contain discursive excess. Orality can be the medium for that excess, but there are
also modes of texuality that fall under censure. In the Han, as we shall see
below, there are specific modes of textuality that are censured for their
prolix and uncontrolled excess, not to mention the numerous censures
for slander and other politically delegitimated speech. By the time of the
Family Instructions, priorities for reading and study have become more
codified; its author urges assiduous study of an expanded canon—
examples of worthy texts are centered on the Confucian canon but also

include many works of history or noncanonical philosophy—but cautions against overindulgence in "literary" writing (*wen*), which is too frequently shallow, insufficiently morally uplifting, or evanescent, like speech itself.[24]

The need to control textual proliferation was recognized quite early, and was probably what was behind the Qin dynasty "burning of the books," which was not at all a rejection of the textual, as is sometimes claimed, but was clearly an attack on "private teaching" (i.e., nonimperial authority) and the uncontrolled and unofficial circulation of textual material. The only texts consigned without exception to be burnt were those that "used the past to criticize the present." Most texts proscribed at large were allowed to exist in the imperial library or under the auspices of officials assigned to their study (Qian Mu 1971). By Yan Zhitui's time, which was over three hundred years after the beginning of the general adoption of paper in the late Han, the physical proliferation of texts was such that the tightly controlled circulation aimed at in the Qin would have required considerable administrative resources. The Han marked the first phase in the transition to the broader and more thorough kind of textual culture that existed in the Liang. The signal achievement of that first phase was the establishment of the classical canon and the writing system with which it coexisted.

The first eighty years of the Han dynasty have been aptly characterized as the period of imperial consolidation (CHC, chapter 2). It was during this period that central political authority was firmly established, especially above and over the regional kings. Great advances in administrative, legal, ritual, and political regularization and standardization came during the reign of Emperor Wu (141–87 B.C.E). Emperor Wu's reign is also associated with the establishment of "state Confucianism," a phenomenon attributed to Dong Zhongshu, generally regarded by his near contemporaries and since as the foremost thinker of the Former Han dynasty, "the leading Confucian," according to the Han historian Ban Gu (HS: 2526). Dong Zhongshu's major work, *Luxuriant Dew of the Spring and Autumn Annals*,[25] is of considerable cosmological scope. Among its foundational organizing principles are the following: the world is a system of correspondences under the authority of heaven; the emperor needs to act in accord with heaven, which demonstrates its will through signs and portents; to rule, the emperor should accord with "nonaction," serving as a silent and tranquil center of power; his primary task is the recruitment of worthy officials; official worthiness can be judged by a candidate's mastery of the Five Classics, which are the foundation of moral, political, and historical knowledge. Dong Zhongshu's work gave a cosmological basis for the existence of a canon, the need for textual mastery, and the need for institutionalizing mastery of the canonical teachings. The role of Dong

Zhongshu and the nature of the "Confucianism" that was officially established under Emperor Wu remain, however, a matter of some debate.
Benjamin Wallacker writes, for example, that

> in a very real sense, however, content-free Confucianism, the tradition of
> Confucius, which was free to accept beliefs and practices from all schools
> and whose own creed consisted almost entirely of simple reverence for tradi-
> tion, did emerge pre-eminent in Han. (Roy and Tsien 1985: 227)

Xu Fuguan, author of a fairly polemical three-volume history of Han
thought, sees Dong Zhongshu's achievement as establishing the particular
characteristic of Han thought itself: a Confucianism that is based on the
authority of the canonical texts and that assimilates yin-yang, five-ele-
ment four-season cosmology that aimed at all-inclusiveness and thus
formed the context for all knowledge of the cosmos, history, government,
and human affairs.[26] Philosophers and intellectual historians are more inclined to judge Dong Zhongshu's work on the basis of content. For our
purposes it suffices to note that a work of grand synthesis like the *Luxuriant Dew of the Spring and Autumn Annals* is thoroughly dependent on
its textual character. A cosmology so saturated with patterning, self-
referentiality, and correspondences is only possible in a wholly systematized textual logic; the centering of Dong Zhongshu's text on canonical
textual mastery is not coincidental at all. His text is positioned, in fact, as
a commentary on the canonical text that was at the center of Han classicism: the *Spring and Autumn Annals*.

The elaboration of this text-centered cosmological system might be
reminiscent of other canonizations in other eras, but we should remember
that such a text-centered system is not the only conceivable means of
transmitting official values. The Homeric poems, the pre-Platonic equivalent of the canon in ancient Greece, functioned in a similar way in a system characterized far more by orality than was the system in Han China.
A generation of classical scholars, Werner Jaeger and Eric Havelock prominent among them, have established the centrality of the Homeric poems
to early Greek "paideia," a term which Kevin Robb prefers to explain as
"enculturation" rather than "education," the more common translation.[27]
Harold Innis has suggested that maintaining an empire on the scale of
Qin or Han China must depend to a greater extent on technologies of
written communication than on orality (Innis 1950). But the elaborate
systematization evident in a work like Dong Zhongshu's shows that Han
China's commitment to textuality was much deeper than simple communication. An officially delimited textual canon can permit institutionalization and control mechanisms of far greater specificity than simple "enculturation": It can structure the content of knowledge and of pedagogy, the

referent system in intertextual composition, the "language" for written communication. "Intellectual work" becomes, at its very core, the affair of the state. Stephen Durrant, in a study of Sima Qian, sees the canonization practice instigated by Dong Zhongshu in this light:

> This was a decisive moment in Chinese history. A canon had been formally established and placed at the centre of a government-controlled educational establishment, and much of the subsequent intellectual history of the Han dynasty concerns attempts by various schools of classic-interpretation to gain access to the power that came with government recognition and sponsorship. (Durrant 1995: 55)

In 136 B.C.E., in response to currents of advocacy like that of Dong Zhongshu, Emperor Wu established the office of the Erudites of the Five Classics (*wu jing boshi*) for the teaching and transmission of specific lines of interpretation of the *Yi jing*, the *Poetry Classic*, the *Book of Documents*, the *Book of Rites*, and the *Spring and Autumn Annals*. Prior to 136, the office of Erudite seems to have been much more general and varied in function, though it usually had some connection with pedagogy, textual mastery of a variety of kinds, or advisorship. There were Erudites at the provincial and local levels as well as in the imperial court. In 124 B.C.E., the Imperial Academy was reestablished. This was the official institution for the transmission of classical learning, and it functioned both as a site for the recognition of imperially sanctioned lines of transmission and for the recruitment of officials. Erudites of the Five Classics were the supervisory instructors there. The Imperial Academy did not differ from provincial and private institutions of learning in content. Study of the classical texts, and of the host of other texts such as the various apocrypha, medical treatises, divinatory or physiognomic texts were carried out everywhere. But it was only through official recognition at the Imperial Academy that the highest level of institutional and symbolic value was realized: for a text, a teacher, or a school or transmission. Durrant and Xu Fuguan both suggest that the imperial government's establishment of an official canon, with bureaucratic office to match, had bad consequences: It relocated scholarship and intellectual inquiry from the private and general sphere to the government bureaucracy, and it encouraged narrow specialization of a kind antithetical to the all-inclusive and synthetic project of Sima Qian or Dong Zhongshu. This may very well have been the case. From the perspective of the Empire of the Text, though, Sima Qian and Dong Zhongshu were not at odds with the establishment of official canonical transmission. In the writings attributed to them, Sima Qian and Dong Zhongshu established that the whole of the imperial project can be founded on textual knowledge. Official canonical transmission might have deviated from their grand synthetic projects in actual practice, but it followed logically from the nature of the claims made for textual authority itself.

The proximity, in Emperor Wu's reign, of the establishment of the canon, the library, of the Erudite positions, and the renewed and redirected Imperial University underscores the fact that canonical texts and pedagogy are intimately tied at inception. Our easy and casual association of the pedagogical scene with textual culture in Imperial China makes it easy to forget that such was not always the case. The archaeology of a common Han name for the canon itself—the Six Arts—recalls that the Imperial Academy was a scene of ritual archery before it was used for text-based instruction. In the *Rites of the Zhou* (probably a Han text in the form we have come to know it but dating from the Former Han at latest) the Six Arts are activities that account for nearly the whole of the "public" life of a gentleman: ritual, music, archery, charioteering, writing, and numbers. By the late Former Han, in the writings of Sima Qian, Dong Zhongshu, and others, the Six Arts are texts: the *Book of Rites*, the *Book of Music* (this is the one not in the list of the Five Classics), the *Book of Documents*, the *Book of Poetry*, and the *Spring and Autumn Annals*. Canonization is a foundational stage in the consolidation of textual authority.

I will use here a concept which I call the text-system. It refers to the material text, including appended exegeses, the contents of that text and its exegeses, the transmission mechanisms for the textual material, and the teachers and students involved in that transmission. At the apex of a text-system was the master, or teacher. A teacher would lend his authority to a particular textual variant and to a particular line of exegesis. References to the classical canon in the dynastic histories are generally not to the simple title of the classic, but to the text-system with which it was associated, as in the Guliang commentary to the *Spring and Autumn Annals*, or the Meng transmission of the *Yi jing*. Two Latter Han texts illustrate the operation of the text-system, the first a memorial in the biography of Lu Pi (37–114):

> Those who argue about a classic are transmitting the words of the primary teacher, and not their own opinions, so they cannot concede points to their opponents. If they do, then the Way is unclear, just as a straight-compass cannot be used if it is crooked. The questionee must make clear the bases of his answers. Speakers must establish the authority of their interpretations. . . . If schools are different, the representatives of each must be ordered to develop his school's line of interpretation, so that the meaning can be seen. (HHS: 884)

An individual interpretation that was affiliated to a school of interpretation had no standing. Xu Fang's famous memorial of 103 C.E. (HHS:

1500–01) shows that explicit and official scholarly filiation was the government's defense against and response to the threat of textual chaos. He traces the classics back to Confucius himself, and the "chapter-and-verse commentary" (about which more below) to Confucius's disciple Zixia. The establishment of the Erudites, the examination system, and the Imperial Academy was all to ensure that the line of transmission was as clear as possible. But by Xu's time, the system was in need of correction:

> I have observed the testing of erudites and students in the Imperial Academy, and all speak from their own minds; none follow the authority of a School's teaching. . . . I suggest that the examinations should be of a particular school's chapter and verse commentary, and should consist of fifty questions. Those who answer the most will be of the highest rank, those who cite text will be the highest experts. If an originary teacher is not followed exactly, or if there are internal contradictions in the answers, it will be judged as incorrect. (HHS: 1500)

The *Collected Biographies of the Scholars* (*Rulin zhuan*) sections of the early dynastic histories all list genealogies of exegetical transmission: A scholar would transmit not only the content of a particular classic, but a particular school of interpretation of a classic. Filiation to a particular line of textual transmission, and the politicosocial ties thus fostered, may have been more significant than identification with the school's intellectual content. This teacher-student relationship had a pseudokinship character that played an important role in the structuring of official life, a topic discussed further in the next chapter.

The establishment of official schools of textual transmission, as well as the association of an Erudite position with a particular school, structured the content of the exegetical work, of which the most common kind has been called "chapter-and-verse" commentary. The term is used to characterize the mode of commentary that elaborates on individual words or phrases to elucidate both the semantic sense and the judgment on the material implied by the use of the phrase. Later in the Han, the apocryphal commentaries, which found portents and prognostications in esoteric readings of the classics, were subsumed under chapter-and-verse commentary (Dull 1966; Anne Cheng 1985; Ngo 1976). Some of the surviving examples take the form of questions and answers, evidence, perhaps, of their origin in symposia or in situations of official examination. As the term implies, "chapter-and-verse" commentaries referred to the actual words of the canonical texts. They could, as suggested above, range considerably in content, and seemed to be infinitely expandable in length as well. Han criticism of the work of the scholastic schools often centered on the prolixity of the chapter-and-verse commentary. Two other modes of classicism were held up as alternatives to chapter-and-verse commentary. One type includes the grand syntheses, found in texts such as Dong Zhongshu's *Luxuriant Dew of the Spring and Autumn Annals* and He Xiu's later *Explicative Commentary on the Gongyang Transmission of the Spring and Autumn Annals.*[28] The other is the explanatory commentary, which is my translation of *xungu*. Explanatory commentary was shorter than the chapter-and-verse commentary, and served primarily to provide philological annotations on the classic texts; its object was more narrowly defined as the meaning of individual words and phrases. Although several biographies in the Han dynastic histories, such as Yang Xiong's in the *Han shu* and Huan Tan's in the *Hou han shu*, state that their subject "didn't do chapter-and-verse commentary, but only did explanatory commentary," the differences in content between the two modes of commentary were not always clear-cut. Although explanatory commentary tended to be shorter and more directed at the words of the classical text, chapter-and-verse commentary could include passages that were equivalent in content and style to the other kind. The dynastic histories seem to associate chapter-and-verse commentary with their particular school of transmission, as in "the chapter-and-verse of the Meng *Yi Jing*." Explanatory commentary seems to have been more "independent." The establishment of the canon and of officially recognized lines of canonical transmission in the early Han set the context for the various rivalries that have been used to characterize Han classicism, foremost among them the Old Text/New Text division. For Qian Mu, the dichotomy between chapter-and-verse and explanatory commentary is the most significant one of Han classicism. He identifies chapter-and-verse with the New Text version and generally with "school of transmission" text-systems, and "explanatory commentary" with Old Text scholarship (Qian Mu 1971: 200 ff).

Since the Qing dynasty, the Old Text/New Text controversy has become the primary lens through which Han thought and Han intellectual policy, particularly with regard to the classical canon, have been viewed.[29] Although there have been both exhaustive studies and cogent summaries of the Old Text/New Text so-called debate in the Han,[30] the sources allow for considerable disagreement about such basic issues as the nature of partisan identification, the degree of difference between the two camps, and even what was at stake.[31] My own view is that an overemphasis on the centrality of the partisan quality of the conflict has obscured other developments even within the restricted area of studies of the classical canon. To summarize the conflict: The "new" in New Text refers to the versions of the classics accorded imperial recognition in the Former Han, so called because they were written in *li* shu—the official Han script. The Old Texts probably also date from the Former Han, and in one common version of the story were purported to have been discovered in a wall of Confucius's former residence in the midst of a prince's remodeling project. These texts were written in the *zhuan* form of script that was common before the Qin writing reform in a style attributed to Cang Jie himself. The best known of the Old Texts, the *Zuo zhuan*, is so designated because of its association with the Old Text version of the *Spring and Autumn Annals*, on which it is supposedly a commentary.

The first name associated with the Old Text classics was the famous Kong Anguo, a descendant of Confucius and a New Text Erudite who tried unsuccessfully to present an Old Text version of the *Book of Documents* for official recognition around 100 B.C.E. Official recognition meant that a position of Erudite would be established for that particular line of textual transmission. The first significant Old Text partisan of record was the bibliographer Liu Xin (46 B.C.E.–23 C.E.), who continued the work of his father Liu Xiang (d. 8 C.E.). Liu Xin promoted Old Text versions of several of the classics, adding several to the previously extant list. These Old Text versions were made orthodox under the emperor Wang Mang's short-lived Xin dynasty, though even then they did not supplant the New Text versions, and they retained some degree of recognition throughout the Han. Still, official recognition remained largely the monopoly of the New Text Erudites. When the Dongguan Stone Classics were carved in 175, an event of seemingly momentous importance that I will discuss below, they were in the New Text versions. But when a new set of classics was carved during the (Cao) Wei dynasty in the 240s, the Old Text version had attained official recognition as well. The work of Zheng Xuan, an Old Text scholar, was the primary authority for the ascendancy of the Old Text versions at the end of the Han, and his exegetical authority remained paramount in classical scholarship through the Tang dynasty.

The history of Han classicism was also marked by three assemblies that debated and discussed official policy toward the classics. These assemblies are known by their location: Shique (51 B.C.E.), Yuntai (28 C.E.), and Bohuguan (White Tiger Hall, 79 C.E.).[32] The Shique assembly began as a discussion of the merits of the Gongyang and Guliang commentaries to the *Spring and Autumn Annals*, but ranged to a discussion of all the classics. Following the assembly the number of Erudites was increased, and there was no longer only a single Erudite for each classic.[33] The Yuntai discussions were about the merits of the Old Texts and resulted in a short-lived revival of the Erudite chair for the *Zuo zhuan,* which had been established at the end of the Former Han and continued under Wang Mang. The reasons for holding the Bohuguan discussions remain unclear, but the record of the discussions remains. It took the question-and-answer format of the Shique discussions, and ranged over the entire field of Han classicism, from textual issues to apocrypha, ritual, and family life. One participant was the famed scholar Jia Kui, an advocate of the Old Text and a favorite of Emperor Zhang, and an influential teacher to a generation of students, many of whom attained high office. No change in official policy resulted from the Bohuguan discussions. What is clear from the surviving records of all of these discussions, though, is that the divisions were not always well marked. A memorial by Jia Kui states, in fact, that there was a 70–80 percent overlap between the contents of the Old and New Text versions of the *Spring and Autumn Annals* (HHS: 1289).

The two versions are based on three areas of difference: the form of the script (whether in Han or pre-Qin writing); the actual content of the text (two versions of the same classic could vary by several hundred characters); and the exegetical tradition that structured a particular text-system's transmission. The first feature—the form of the script—is rarely re-marked upon by contemporary scholars, but it seems to have been a significant concern in Han writings.[34] This emphasis should remind us that the graphs were not simply transparent indicators of content. Examinees in the Han were tested on their ability to read different forms of script, and the weight attached to that competence suggests that the variant forms were not conceived as simple variations of the same thing but as having distinguishable material presence in themselves. The matter of different wording seems to have been less of a concern than one might expect: a lexical variant was more often cited as an example of faulty transcription than as expressive of a different content. The exegetical tradition was an important distinguishing feature but one that can easily be miscategorized. It is necessary, I believe, to treat exegeses within the context of the nature and practice of "schools" of thought, which is one of the parameters of the text-system.

The "school of thought" category has been an important one in Han and pre-Han intellectual history. Classical study and textual transmission were organized into clear lines of filiation. In recent scholarship on Han classicism, two terms are frequently used: master-filiation (*shifa*) text-systems and school (*jiafa*). The first refers to an exegetical tradition or a line of textual transmission that traces its roots to a specific teacher. The second refers to a more general "school of thought" that derives less directly from the thought of the original master of the school but characterizes all who are identified as members of a particular school. Scholars are far from united in accepting these as two separate phenomena. The dichotomization of master and school, mentioned above, is most closely associated with the late Qing classicist Pi Xirui, whose work has shaped the study of Han classicism for most of this century (Pi Xirui 1925). Pi Xirui theorizes that there was a tendency over the course of the Han away from "master" filiation and toward "schools." The *Collected Biographies of the Scholars* in the *Hou han shu* suggests, however, that this is an oversimplification, and many scholars treat the two phenomena as one. The existence of schools had an official and an unofficial character. Certain schools were recognized at court as official text-systems, but there were other text-systems, consisting of a master, an exegetical tradition, and a school of followers, outside of the court. The existence of the schools was probably a consequence of political initiative, material necessity, and the tendency for text-systems and their social groups to form textual communities, a phenomenon noted in many cultures prior to the rise of the figure of the individual reader, as in the modern period.

Schools of textual transmission, as well as institutions of learning (*xue*), were based on written texts but probably operated primarily in an oral mode. Mastery of a given text is expressed throughout the dynastic histories as the ability to "recite" it. The dynastic histories also attest in numerous anecdotes to the difficulties of obtaining material texts, even for men of means,[35] throughout the Former Han. References to book markets all date from the Latter Han and may have been a consequence of the more widespread adoption of paper (about which more below). It is a testimony, perhaps, to the power of textual authority within the text-system that the oral transmission of textual material, in the form of lectures, interrogations, or skill at recitation, is rarely mentioned. This is in contrast to the European medieval period, where there is substantial record of the oral dimension of textual culture. It is difficult, then, to offer more than tentative hypotheses about the oral culture of the text-systems. One possible consequence of the primarily oral medium of transmission, especially in the Former Han, was that the authority and integrity of a text became inseparable from the authority of the teacher. This extended from textual content to exegesis and was a defining feature of the text-system. The material text, though it was in one sense the determinant of a particular sociotextual matrix, shared ultimate authority with the founder or head of an exegetical tradition. Throughout most of the Han dynasty, the roles and relative authority of all who stood in relation to a text were highly codified. The authority of a particular text, likewise, was determined by the political and social milieu that structured its transmission, reception, and interpretation. I suspect that the "oral" character of transmission began to attenuate as the dynasty approached its close and as the empire of the text became more fully textual. (That is a hypothesis that I treat at greater length below.)

I have already suggested that the oral/literate dichotomy in thought that we associate with the work of Eric Havelock[36] and his followers might not be appropriate to a China that always gave discursive prominence to the textual. Havelock summarizes a 1978 article, "The Greek Concept of Justice from Its Shadow in Homer to Its Substance in Plato," as

the twin proposal that the notion of a moral value system which was autonomous, while at the same time capable of internalization in the individual
consciousness, was a literate invention and a Platonic one, for which the
Greek enlightenment had laid the groundwork, replacing an oralist sense of
"the right thing to do," as a matter of propriety and correct procedure.
(Havelock 1986: 54)

I have already noted evidence from the the Warring States period suggesting that ritualized violence and blood oaths were replaced by text-based
ritual. If Havelock's notion of oral and literate forms of consciousness has
analytical value for the Chinese case, and I am not certain that it does, it
would support our understanding of Warring States developments. The
phenomenon of oral textual transmission I refer to in the Han dynasty
was more similar to textual culture in the early medieval West, where texts
were more commonly "listened to" than read. Speculations about the oral
transmission of textual material, though, allow us to keep the social character of textuality in focus. The school, either the pedagogical institution
or the text-system, was not an environment whose product was the
"reader" but was primarily a system whose central analogue was government itself. From an early date, imperial government recognition of official schools of transmission was a central feature of the organization of
the empire of the text.

To recapitulate, the following dichotomies are commonly used to characterize Han classicism:

New Text	*Old Text*
chapter-and-verse commentary	explanatory commentary
"master" line of transmission or "school of transmission"	"unofficial" study

The notion of "unofficial study" is my own. It conveys the sense that
although Old Text or "explanatory commentary" practitioners sought
and occasionally received the official recognition primarily accorded to
the New Text school, this type of commentary was largely carried out
outside of established bureaucratic practice. There is an implied temporal
dimension to this organization as well, with the categories on the left side
giving way, by the end of the Han dynasty, to the categories on the right
side. Pi Xirui, as mentioned above, further temporalizes the evolution
from "master" to "school of thought." As is the case with Pi Xirui's
dichotomy, none of the above dichotomies is entirely clear-cut. Qian Mu
has demonstrated convincingly that the two supposed camps had far more
in common than was admitted by the Qing partisans of the New Text
school (Qian Mu 1925). He also shows that the texts or commentaries

themselves are not always neatly divisible into one or the other camp: Some identifications of a particular position as Old or New Text seem to have been made after the fact.

Jia Kui (30–101) was a respected scholar of his time. Although he never achieved high office, he had a reputation throughout the Latter Han as an eminent Confucian. His father had studied Old Text classics with Liu Xin, and Jia Kui continued the tradition. But he also taught the Elder Xiahou transmission of the *Shang shu*, a New Text transmission, and was an expert in the Five Schools transmission of the Guliang commentary on the *Zuo zhuan*, also a New Text transmission.[37] Jia Kui is not the only example of this kind. The evidence suggests, in fact, that all histories of Han classicism that rely on dichotomies such as those represented in the above chart or posit some kind of "bitter rivalry" between the two schools are going beyond what is warranted by the evidence.

In the final century of the Latter Han, classicism was dominated by figures who further blurred the dichotomies, scholars like Ma Rong, Zheng Xuan, and Cai Yong. Even the New Text partisan He Xiu, in his commentary on the Gongyang commentary, returns to the "grand syntheses" that marked the much earlier work of Dong Zhongshu.[38] The ascendancy of Zheng Xuan (who was offered and refused the post of Erudite) is regarded as marking the final victory of the Old Text side, but in my opinion it is one of many indications that the nature of classicism and textual culture in general had altered. My own sense of the matter is that by Zheng Xuan's time, the Old Text/New Text division was no longer an issue and that his ascendancy marked less the "victory" of the Old Text partisans than the consolidation of a new orientation toward a pure textuality—as opposed to the text-system at its most developed—characterized by oral or oral-based textual transmission. This transformation was significant both at the level of imperial government and at the level of family and clan instruction, which also had become more text based than it was earlier in the Han (Yu Qiding 1987: 156–165).

Texts in Their Place: Han Bibliography

The transformation to a more wholly text-centered classical canon was both abetted and signified by imperial efforts in bibliography, cataloguing, and bookcollecting. By the end of the Former Han, imperial court textual culture began to acquire the basic character that it would retain at least until the Song dynasty. The court collections aimed both at universality—all types of writings in the empire would be represented there[39]—and at normativization—court officials would determine the correct and official version of a given text.[40] Before the Han, texts seem to have pos-

sessed a power that could exceed their actual content. In characterizing
Warring States recordkeeping as the province of the *"scribes-devins-no-*
taires-annalistes, représentent l'organe de coordination [de la cour] tout à
la fois spéculative et normative,"[41] Leon Vandermeersch is one of many
scholars who have limned the talismanic, sacred character of preimperial
textual culture (Vandermeersch 1977–80, 2: 487). The contents of the official records also had strategic content, according to the dynastic histories. They were secrets, keys to the administration of the state. The *Han*
shu records that when Liu Bang, the future Han emperor Gaozu, conquered the Qin capital at Xianyang,

> his army commanders struggled to get to the storehouse of gold and silk and
> treasure in order to divide it up. Xiao He [Liu Bang's ally], however, first
> went to confiscate the laws, decrees, charts, and writings of the Qin officials.
> Liu Bang thus knew of all the impenetrable areas and passes throughout the
> empire, of population figures, strong and weak strategic points, and of all
> the worries and sufferings of the people. (HS: 2006)

Thus, the book tells us, Liu Bang was able to defeat his main rival, Xiang
Yu, who was close at his heels. We know from voluminous textual and
archaeological evidence that recordkeeping in the Han was minute and
detailed. But as the early imperial bibliographic enterprise progressed, the
work of textual acquisition was not solely a function of informational
content, as suggested in the anecdote above. Qin dynasty efforts at bibliographic control revealed that texts were seen as conveying power that was
neither informational nor "sacred." This power was derived from their
ability to serve as nexus for authority, an authority that, if uncontrolled
or independent of the organs of government, could threaten the political
authority of the central state.

The Han effort at bibliographic control is a continuation of the spirit
of the Qin policy, which recognized that authority over the text-systems
needed to be consolidated at the imperial center. Although there are scattered records of bibliographic policy before Emperor Wu's reign, the *Han*
shu Yiwen zhi locates the beginning of the real textual recovery work at
that time.

> So [Emperor Wu] established a policy of collecting writings, created the post
> of official copyists, and, extending even down to the level of the various
> schools of philosophers and their commentaries, had them all stored in the
> Bifu. By the time of the Emperor Cheng, many writings had been lost, so
> Receptionist Chen Nong was dispatched to look for missing writings
> throughout the empire. Grand Master for Splendid Happiness Liu Xiang
> edited and compiled the classics, commentaries, philosophical works, poetry,
> and fu; Infantry Commandant Ren Hong edited and compiled military texts;

Grand Astrologer Yin Xian edited and compiled works on astronomy, ca-lendrics, and divination; Attending Physician Li Zhuguo edited and com-piled works on medical formulas and cures. When each writing was com-plete, Liu Xiang would make a list of the *pian* [n.b. this term will be discussed below; here it could mean chapter], summarize the main ideas, and record and memorialize to the throne. When he died, Emperor Ai charged his son Liu Xin, Commandant-in-Chief of Chariots, to finish his father's work. Liu Xin amassed all of the writings and presented his Seven Categori-cal Summaries to the emperor. (HS 30: 1701)

The classification system of the Han divided works into (1) classics and their commentaries; (2) philosophical works; (3) poetry and *fu*; (4) mili-tary texts; (5) astronomy, calendrics, and divination; (6) medical formulas and cures.[42] When considering this effort, it is important to reflect upon our contemporary assumptions about book organization. It is not self-evident that books should be catalogued at all, much less by subject cate-gories. In the medieval West, books were most frequently catalogued ac-cording to their owners' names, not the books' authors or contents, which could be quite various. Modern bibliographic work reveals most of its ideological assumptions in its classificatory categories: Literature, for example, as we know it today, is a relatively recent arrival on the scene, as are most of its subdivisions. The first bibliographers of record in imperial China, Liu Xiang and his son Liu Xin, were not only cataloguers but editors, compilers, commentators, authors, and even, as we have seen, par-tisan advocates of particular schools of transmission. These functions were not separable. Authorship was an evolving category in early imperial China, and what modern thinking would call derivative work— commentary, annotation, editorship—was not so considered in the Han.[43] The Lius' bibliographic work was to be as influential in the history of imperial bibliography as Sima Qian was to be in historiography. Their contribution to the construction of the authority accorded to the classical texts in their textual form, as opposed to their orally or institutionally transmittable form, was part of a process joined one hundred years later by Xu Shen's dictionary, which was explicitly conceived as an aid to a reading of the entire textualized canon. There is no point, of course, at which the text-system ends and the text emerges in its unencumbered purity. I am suggesting, though, that within the text-system one can ob-serve an evolving orientation toward the authority of the material text itself, with less dependence on its social, official, or pedagogical determi-nants.

The canonization process begun under Emperor Wu clearly had its ar-chitectural counterpart in the establishment of the imperial library, the Bifu, the name of which probably signifies that it was a restricted area.[44]

That the collection had deteriorated so much, according to the passage above, in the fifty years between the reigns of Emperors Wu and Cheng suggests that the collection was not only a repository, or a source for reference, but was actively used. This is further indicated in the "*Fu* on the Western Capital," by Ban Gu:

> There were also:
> Tianlu and the Stone Canal Pavilions,
> Those repositories of documents and writings.
> Here were commanded:
> Elders, diligent in instruction,
> Famous scholars, preceptors, and tutors
> To lecture and discourse on the Six Classics,
> To examine and compare discrepancies in the texts
> (Knechtges, trans. 1982: 127)

This describes some of the activity that characterizes the text-system—the work of teaching and discussion that took largely oral form but was centered on a written text. The workings of the text-systems were becoming more standardized in the Former Han. The suggestion here is that the authority of the texts had been established to the point where physical proximity to their officially recognized versions itself conveyed power and authority to the teachers and students. But the texts also acquired their power and authority from their physical presence at court. In other locations they were invested with a different kind of authority. There are numerous references to private collections in the *Han shu*, and, unlike during the Qin dynasty, the private collection of books does not seem to have been viewed as a threat to central authority. Liu De, Prince Xian and father of Liu Xiang, was, like Liu An, the king of Huainan, a prominent book collector.[45]

> Liu De received valuable books from the people. Books given to him had to be written well and carefully, and he would keep the authentic texts, paying for them with gold and silk. Thus philosophers and experts from throughout the empire, thinking nothing of distance, would offer old books from the ancestors to the king. Thus he had many books, as many as the Han court. (HS: 2410)

A surviving fragment of Liu Xiang's bibliographical notes on the *Guanzi* shows that the Lius' bibliographic work was dependent on private collections and that the work of collation often involved consultation of editions received from several different sources, who were named in the notes as the owners of the texts (Van der Loon 1952: 360). Only the text as combined, collated, and assembled at court, though, had full auratic value.

The idea of a separate space for collected texts, with an authoritative classical canon at their center, marks another kind of departure from an earlier conception of court textuality. In the Han, the texts become dissociated from their filiations to specific bureaucratic offices, and conceived more broadly as the totality of knowledge and source of official expertise. Classical instruction would prepare its recipients for *all* offices. Qing thinker Zhang Xuecheng imagined a biblio-bureaucratic utopia, where texts, instruction, and bureaucratic duty coincide perfectly:

> With offices came laws, and so the laws were embodied in the offices. With laws came books, and so each office preserved its own books. With books came learning, and so teachers perpetuated this learning. With learning came professional traditions, and so disciples practised these professions. The offices, their special functions, the learning, and the professions all had a single source, and government in the empire consisted in a unity of letters. Since there were no writings of private parties, it followed that the divisions of administrative responsibility corresponded to the divisions within bibliography, and there was never any system of bibliography apart from this. Writings of later times must be traced back to the Six Classics. The Six Classics are not the books of Confucius, but are actually the old statutes of the offices of Zhou.[46]

The *Yiwen zhi* shows that Liu Xiang's records filiated the philosophical schools' writings to particular pre-Qin administrative offices, but this was not the system used for the Six Classics. Han bibliographic practice seemed to aim not toward the synthetic, canonical reductionism of Zhang Xuecheng's particular classicism, but toward standardization, authoritativeness, and comprehensiveness, which seem to have been the primary requirements of the era of establishment of textual culture.[47]

Archaeological discoveries in this century have laid to rest an anxiety about pre-Qin texts that has surfaced frequently since Kang Youwei registered his suspicion that bibliographers Liu Xiang and Liu Xin had played a role in the formation of the classical canon that was much closer to "author" than to "bibliographer."[48] Pre-Liu Xiang versions of various texts have been found, and their deviation from received versions of certain texts has been slight enough to claim that the Liu's work on the classical canon was in fact closer to "bibliographer" and "cataloguer" as we understand the terms today. On other texts, though, their work was more substantial. Surviving evidence suggests that Liu Xiang, and probably Liu Xin as well, seem to have been largely responsible for the received forms of several texts, for example, the *Guanzi*. If descriptions of the excessive length of chapter-and-verse commentaries are accurate, then the Lius might easily have done considerable editorial work on the exegetical literature. It is clear that the Lius did not seek a copy of every book in the empire. They sought only what they determined to be the representative version of the particular text or commentary that they wished to include. In Liu Xiang's *Separate Notes* (Bielu) he records:

> When one person reads the book and accords the former and latter parts of the text looking for errors and correcting them, that is "revision" (jiao). When one person holds the book and one reads the book, like enemies in combat, that is "collation" (chou).[49]

This passage implies a final version that might differ from both of the source versions.

Judging where the Lius stood on the author-bibliographer continuum ultimately requires a judgment about what constitutes the fundamental integrity of a "book." This is not an easy judgment to make. There are difficulties presented by the material dimension of Han texts, which I will address in a later section of this chapter, but bibliographic terminology is somewhat obscure as well. The works listed in the *Yiwen zhi* seem to have consisted mainly of bamboo and silk. The terms *pian* and *juan* are used to indicate the length of, or the number of units within, a particular record. The difficulty is that these terms can have several senses. Number of units of writings or drawings on silk are always expressed in *juan*, but the term is also used with texts written on multiple bamboo strips. It seems to be a general term that could be translated as "roll." A *pian* can refer both to a physical unit of text (the bamboo classifier suggests that it might be a given quantity of bamboo strips) and to a unit of text corresponding to an English word like "volume," "section," "chapter," or "version." Song scholar Zheng Qian notes that the *pian/juan* distinction seems to have been clearer in some sections of the *Yiwen zhi* than in others, with the sections on the classics and the philosophers showing the most overlap between categories.[50] It is difficult to determine from the *Yiwen zhi* what, exactly, the basic textual units were: chapter, section, or work. Liu Xiang wrote a notice on each *pian* and memorialized the notice to the throne; a *pian* must, therefore, have had a certain coherency. Most titles consist of multiple *pian*, but it is nowhere clear how the contents of a title were finally determined. This is an area that was subject to considerable variation in preprinting days. Arguing ex nihilo is risky, but it is possible that at Liu Xin and Liu Xiang's time the social life of a given title was such that its material unity was but one factor of its totality. The bureaucratic office, the pedagogical operation, and the exegetical and transmission system that surrounded a text was as much a part of the text's existence as the bamboo or silk.

Textuality Takes Command

The discussion of the relative merits of different text-systems, particularly the Old Text/New Text division, accelerates in the Latter Han, following the completion of the Lius' initial bibliographic work. Although the Old Text/New Text division was later claimed to have been the main issue of Han classicism, semiotic principles suggest that any story of factional conflict must take one of a limited number of narrative forms. To say "Old Text/New Text conflict" is, regardless of the supporting evidence, to generate something like the actual narrative that most scholars have continued to circulate. But an overinvestment in that fairly stock narrative might obscure a different, though perhaps more important story. Let us start from the most partisan side of the conflict: the charges leveled against the New Text partisans in pro–Old Text writings. Xu Shen's *Shuo wen*, the *Han shu*, primarily authored by his contemporary Ban Gu, and the writings of bibliographer Liu Xin are representative examples of Old Text partisanship. The passage above (p. 39) from the postface to the *Shuo wen*, "one must follow the old writings and not distort everything," is something one might expect in the context of the Old Text claim for the authority of comparatively greater antiquity. The next line, though, is a direct invocation of the textual: Invoking Confucius as commentator on textual transmission, Xu Shen's postface here makes the claim that primary authority in reading and understanding a text lies not in the filiation to an authoritative school of interpretation, or in the official recognition of a school of interpretation in the Classical Erudite system, but in the physically extant written text. Contrasted to this are "pronouncements," *oral* teachings, which are substandard, heterodox, and confused. Immediately following is the statement that *written* language is the foundation of classical learning. Old Text partisan defenses of the authority of the *Zuo zhuan* rested largely on its author's purported firsthand knowledge of the master's teachings. This was not framed as a defense of oral transmission, however. The Zuo transmission was more reliable precisely because it had *not* passed through generations of oral transmission, but had taken written form earlier. This emphasis on the textual form itself is new, and is part of the orientation toward the centralized and standardized textuality that I am claiming for the period. Below are some further examples from Ban Gu's "Summary on the Classics" in the *Yiwen zhi*, the Liu Xin text being a letter included in Ban Gu's biography of Liu Xin in the *Han shu*:

> Scholars of antiquity were able to master the tradition of any single classic in three years, even while tilling their fields and maintaining their families. They could master the basic point, since they applied themselves to the clas-

sic's text. Thus, they could devote little time to study, but still "amass considerable virtue" (cf. *Yi jing*), and thereby, at thirty, command firm mastery of the Five Classics. When in later generations after the texts of the Classics and their Commentaries had become corrupt, and full of gaps, the Erudites no longer kept in mind the saying "Inquire well, but leave aside the irresolvable questions," (Analects). Rather, they left the actual text behind, avoided questions, and, in their zeal for florid and empty lofty analyses, destroyed the integrity of the graphs of the texts. Explanation of a five-graph phrase could reach 20,000–30,000 words. This tendency accelerated with time so that later, if a youth devoted himself to a single classic, he would be a white-haired old man by the time he could say one word about it. They took refuge in their accustomed ways, and calumnied anything they hadn't seen. They rendered themselves in the end isolated and irrelevant. Such is the the disaster of the scholars. (*Yiwen zhi:* 1723)

In the past the scholars who edited texts didn't consider the lacunae caused by defective texts. With great irresponsibility and mindless conformity with the vulgar, they broke up passages and took graphs apart. Their obscure pronouncements and prolix analyses multiplied. Scholars could grow old before they could fully exhaust the teaching of a single classic's commentarial tradition. They trusted oral transmission and rejected written records. They affirmed worthless teachers and denied the teachings of the ancients. . . . They preserved and guarded these superficial and defective texts, fearful of exposure and the spoiling of their self-interested projects. They had none of the public spirit that would lead them to follow the good and serve principles. Some were jealous at heart, and loath to examine their real feelings. But their sycophantic coteries marched in step, with their yes's and no's in unison. They shut out the Old Texts, regarded the *Shang shu* as complete, and said that the *Zuo zhuan* was not a commentary on the *Spring and Autumn Annals*. What a pity! (HS: 1970)[51]

The first passage is not the explicit attack on oral transmission that we find in the second. It consists mainly of the antiobscurantism and antipedantry that characterized most attacks on the chapter-and-verse excess. The concern in both the Ban Gu and Liu Xin selections is for the integrity and wholeness of the classical texts, and, by extension, with the integrity and wholeness of the whole classical canon. Hairsplitting obscurantism is guilty on several counts. It leads to overspecialization on a single text at the expense of wider mastery and the attendant level of "spiritual power"; it engenders a prolix exegetical effusion that overwhelms, in quantity of writing, the classical texts themselves; and in devoting excessive exegetical energy to a single word or phrase, it compromises the textual integrity of the individual classical work. Liu Xin's letter even suggests that the supposed *physical* deterioration of the classical texts was a consequence of the lax standards during Emperor Cheng's reign. Already by Liu Xin's time, and more markedly later in the Latter Han, the text-systems of the schools of transmission had become too elaborate and multifaceted for textual authority to be clear.

The various arguments against the New Text transmission set out the following set of dichotomies (bearing in mind that the case presented here is wholly from the anti–chapter-and-verse position):

orthodox	*heterodox*
fidelity to written text	fidelity to line of exegetical transmission
generalist	specialist
tolerance for unclear unknowable words or passages	overly speculative exegeses; needless exhaustiveness
"public-spiritedness"; openness to dialogue	cliquish closed-mindedness
economy of exegetical production	exegetical excess

The anti–New Text position, represented on the left side of the list above, was an implicit argument in favor of textual authority. Textual authority in general was not predicated solely on the sheer volume of textual production overall, although the increasingly common use of texts for minute record keeping is a related phenomenon.[52] The prolixity of New Text exegetical production is blameworthy because it contributes more to the authority of a particular school than to textual authority in general. The suggestion in the passages above, in fact, is that the New Text exegetical prolixity is a function of insufficient authority accorded to the primary texts themselves, which must be the root of all textual authority.

At stake here are the parameters within which the categories of the official and the private are determined; this is a negotiation that must be made by every governmental power. In the Latter Han, in passages like those quoted above, there emerges a position generally associated with Old Text scholarship holding that textual authority and integrity, rather than person-centered transmission systems, are better guarantors of a true "public" life. The Xu Shen and the Ban Gu passages refer explicitly to points at which the classical texts resist, or should properly resist, exegesis: Xu Shen cites the passage from the *Analects* about scribes who will not leave a blank, and Ban Gu, the passage about putting aside the points that are in doubt. Here, somewhat paradoxically, is a demonstration of true textual authority: The canonical texts will exceed the abilities of their interpreters. A classic should not be reducible solely to its interpretation.

The Dongguan Stone Classics, in New Text versions, were carved in 175 C.E. under the supervisorship of Cai Yong. By the latter half of the second century, though, the ideology of textual authority reigned supreme. This was the period of Ma Rong, Zheng Xuan, and Cai Yong himself. They represented a new position for the scholar-official, one to which the Old Text/New Text controversy as formulated in the Bohuguan discussions had little application. A classical canon-centered textuality itself had triumphed over oral transmission, over the authority of a particularist interpretation, over localisms, over the text-systems composed of master, students, reciters, listeners, texts, and commentary. Canonicity, as it had been understood since the Han, had subtly changed form and had itself become a more fully textualized function. The fact of canonization no longer rested on the administrative recognition of a particular school of transmission or on the establishment of an Erudite position (although Erudites continued to exist) but on the idea of the full scope of representational power that inhered in the canonical texts themselves, as a repository of cultural values and as material objects. Social and political life, from the administrative to the apparently personal, was apprehensible in its entirety through the canonical texts.

Today, in the last decade of the twentieth century, questions of canonicity have been framed largely in conflictual terms of inclusion and exclusion. Harold Bloom's survey, *The Western Canon*, avowedly rejects both the attack on the western canon for its role in the strengthening of ruling-class hegemony (the position of the "school of resentment") and the defense of the canon on the grounds of a societal need for transmitting the essential civilizational values found in the canon's timeless truths. Still, in arguing for an aesthetic canon, Bloom also defines the corpus in terms of struggle, namely, the canonical texts' struggle with one another for inclusion. As we have seen in the history of Han classicism, the struggle in early imperial China was not primarily over simple inclusion in the canon but over official recognition of an exegetical tradition. The *Zuo zhuan*, itself proposed for inclusion as an Old Text transmission in the Han, took the form of a commentary on the *Spring and Autumn Annals* (although that may not have been the form taken by the text originally).[53] The discursive prominence accorded to commentary shaped the entirety of the textual scene. Intertextual relations were presumed from the start, and the entirety of writings within a school of transmission referred of course to the original classics. Early Han bibliographers also categorized writings by "school." By the end of the Han, though, "school" has an expanded sense, referring to something not unlike the earlier school-of-transmission text system, but now more fully textualized.

Near the end of the Han, two letters, Cao Pi's "Letter to Wu Zhi" and Cao Zhi's "Letter to Yang Dezu," use the phrase *cheng yijia zhi yan* "to establish one's own school of thought" as signifying the highest praise accordable to a written text. The source of the expression is probably Sima Qian's well-known "Letter to Ren An," in a section describing the composition of the *Shi ji* itself. In Cao Pi's letter, as he reviews the work of his contemporaries, only Xu Gan's *Discourse on the Central*, a text discussed at greater length in chapter 4, is said to have achieved the status of "a school of thought," which is now associated with a textualized temporal permanence: "Xu Gan wrote the *Zhong lun* in twenty-odd chapters, which has become a school of thought. His phrases are classical and refined, worthy of being transmitted to posterity. The man will be immortal."[54] Cao Zhi uses the phrase following an expression of disdain for belletristic writing in describing his second priority for his life's ambition, should he be unable to realize his first ambition of service to the state.

> But if my ambition bears no fruit and I cannot put my ideals into practice, then I will, like Confucius before me, collect material from the historians' draft records, judge what is good and what is bad in the morals of our times, determine when goodness and justice have been attained, and thus set up the words of a school of thought. Even though they may not be treasured eternally in some famous mountain,[55] they may be handed down to those who have the same tastes as mine. But this is something I would like to do when my head is white, not something I should talk of today! The reason I am not ashamed of saying these things is because I am confident that you understand me, as Hui Shih (understood Chuang-tzu).[56]

Both Sima Qian's historiographical project and Cao Zhi's letter look to Confucius, as author/compiler of the *Spring and Autumn Annals,* as a model. This was the central text of the Han canon and was the subject of most exegetical debate. Cao Zhi's letter shows how the textual scene has changed. By the time of the letter's composition, Sima Qian's *Shi ji* itself had reached near-canonical status; it is a source of intertextual reference in much of late Han prose and poetry. Sima Qian's own work constituted a bid for textual immortality at a time when the project of textual consolidation had just begun. By Cao Zhi's time the scene of writing implicitly recognizes the ability of a text to find a community of readers over time in the absence of its author and separated from each other. "A school of thought," by the end of the Han, requires neither academy nor Erudite, but simply a textual existence.

Written on Bamboo, Silk, Wood, Stone, and Paper: The Materiality of the Text

> Works and discourses exist only when they become physical realities and are inscribed on the pages of a book, transmitted by a voice reading or narrating, or spoken on the stage of a theater. (Chartier 1994: ix)

Roger Chartier's reminder, which sums up the work of a recent generation of "new philologists" working with written materials from the West
of antiquity and early medieval times, turns our attention to physical form
as a necessary determinant of content. In a recent essay that is part of this
tradition of scholarship, D. F. McKenzie cites with approval John Locke's
*An Essay for the Understanding of St. Paul's Epistles. By Consulting St.
Paul Himself*, which "quite explicitly addresses the question of intention,
and the role of typographic form in obscuring or revealing it"(McKenzie
1985: 46). Locke's complaint is that dividing the Scriptures into chapters
and verses allows the text to be treated as a collection of fragments, which
disrupts those sections that originally might have composed sustained,
unitary, and coherent arguments. The potential for the scriptural fragment to be used for certain polemical purposes would be compromised,
though, were the text arranged as a continuous argument. Locke is aware
that the stakes in typography can be high. McKenzie cites the parliamen-
tary debate over gay rights in New Zealand, where "members shot biblical verses from one side of the house to the other like paper darts in a
school room" (McKenzie 1985) as a confirmation of Locke's reservations
about the possibilities for distortion inherent in the fragmentary typography of the Epistles. McKenzie's argument, one that Roger Chartier devel-
ops as well, is that a renewed attention to the materiality of the text rein-
troduces questions of the author and intentionality into critical discourse,
after their successive banishments by New Critical, structuralist, and
poststructuralist criticism. Further, this materially based evidence of author or intent is less compromised ideologically than in its earlier incarnation.

I bring up this example from the West because it reminds students of
China of the ways the canonical classics have been used since the earliest
times. No text, perhaps, was used in its fragments to such an extent as the
Book of Songs, a fact scarcely reflected in its typographical arrangement.
McKenzie's eagerness to locate typographical evidence of authorial intention obscures those aspects of the social life of texts that influence or
predetermine what typographical arrangements are able to take place. It
is generally accepted that the codex, the earliest form of the book as we
know it today, gained its ascendancy in Roman times because it was favored for use in the Christian community.[57] This was in part due to ease
of reference to specific parts of the text, i.e., for partial or fragmentary
reading. Perhaps, then, Christian textual culture encouraged the fragment
from its inception. A visit to any Bible study class in the United States
today would confirm that partiality toward the fragment flourishes and
that polemical use of the fragments characterizes a politicized Christian-
ity. Anecdotal evidence about use of the Chinese classics in the early imperial period suggests, however, that both the whole text and the fragment

were valued and circulated, albeit in different situations. Reading a typo-graphical intentionality might prove to be as problematic as the authorial intentionality it was intended to replace. To paraphrase Marx, men arrange and compose their own texts, but they do not arrange and compose them just as they please, under circumstances chosen by themselves.

Records of the acts of reading and writing are fairly common. Unfortunately, in the case of early imperial China, the records of the materiality of texts, as well as physical descriptions of human handling of the texts, allow for too few conclusions about material textual culture. We read of a group of literati composing spontaneous pieces on command at an out-ing, of poor scholars who stay up all night reading, of officials carrying writing materials into battle. T. H. Tsien, in *Written on Bamboo and Silk*, has given a comprehensive picture of textual materiality in the early imperial period, one that, impressively, has required little modification following recent archaeological investigation. Yet significant questions remain. The material contents of the imperial library are not always clear. We are often ignorant about whether a writing was on silk, bamboo or wooden strips, or wood tablets. A fragment commonly cited in bibliographic history reads:

> Liu Xiang has served the Emperor Cheng for more than twenty years in the custody and collection of books. They were first written on bamboo because writing could be changed easily by shaving the tablets. When texts were ready for copying, they were written on silk.[58]

Silk, however, may still have accounted for only a small percentage of the collection in the library, even if one is generous in assigning *juan* figures to silk rather than bamboo. Each material had advantages and disadvantages. Silk was the most expensive material, but it took ink easily and allowed size variation to accommodate maps, charts, or drawings. It is recorded in the *Chuxueji*, a seventh-century encyclopedia, that writings on silk were cut to the length of the texts themselves.[59] It was easily transportable, and, as the passage cited above suggests, silk was used for presentation copies as well. Yang Xiong's "Reply to Liu Xin" reports that in compiling the *Fang yan*, he traveled with four-inch-wide white silk and a brush to record his data, copying it onto wood with lead when he returned home.[60] Bamboo, cut into strips that held one, or at most two, vertical lines of graphs, was easy to transport and inexpensive. It was probably the most widely used writing material in the Former Han, and it remained in use throughout the Latter Han and beyond. It was used extensively for record keeping and for official versions of texts in collections. Bamboo, like wood, could be scraped clean, and new text could be written on it. Wood was also inexpensive and easy to use. It was used commonly for short documents in block form, with multiple lines of texts, or it could be cut into strips like bamboo and bound together with cloth or cord for longer or shorter texts. Bamboo and wood were frequently cut into officially mandated standard sizes depending on the nature of the texts (Tsien 1962: 104–7).

Bamboo and wood, when cut and prepared for writing, were used only for purposes of writing. Silk and paper are distinctive in that they were used for many purposes—quotidian, official, and ritual. Silk was of course a common currency in the Han. Although there were specific silk preparations that were preferred for writing, the material's status as a medium of exchange could easily have contributed to the ability of silk texts to serve as presentation copies. That paper predates the supposed invention by Cai Lun is now widely accepted. The HHS mentions that paper and bamboo versions of the *Zuo zhuan* were given to a group of Jia Kui's students in 76 C.E. (HHS: 1234). Ts'ien quotes a letter by Cui Yuan (d. 143) saying that "I am sending you the works of Xuzi in ten rolls. Being unable to afford a copy of silk, I provide only a paper copy" (Ts'ien 1962: 139). There is not, however, widespread evidence that paper was a low-prestige material. In the later part of the Latter Han, in fact, it is often unclear whether paper or silk is being referred to. It seems likely that a widespread adoption of paper was in part responsible for burgeoning textual circulation toward the end of the dynasty, although this cannot be proved because paper survives less well than any other medium of writing.

Reading texts on scrolls—whether of silk, paper, or bamboo or wood strips threaded together—is most efficient when the texts are short or consist of familiar material that is reread. Expandability, however, would seem to have been an inherent possibility of the silk or bamboo scroll. It is not surprising that so much textual production would be in the form of commentary, which, like a lengthening scroll itself, could be an extension of the classical text. It is possible that the complaints against the prolixity of chapter-and-verse commentary were reactions to the possibility for nearly infinite expansion of scrolled material and a preference for shorter rolls of cloth or paper, which must have been easier to handle. The evidence suggests that as the Latter Han progressed there was a greater proliferation of writings that could fit on an easily handled piece of cloth or paper. *Fu* (rhyme prose), for example, were generally shorter at the end of the Han than they had been during the reign of Emperor Wu. Letters, a flourishing literary form throughout the Latter Han, were also generally a short form. A virtue of the scroll format, for any of the scrolled materials, is ease of copying, a central activity in early imperial textual culture. A scroll is easy to lay flat and adjust in width, thus permitting writing material to be placed at its side.

Materially inclined textual historians argue, with reason, that a consideration of the physical character of texts gives useful indications of the social life of the texts: the actual human use of the textual material. In manuscript culture, when one physical text is presumed to have many readers—or, in most cases, listeners—the social character of the texts exceeds its physicality. But what about texts that were read rarely, if at all? The wood strips from Juyan, a cache of administrative records from a frontier post, dating from 100 B.C.E. to 100 C.E., for example, have been subject to exhaustive study, and have even been partially translated into English. It is likely that they have had many more readers in the twentieth century than they had during the two centuries of their composition. Administrative texts—records of proceedings, inventories, legal codes, and so on—form a category of writing that designates texts designed primarily not for reading, but for monitoring and administration, regardless of the texts' physical character or mode of reproduction. This category of text—and I would suggest that the Juyan strips belong in it—is one I would characterize as the "not unwritten," texts that exist because they are ordered to exist—texts whose absence would subject the author to blame or punishment and whose existence itself is thus not primarily communicative, but performative of adherence to a regime. The not unwritten text is, because of its very existential performativity, less conditioned by its materiality than are reader-directed texts. Its primary function, like bureaucratic records, was to exist.

Canonized texts were texts to be read and consulted, but they were also texts whose physical existence was often the consequence of imperial or official command. Their physical existence undoubtedly had multiple functions, but I would hypothesize that the primary function in the Han was auratic. The physical existence of the authoritative versions of the texts signifies intellectual and ideological authority, and it signifies the location of the texts as a center of transformative power. This was of critical concern at the imperial court, but the records of private book collections, such as those belonging to Liu De from the Former Han and Cai Yong of the Latter Han, suggest that these scholars' ability to attract followers and students was partially related to the size of their libraries. Scholars who sought the source versions of authorized classics would naturally be drawn to their presence. The authoritative versions of the classics must have been used regularly for reading as well, before groups or by individuals. The material form of the authorized versions would clearly be more of an issue than with other kinds of texts. The arguments cited above against chapter-and-verse commentary did have a material dimension: There was an implicit complaint about the length of the exegesis in relation to the classical text. The primary polemical concern, though, was for the "correctness" of the classics.

Textual integrity was stated as an imperial concern in the Western Han;

it was one of the impetuses behind the construction of libraries, the establishment of official schools of transmission, the bibliographic work of Liu
Xiang and Liu Xin, and the discussions held at Yuntai, Shiquge, and the
Bohuguan. How then, one wonders, was textual integrity so easily compromised? Texts became lost in times of political disturbance. Imperial
collections were destroyed between the Qin and Han, in the Wang Mang
interregnum, and in the Dong Zhuo usurpation toward the end of the
Han. In the Latter Han one reads of concern over the deterioration of the
texts and the subsequent need for new, authoritative versions in the reigns
of Emperors He, An, Shun, and Ling. An authoritative version of a text,
it seems, could become unavailable in fewer than ten years, even without
political unrest or natural disaster.[61] The different materials exposed the
texts to various dangers. Bamboo and wood, which needed to be bound
together if the texts were composed of multiple pieces (which was nearly
always the case with bamboo strips), frequently lost their binding material, and the texts that they had constituted became scattered and corrupt.
Silk was sometimes commandeered for other uses. The HHS records that
following Dong Zhuo's destruction of Loyang and all of the libraries
there, "volumes, bamboo records, and writings were scattered and lost.
Charts and writings on silk, if large in size, were used as tent covers; if
small, as bags (HHS: 2548). (In another context, Yan Zhitui remarks that
he never used paper with quotations or commentaries from the Five Classics for toilet purposes. Teng 1968: 20–21.)

Still, it is puzzling that despite massive evidence of imperial concern
over textual integrity, particularly in the Latter Han, a stable and permanent solution was not proposed until 175 c.e., with the carving of the
stone classics. That may have reflected the residual power of the schools
of transmission: The more a text was embedded in its text-system, the
more it was subject to the human vagaries of death, exile, and absence.
What, though, of the mental existence of the classics, lodged in the memories of those scores of scholars whom the histories allege could recite the
canonical classics after one look or at an astonishingly early age? Ray
Bradbury's novel *Fahrenheit 451* is set in a bibliophobic dystopia where
all printed matter is burned by agents of the state. Hidden in the countryside is the underground resistance, where each member has committed a
book to memory with the intent of transmitting its contents to succeeding
generations, thus ensuring the viability of textual culture beyond the dark
times. Han writings and the later dynastic histories suggest that every
literate person had committed the canonical classics to memory. But there
is no evidence that these memories were ever tapped in times of textual
degradation. Following either a singular catastrophe or a gradual deterioration, the desired solution was to seek texts from private collections.
Oral transmission was, as I have stated earlier, criticized and distrusted

by the major proponents of textual culture. Bradbury's figure of the memorists embodies the position that is criticized by bibliographic theorists and historians like D. F. McKenzie, as well as in the work of the new philologists: A text's existence is reducible to its "content." The Han priority accorded to the material text is clear.

All of the written evidence from the Han suggests that textual anxiety largely concerns distortion of content. The only significant formal concern expressed is over graphic style. But this is perhaps indicative of a difference between alphabetic writing and the sinographs. In the West, in antiquity and in early medieval times, the practice of reading aloud, even when reading to oneself, was common enough for its omission to be worthy of note, as in the oft-cited passage in Augustine's *Confessions*. Alphabetic textual culture contains, besides the letters and vowels themselves, numerous indices of pronunciation to an extent that the sinographs do not. Although there are indications that standards of recitation-pronunciation were under way toward the end of the Han, a development that by the Tang dynasty would be fully developed, one must assume that the worlds of the oral and the textual did not closely coincide over the course of the Han. Recitation from memory and oral declamation seem to have been in different spheres from the textual, which was a form of authority that had its roots in nonvariability and consistency.

In Western "new philology," much of the materiality of the texts studied, such as typographical layout, punctuation, orthography, and capitalization, allows for hypotheses about the complex interaction between text and body, particularly eye, mouth, ear. The more textuality becomes subject to convention and standardization (orthographic, typographical, etc.), the fewer clues its materiality provides. The graphic standardization realized over the course of the Qin-Han was part of a project that implied a more independent and stable materiality than that provided by, for example, an alphabet prior to orthographic standardization. The letters of an alphabet, given their references to vocalization and their function as combinatory elements, require that standardization take the form of a regime of combination that postdates the existence of the letters themselves. The sinographs, on the other hand, appear in their official versions as evidence of prior standardization. So the physicality of the sinographs has more of the ideological work of materiality already performed. The quotation on the first page of this chapter—"the government of Kings Wen and Wu [of the Zhou] is laid out on the wood and bamboo tablets," makes a claim for a performative materiality—one that gives an indication of the stakes in the authoritative written versions of the texts. The Han was an age of omens and portents. One of the most important tasks of court scholars, across the New Text/Old Text and other divisions, was to read the material world for signification. The canonical texts were already supramaterial in that they were signifiers par excellence. Attention to and anxiety over their actual materiality—the coherence or incoherence of the sinographical content—was to be expected. Because one of their primary functions was simply to exist, their layout, arrangement, and division structure were less urgent issues.

The signal event in the material history of late Han classicism, and one that emblematized the supramaterial character of the official version, was the carving of the classical canon in stone in 175–183 C.E. The records of this event allow for some insights into late Han material textuality.

> Cai Yong felt that the classics, due to the length of time since the days of the sages, had suffered many errors in graphs, and that ignorant scholars had made incorrect interpolations, thus misleading scholars in times that followed. Therefore, in 175 C.E. Cai Yong . . . [with a group of other officials] memorialized a request to make a definitive and standard edition of the graphs of the Six Classics. Emperor Ling assented. Cai Yong then wrote the texts on the stone tablets, and had workers engrave them and set them up outside the gates of the Imperial Academy. Thereby, future scholars and those who wished to study later would all have access to the correct versions. When the tablets were done and erected, those who came to look at them and copy from them numbered in the thousands of carts daily, blocking the streets and alleys of the city. (HHS: 1990)

The text translated above from the HHS, which may have been based on access to a copy of the actual memorial Cai Yong wrote, specifically mentions the *written graphs* of the classics as defective. This is a memorial, then, that is wholly addressed to the textual form. The number of "readers," even allowing for exaggeration, are impressive, but so is their activity: copying.

It is easy to overlook the role of copying in a manuscript culture. The common word "to write" (*xie*) seems, in the Han, to have meant primarily "to copy." A common trope in biographies of poor scholars shows their subject going to great sacrifice in order to copy texts. Although there are equally great numbers of anecdotes of young scholars who are so brilliant that they can recite a text after one reading, such feats of memory do not seem to have obviated the need for copying. The number of copiers of the Stone Classics, and other anecdotes about copying in the histories, also make it clear that there were many public servants whose job was copying texts, and that it was also widely practiced among educated people. Nearly every user of a book was also a writer, or copier, of many of the books in his possession. The figure of the reader/copier was not limited to China. Manuscript books in Europe are unique editions, of course, and many medieval manuscript codices are composed of diverse and extraneous material that is bound between the book's covers solely due to the writer's whim. Although the word *zhu* "to compose" is frequently used for "original" compositions, and never for copying, "original" compositions in the Han, as we shall see in a discussion of intertextuality in chapter 4, are often pastiches of preexistent texts. The boundary between copying, annotating, commenting, and composing must have been quite fluid. If reading commonly implies copying and copying is on the continuum of writing, then that suggests a reconsideration of the boundary between writer and reader.

Reading and Writing

To study (*xue*), as I mentioned in the previous chapter, is to imitate; what became the common word for "to write" meant, in the Han, "to copy." The classics were reproductions, re-presentations. If writing is, at some of its core levels, always a *re*writing, then the scene of writing always has the scene of reading embedded within it. Of course, any writer, anywhere, must also be a reader and must use the various linguistic conventions learned and absorbed in the reading process. Recall, though, the de Certeau passage earlier in this chapter about the "freedom of the reader." This makes an argument for a pure scene of reading that doesn't presume reading as a prelude to writing. Is there a position of the pure reader, the free reader, in this formative period of the Empire of the Text? The fact that the reader can leave no record of her activity that is not inscribed in a written text should not make us despair of answering the question. Textual indices of reading suggest, for the most part, a scene that is thoroughly embedded in textual circulation, that is inseparable from writing.

Over the past few decades, Chinese literary study in the United States has been particularly concerned with the issue of fictionality in literary writing. There is a broad consensus now that the truth/fiction dichotomy as we once deployed it here in the West is a singularly inappropriate category to import to the study of Chinese writing, particularly poetry. Stephen Owen has made the point in many of his writings that *shi* is not poetry, that in a *shi*, unlike in a "thing made" (i.e., a poem), we are always reading "verbal manifestations of [the poet's] inner states" (Owen 1985: 63). To illustrate what he clearly regards as a significant difference between two systems of reading, Owen gives this example:

> There is a famous painting of Saint Sebastian by Antonella da Massina: the saint appears in a full-length frontal view, his body transfixed with arrows. If the painting were a T'ang poem, the traditional reader would recoil, not only at the grotesqueness of the subject matter, but also from the immediate recognition that the poet/painter was standing among the executioners. If

what is seen is presumed to be historical experience, then the point of view
is implicated in the view itself. (Owen 1985: 63)

Owen does not refer here to the plethora of critical works, following
Lacan's analysis of the gaze in "The Mirror Stage" and other essays, that
explore ways in which visual material constructs and offers specific subject positions to the viewer. He need not, since there is no reason for every
critic to acknowledge this work. But to anyone familiar with this body of
criticism, Owen is making quite a leap in assuming a particular principle
in the structuration of the viewer's subject position: that the viewer/reader
and the painter/poet are interchangeable, and that the painter/poet, in his
work, operates from and creates a "point of view" that can be occupied
by the viewer/reader. The viewer who is *not* a Chinese "traditional
reader" would presumably not identify the artist's "point of view" with
the invisible executioners. But, and this is more central to my argument,
would such a viewer identify his or her own point of view with the artist's? Identification, were it to take place in the psyche of this viewer,
might be with Saint Sebastian or might develop in the various directions
that analysts of the gaze have theorized.

Owen is confident that the "traditional reader's" subject position is
determined in advance. One defining feature of this "traditional reader,"
then, is the ability to identify with the "traditional writer." Once this
identification mechanism is in place, the question of fictionality too has
been decided in advance. Fictionality involves a three-way construct: the
author, the reader, and the Other, or however one wants to refer to the
location of standards of truth, convention, or mutual intelligibility. The
reader who has already identified himself or herself with the writer un-
does this triangle. I think, however, that Owen has a valid point: In certain
phases of textual history this identification did indeed take place. But to
avoid any pretense of understanding the psyches of those long dead, I
would frame it thus: In early imperial China, in the age of manuscript
textual culture, the position of early imperial reader is fundamentally interchangeable with the position of early imperial writer. I specify the
time, the place, and the technology of textual reproduction in order to
underscore my belief that this identificatory ability cannot inhere in
"reading" as a generalizable phenomenon across time and space. If we
imagine a scene of reading, for example, where the predominant textual
material is presumed to be authored by the God of one of the eastern
Mediterranean monotheisms, the reader would be offered neither identification nor authorial interchangeability. Even in this situation, though,
there could exist, given the right social determinants, the freedom of the
reader that de Certeau evokes. Ultimately, the issue of fictionality is only
in need of determination when the positions of reader and writer are

clearly demarcated—when there is at least the theoretical possibility of "pure" readership. The truth determination requires the ontological separability of reader, writer, and text. Since reading is an intangible process, it is difficult to write or uncover its history, so my claim here must be at the level of hypothesis. All evidence suggests, though, that in early imperial China the position of pure reader did not exist, and that every early imperial reader was, implicitly at least, also a writer. Owen posits that when we read *shi* poetry, "what we actually do is read the poet in the act of reading the world, see the world through his eyes" (Owen 1985: 73). But if the poet's reading was expressed in his writing, where is the reader who doesn't write? When does the writing stop?

Han government depended on textual production, largely in the form of memorials and reports. Orders, decrees, and other genres from the center informed officials throughout the empire of policy and procedure. In principle, government policy also allowed and encouraged the free flow of texts to the center: There were few or no restrictions of rank put on the right to memorialize directly to the throne. Even anonymous memorials to the throne were permitted. This theoretical freedom of access did not exist throughout imperial history. I am not implying here that the Han was characterized by "freedom of speech." Slander laws prohibiting criticism of the empire were in existence throughout almost the entirety of the Latter Han, when memorial access to the imperial court was supposedly at its height. Still, it was presumed that writing was the major part of the work of all officials. In classical study as well, we have seen that study engendered the production of commentary, which in its chapter-and-verse form would be voluminous. Omen reading and interpretation, an area of immense importance throughout the Han, can be viewed as a textualization, a writing, of the phenomenal world. To be an official in Han China—and such was the goal of all literacy and education—was to read—written texts as well as the textual analogue that was the social and natural world—and to produce texts.

It could be argued, of course, that the same textual saturation inheres in the working world today and that, by my standards, anyone who writes an office memo is a writer. This is where Foucault's notion of the "author function" is useful: In a given regime the author function will be applied to certain discourses and not to others. In a "civilization like our own"

> a private letter may well have a signer—it does not have an author; a contract may well have a guarantor—it does not have an author. An anonymous text probably has a writer—but not an author. The author-function is therefore characteristic of the mode of existence, circulation, and functioning of certain discourses within a society. (Foucault 1979: 141–60)

The author function also applies to a critical reading of texts: Certain critical practices require an author for the intelligibility of certain genres of texts. We bring certain expectations of unity, such as stylistic unity, development, and maturation—to a collection of literary texts ascribed to a specific author. We expect to be able to say something, for instance, about Li Bo's poetry as a whole. One of Foucault's determinants for the rise of the author function is penal authority:

> Texts, books, and discourses really began to have authors (other than mythical, "sacralized" and "sacralizing" figures) to the extent that authors became subject to punishment, that is, to the extent that the discourses could be transgressive. (Foucault 1979: 148)

Han writers could be punished for words in violation of the slander laws. But being punished for criticizing imperial policy when one of the "author's" professional responsibilities is writing memorials about imperial policy is a far different matter from heresy, for example, as it is was known in medieval Europe. There is no equivalent to heresy in Han China, and this is, I believe, a consequence of the particular character of textual culture. The judgment of heresy implies that the heretical text be separable from the author as a readerly text—one capable, for instance, of leading other readers astray—and then be *re*assigned to the author's responsibility. The independent existence of the textual content as a thing read is the crucial intermediate step. In the slander law violation, on the other hand, the text does not exist to create a scene of pure reading. The memorial to the court was a performative act; the punishment was performative as well.

Writing only creates the scene of pure reading under specific conditions, and I am arguing that those conditions did not exist within official textual culture in the Han dynasty. The activities of reading, studying, copying, transmitting, and creating knew no clear boundaries, and formed no discrete categories. What they had in common was that they all constituted adherence to the regime of textual authority. One reason de Certeau can speak of the "freedom of the reader" is that the pure reader is also ultimately free from de Certeau: the reader's activities, immaterial as they are, are ultimately inaccessible to language except through an act of reinscription. The figure of the reader is thus susceptible to a vast array of critical projections. My understanding of Han textual culture is an experimental one that views every one of its members as a writer in the broad sense of the word, which encompasses reading, copying, transmitting, and teaching. This understanding has some consequences. It requires a modification, for example, of what has become the consensual understanding of the figure of the literatus—the *shi*—in late Han times, that a large number of the *shi* were characterized by a posture of "dissent." In the Empire of the Text, there is no dissent. To write at all is to perform allegiance. Let us turn now, then, to the *shi*, to whom I will hereafter refer as simply the shi, unitalicized, and no longer as "literatus" or "scholar-official," for reasons that will become clear in the following chapter.

Notes

1. *Doctrine of the Mean*, chapter 20. Sibu beiyao ed. See the glossary entry "Ai gong . . ." for original text.

2. The expression "lay out [or carry out] government" (*bu zheng*) occurs first in the *Book of Songs*: "*Bu zheng you you/bai lü shi qiu.*" Carry out government in a gentle manner/100 blessings gather round. (Mao 304). This text, and the way the text is quoted in the *Zuo zhuan*, shows that the sense of *bu* "to lay out" is clearly active and not representational.

3. I am leaving this term, which has been translated "scholar-official," "literatus," etc., untranslated.

4. Alfred Sohn-Rethel (1978). See also Slavoj Žižek (1989), especially chapter 1: "How Did Marx Invent the Symptom?"

5. This interpretation of Althusser derives from Slavoj Žižek (1994), 24ff.

6. Bourdieu (1990). This understanding of the canon dispute comes from John Guillory (1993).

7. Harvey Graff (1987). Most scholars of literacy emphasize that it is neither innocent nor self-explanatory. See also William Harris (1989) and Rosalind Thomas (1992).

8. This topic is discussed at greater length in chapter 3.

9. Claude Lévi-Strauss (1974), 331–43. Derrida (1976), 101–40. Joel Kuipers's argument is also an implicit attack on the Lévi-Strauss position.

10. Quoted in Martin Irvine (1994), 1.

11. Although Derrida does make the connection between Rousseau's idea of writing as a dangerous supplement and the supplement as an economic term, this is at the most abstract level.

12. Unless I specify otherwise, references to the dates of composition of Han and pre-Han texts are from Michael Loewe, ed. (1993).

13. QHHW, 740b. Studies include Boltz (1994), Miller (1953), and Thern (1966).

14. This, and other *Yi jing* translations in this passage, are from Wilhelm and Baynes (1967), 166–7.

15. Boltz (1994), 138–43, shows convincingly that *wen*, by the Qin-Han period, had a technical usage in lexicography, distinguishing the simple character—monosomatic, in P. Boodberg's coinage—from the compound character, for which *zi* was used. This accords with Xu Shen's passage here, where simple semantic categories are suggested.

16. Tomosomatic or syssosomatic, in Boodberg's terminology. See note 15 for the *wen/zi* differentiation.

17. Most editions omit this sentence. Ding Fubao restores it, based on the preface to the *Book of Documents.*

18. In "The Pit and the Pyramid: Introduction to Hegel's Semiology," in Derrida (1992), 95–108.

19. It is possible that even the various (though not numerous) references to regional dialects refer to regional variants in written form rather than to speech.

20. One indication of the place of orality in the *Shuo wen* is in the numerous "read like" specifications, which, in the formula "A is read like B" presumably means that A and B are homophones. Although there have been numerous philological studies on the "read like" phenomenon, it should be stressed that the verb "read" probably indicates not a standard pronunciation of a word in the spoken language, but directions for oral recitation or reading of a text. See Coblin (1978).

21. A somewhat paradoxical feature of the *Shuo wen* is that it is simultaneously the earliest surviving formal recognition of the "phonetic" element—the vast number of graphs are of the "formulating the sound" category—and, if we are to accept Boltz's hypothesis, a continuation of the prescriptive tendency against late Warring States desemanticization or phoneticization. Following Foucault, the entry of a category like "phonetic" into discourse can be understood as accomplishing its containment rather than a recognition of its "appearance." These two disparate positions on the "phonetic" in the *Shuo wen* are not, then, as contradictory as they might seem.

22. Chen Yinke has hypothesized that Yan Zhitui himself was a principal oral source for the standardization of pronunciation in the *Qie yun* rhyming scheme. This was supposedly because of his maintenance of a Loyang accent while in exile in the South. Quoted in Teng (1968), xxviii.

23. This is also the source of the value of speech—the conversations of the neighborhoods and alleyways—as a diagnostic tool. The gathering of and interpretation of popular speech, a practice that originated in Zhou times, treated speech or singing as portents; there was something about it that accorded with the more cosmological patterning of weather, or other manifestations of nature.

24. For example, "Moreover, what after all is the use of the T'ai-hsüan now? This book is only good for covering a pickle jar." in Teng (1968) 94–95. The *T'ai-hsüan* [Tai xuan] is a work by the Han author Yang Xiong that was a rewriting of the *Yi Jing.*

25. This is a much-studied text, and summaries can be found in any history of Chinese philosophy. A very cogent discussion is in Anne Cheng (1985), 7–66.

26. Xu (1977–79) vol. 2, 256–57. It is very important to Xu to situate the importance of Dong Zhongshu's thought within the context of Dong's own outstanding character. He systematized intellectual work as he did, Xu argues, because of his genuine concern for the well-being of the country and of the people.

27. Kevin Robb (1994), 41. Robb also advances the theory, which provides an interesting comparison to the remarks above on Xu Shen and graphic standardization, that the Greek alphabet itself was a product of the Homeric poems; that the Greek vowels, which represented the major Greek alphabetical innovation over its Phoenician predecessor, were deployed in order to properly represent Homeric

hexameter; and that the first Greek writing was the ritual inscription of fragments from the Homeric poems. In both the Greek and the Chinese cases, then, one could argue that the texts precede the writing systems themselves.

28. Anne Cheng (1985) is a study with partial translation of this work.

29. A good summary of Qing dynasty discussion on Old Text/New Text controversy is in Kai-wing Chow (1994).

30. See Tjan (1949–52); Robert P. Kramers, "The Development of the Confucian Schools" and Ch'en Ch'i-yun, "Confucian, Legalist, and Taoist Thought in Latter Han," in CHC, 747–807; Ch'en Ch'i-yun (1975) and (1980); Anne Cheng (1985), 67–154; Qian Mu (1958); Pi Xirui (1925).

31. Discussion of the Old Text/New Text division has been complicated by the Qing dynasty philologists' resurrection of the discussion in a context that had more to do with currents in Qing intellectual history than the original Han dynasty context; like many historiographical issues, the haziness of the actual content of the original dispute seems to have been useful in maintaining the conflict's valence for later struggles.

32. See Tjan, Qian Mu, Pi Xirui, Anne Cheng. Tjan has a translation of the Bohutong discussions that includes some of the Shiquge discussions as well.

33. Pi Xirui sees this as marking the transition from "master" line of transmission to "school of transmission" (about which more below).

34. Qian Mu, however, demonstrates convincingly that many of Sima Qian's mentions of the term "Old Text" refer to the form of the script.

35. For quotations see Yu Qiding (1987), 184 ff.

36. Eric Havelock, *The Muse Learns to Write*, is a summary of a lifetime of work.

37. HHS, 1234. The Five Schools refer to five Guliang teachers from the Former Han, including Liu Xiang.

38. This is the thesis of Anne Cheng (1985).

39. But the court did not, as I shall explain below, aim for a copy of every extant book in the empire.

40. The classicist Jesper Svenbro suggests a parallel with ancient Athens that illustrates the conflation of physical location of texts, textual transmission, and textual authority:

What can the reason be for Plato's ability to write when the reasons for not writing produced by Socrates appear to be universally valid? The difference is that Plato has foreseen how to defend and control his writings, even well after his own death. Like Epimenides, he has concerned himself with the location of his inscriptions, and in particular, with the location where his writing will be deposited. Plato was the founder of the Academy; and what was the Academy if not the institution that, for close to a millennium, guaranteed the protection of Plato's works? . . . Once the Academy had been founded, Plato could risk doing something that Socrates could not. He could commit his words to writing, in the firm conviction that he had made sure that his readers would be engaged in the same quest as himself, and that, after the appropriate training, they would be ready to come to the aid of his lógos gegramménos (written speech). Jesper Svenbro (1993), 215–16.

41. "Scribes-diviners-lawyers-historians, representing at once the normativizing and speculative functions at court."

42. The seventh of the Seven Categorical Summaries was an additional summary that covered the entire collection.

43. This topic is discussed further in chapter 4.

44. Books were stored not only in the Bifu. The *Han shu bu zhu* notes that one hundred years after Emperor Wu inaugurated the collection of books, mountains of books had been amassed. A fragment from the Seven Categorical Summaries records that: Outside [the inner palace] there were the collections of the Chamberlain for Grand Ceremonials, the Grand Astrologer, and the Erudites. Inside there were the storehouses of the Yange, Guangnei, and the Bishi. Quoted in Chen Guoqing, ed. (1983), 4–5.

45. Prince Xian, whose collection also included Old Text versions of the classics, is mentioned as another source of the Old Text versions besides those buried in the wall. He also appointed Confucian Erudites at his court. This seems to have been common in the feudal princely courts.

46. The translation is adapted from Nivison (1966): 60.

47. In the essay "Principles of Editing and Collating," Zhang Xuecheng states his belief that in Liu Xiang and Liu Xin's time there were several standards of writing, and that variant versions were tolerated, as long as they didn't influence textual standardization at the center. Zhang postulates the category of "Central Writing," which differs from "outside writing" and writing between officials. There seems to be insufficient evidence to assume that these were meaningful categories in the Han. But the importance he places on standardization at the center accords with my own understanding. In Zhang Xuecheng (1936 rpt.), 13–16.

48. In Kang Youwei, *Han shu Yiwenzhi bian wei*. Excerpts reprinted in Chen Guoqing (1983), 244–46.

49. Quoted from Ying Shao's *Fengsu tong yi*, in the Li Shan annotation to the Fu on the Wei capital in the *Wen xuan*, j. 6, 22a.

50. Also quoted in Chen Guoqing (1983), 237.

51. There are partial translations from these passages, with readings that diverge from my own, in Tjan (1949–52), 142–44.

52. We know from the archaeological record, for example, that local officials were obliged to and did keep written records of their administrative work in minute detail. See Loewe (1967).

53. For a review of the literature on this see Loewe, ed. (1993), 68–76.

54. Adapted from Holzman (1974), 124.

55. This expression is also from the letter to Ren An.

56. Trans. Donald Holzman. In Holzman (1974), 21.

57. See Roberts and Skeat (1983), especially chapter 8.

58. From the *Taiping yulan*. In Tsien (1962), 128

59. Quoted in Tsien (1962), 127.

60. QHW 52:9a (411). The silk specified—*you su*—was white and smooth, and was of the kind used expressly for writing.

61. DHHY lists examples from the HHS, 172–73.

2

The Shi

Who Were the Shi?

Were the shi a class, a social formation, an occupational category, the literate? Patricia Ebrey is not referring to the categorical difficulty when she points out that "there is no widely accepted description of Chinese social structure for the pre-Sung period"(Ebrey 1978: 120), but the fundamental issue of classification is certainly a primary reason for this lack of consensus. Many scholars have commented on the conceptual inadequacy of the term, since it does not always refer to a group with a specific relation to modes of production, wealth, or even necessarily to actual political office.[1] In many respects, the shi are at the heart of the debate about early imperial social structure, the question of feudalism, and periodization in general. The debates in Chinese historiographical circles in the twenties and afterward, beginning with the work of Tao Xisheng, often centered on the character of the shi and the question of their social role or roles (Pilz 1991; Dirlik 1978: 114 ff; Tao Xisheng 1954). I am more interested in exploring the difficulty of reaching a normative definition of this group than in "solving" what is probably an insoluble definitional problem. This difficulty, as my discussion in the previous chapter should suggest, has something to do with issues of representation and textuality, an area to which, naturally, few social historians in China and elsewhere have devoted much attention. I would like to suggest, though, that Patricia Ebrey expresses a minimal but general consensus as follows, one that would be acceptable to scholars holding a variety of positions on the structure of early imperial society, periodization, landholding, or central authority: "The term *shih*, from the time of Confucius at least, was used to refer to those qualified, morally and culturally, to be officers of the state"(CHC: 631). The determination of these "moral and cultural qualifications" was a central subject in preimperial and early imperial textual practice. Although "moral" and "cultural" are malleable terms, there are a few strict parameters governing eligibility for inclusion in the shi category. Eunuchs, for example, who frequently served as officers of the state, could not be considered shi, not even the "virtuous eunuchs," of whom there were many (Jügel 1976). Neither could women, who were generally barred from official titleholding as well. It could be argued that the determination of the "moral and cultural qualifications" was indeed the central concern of "Confucian" thought and was also the principle that informed biographical writing in early historiography. Bibliographic subjects were often grouped to illustrate certain behavioral or life-course types. The "exemplary life" is central to the didactic quality of early historiography and other forms of life-course representation. All social roles depend on external recognition and differentiation: A person is gendered male within the social system of gender differentiation and in contradistinction to those gendered female. But the term "moral and cultural qualifications" suggests that inherent in the determination of this particular group—the shi—were the primary concerns of elite ideology itself: "morality" and "culture." Recognition of a man as a shi was the social practice of imperial ideology. I am not suggesting that determination of the shi was wholly subjective and external. Although not every shi was part of the propertied elite, male members of the propertied elite (with the exception of eunuchs, who were arguably not "male") were classifiable as shi. As a distinguishable group, though, the shi were more identified than any other with early imperial official ideology as expressed in its philosophical/moral/cultural content, and in the mode of that ideology's circulation. This is the primary way in which shi are differentiated from other groups: Farmers, tradespeople, and merchants are identified not in ideological or idealist terms, but through their function. In the strict definitional sense the shi are not simply equivalent to officials. They are officials but are also potential officials or ex-officials.[2] Their definition thus exceeds the strictly functional and depends on qualities that we could call "internal" or "subjective." Even when office was heritable or for sale, those who attained office by those means could be deemed after the fact to have satisfied the moral and cultural qualifications to hold office, or, in some cases, they could be criticized for not having those qualifications. When office was obtainable through examination, implicit in the structure was the idea that the examination system revealed something inherent in the candidate. When the exemplary and requisite qualities of a shi are listed, in pre-Qin or in later texts (Ebrey's example is Huan Tan's [43 B.C.E.–28 C.E.] *Xin lun*), the qualities are always on the highest level of generality, or, as Ebrey puts it, "essentially subjective" (CHC: 632).

If we are to define the shi as actual, potential, or former uncastrated male officeholders—and I think that this is a good minimal definition—there is one objective qualification that does seem to characterize the group as a whole: literacy. Officers in Han government had to know how to read and write. This means that they had to have received instruction in the canonical texts and to have acquired the characteristics of textual culture as outlined in the preceding chapter. There was to be no deviation from this requirement for the remainder of imperial history. Even if standards actually declined to the level that Yan Zhitui complained of, where nearly illiterate aristocrats would pay others to take examinations or compose writings for them, the fact remains that for officeholding, the *formal* requirement of canonical literacy, and all that that implies, was firmly in place. The category of the shi is simply inconceivable without the textual medium. Men considered as members of this category composed texts; they were, for the most part, the subjects of the texts; and, as a group whose functioning depended to some extent on external recognition, that recognition was in the form of texts. Han sources are overwhelmingly concerned with the shi category, who thus form the primary social content of Han history. Even archaeological evidence, which is overwhelmingly the material remnants of elite society, has primarily served to expand our understanding of the shi. Nearly everything that we know about other groups in Han society, groups who form the vast numerical majority—women, peasants, slaves, etc.—is refracted through the textual culture that was in the hands of the shi. The inseparability of textual authority and imperial officeholding became codified in the Han, and continued, in a general way, throughout Chinese history. The shi, self-defined or externally defined, were no less subject to history than any social formation, real or phantasmatic, but the connection of the category to textual culture did not change. In what I am calling the *parallel history* of the Empire of the Text, the shi were the population.

A Brief Social History of the Latter Han Shi

There are many studies of the shi in Han social, economic, and intellectual history. The shi of the Latter Han and medieval period are, I suspect, the most widely studied group in the pre-Sung period. Patricia Ebrey's chapter in the *Cambridge History of China* includes an excellent survey of the current state of scholarship on Han shi, and I refer readers to that convenient source. In the brief summary history that follows, I review those aspects of the shi in history that I believe would benefit from theoretical elaboration, and on those aspects which I will use in describing the nature of the shi in the Empire of the Text.[3]

The aristocratic elite of powerful families, which dominated local agricultural production and officeholding in China throughout the period of division and into the Tang, was still in an inchoate state in the last years of the Han. The close connection between membership in these families and officeholding during the Eastern Jin dynasty and beyond is well documented.[4] Although many scholars have noticed a definite trend toward a lineage officeholding aristocracy in the late Latter Han, particularly at the commandery level and in local recommendations and appointments, the character of the ruling elite is still much more fluid and certainly without the institutionalized character of the post-Han period, though by the end of the Han the social, political, cultural, and economic character of these families had largely been set.[5] In the following sections I discuss the issues of representations of the "shi," a term that is used by many but not all social historians of the late Han. "Great family" is a term preferred by some of the social historians who object to the imprecision of use of the term "shi." Nearly all historians, for example, Mao Hanguang, acknowledge some degree of overlap succeeding historical categories: "The 'shi-ization' of the local aristocracy and the aristocratization of the shi represented the late Han tendency toward the codification of the medieval aristocracy" (Mao Hanguang 1988: 77).

Wealth in land was the primary indication of great family status throughout the Han, and the expansion of great family landholdings was usually at the expense of the individual peasant cultivator (Ch'u 1972, chap. 4). During the Western Han the landed aristocracy grew steadily in political and economic power as the amount of land under its control increased (Yang Liansheng 1936: 1007–23). By the time of Wang Mang's interregnum (9–23 C.E.), the power of the landed aristocracy had become firmly entrenched despite repeated government measures to weaken or control it, at least on the formal level. Wang Mang's attempted reforms sought an increase in government-held land, as well as other measures designed to weaken this power, but he was defeated by a combination of peasant unrest and strong great-family resistance (Yang Liansheng 1936: 1007–23). The emperor Guangwu (reigned 25–58 C.E.), first emperor of the Latter Han, is portrayed in historical literature as representing the interests of the powerful landholding families, from whose ranks came most of his officials. Indeed, most of the highest officeholders and imperial consort families of the Latter Han came from the ranks of the landed aristocracy. This was not a stark contrast to the Former Han but was a consolidation of an evolving tendency. It is no surprise that those who figured in textual circulation were primarily from this socioeconomic group. In that sense, Yang Liansheng is correct to imply that the shi in the Latter Han were simply one identity of the landed aristocracy.

The great families of the Latter Han were social units of enormous size. Their retinues included tenant farmers, traders, private armies, and a large group of dependents of varying social levels. The rise in the number of these retainers attached to the powerful families of the Latter Han has been interpreted both as a cause and as a result of the weakened central government. Droughts, plagues of insects, an insecure countryside, and a land tenure system that favored large landowners drove many farmers from their own land. In 153 C.E. there were hundreds of thousands of displaced families, to whom the central government could give only partial relief (Yang Liansheng 1936: 1025). The political and social instability of the time enabled wealthy literati to attract large numbers of retainers, from literati as well as other social classes, to their estates (Yu Yingshi 1959: 69–70). The most common type of retainers, known as "guests," varied greatly in function and status, ranging from an official's personal advisers to semislaves.[6]

The "guest" formation is very similar to feudal structures of seignorage in Europe and Japan. Given the distinctly nonfeudal character of Chinese scholar-officialdom, however, it is not surprising that many of the dependent or semidependent relationships among shi in the late Latter Han were of a nonfeudal character.[7] Two types of relationships, the disciples (*mensheng*) and "former officials" (*guli*), were newly significant social phenomena during the second century. There was some overlap between the two terms. Basically, disciples were men of any age who had accepted someone as a teacher. The teacher-student relationship varied in levels of formality, from an informal relationship without any actual teaching,[8] to a scholar's formalized filiation in a line of text-system transmission. It could occur between a student and a teacher at the local level, or as an alliance between an individual and a powerful local person; within the Imperial Academy at Loyang or as an alliance with some other powerful person at the capital. "Former officials" were those who had passed an examination under a particular recruiting officer, or, more importantly, had been recommended for office by a particular official. Han administrative service depended on local recommendations or on the direct employment of subordinates by those officials with the requisite bureaucratic status. Thus the importance of these ties of obligation was very great. Yang Liansheng points out that at a time when a fixed period of mourning for one's parents had not been established, "former officials" were required to mourn the death of their sponsors for three years (Yang Liansheng 1936: 1035). It has also been claimed that a measure of this relationship's importance was the not uncommon practice of declining an appointment in order to avoid incurring the attendant personal obligations (CHC: 641).

Two primary sets of antagonists served to define the shi in the late Latter Han: the eunuchs and the distaff relatives. Eunuchs were indeed a special case. They were marked physically and, in some cases, by their official function. The tendency in the Latter Han, though, was toward a greater integration of the eunuchs into all levels of the power structure (Jügel 1976: 143–146). In the 130s, eunuchs were allowed to pass on titles to their adopted sons and thus operate in nearly every respect like members of a lineage group. Establishment of regional power soon followed, as did financial benefits from selling offices. In 133, against non-eunuch objections, eunuchs were permitted to judge candidates designated "filially pious and uncorrupt" (*xiaolian*) (DHHY: 52–53). The eunuchs' definition as a social formation was physiological. Had they been identified by official function alone, by the last seventy-five years of the Latter Han their social roles would have been indistinguishable from those of the shi at large, except for those positions in the inner quarters for which their castration had originally been a necessity. The image of eunuchs in the dynastic histories and in shi writings has been overwhelmingly negative. But the not infrequent biographies of "virtuous" eunuchs indicate that the category of eunuch did not necessarily carry individual opprobrium with it. Defined as a group, eunuchs were able to act in their collective interest when the situation demanded it. The apogee of their power came with their victory over a group of court shi during the Affair of the Proscribed Factions (about which more below).

The distaff relatives form a different kind of category, one not as dissociable from the shi as the eunuchs. Until the reign of Emperor Ling (168–196 C.E.), nearly all imperial consort families in the Latter Han were from the highest echelon of the great families. The particular arena of their exercise of power—the emperor's court—caused them to form various kinds of alliances: with or against eunuch factions, with or against other families. Although the category of "distaff relative" was used pejoratively in the Sima Qian's *Shi ji*, it was not used as a categorical pejorative in the Latter Han. Unlike the eunuchs, the distaff relatives did not form a discrete, diachronous group with interests that could stem from their particularity. Distaff relatives, rather, acted as singular clans with particular clan interest. There was certainly factional struggle between certain distaff families—the Dou, Deng, and especially the Liang are familiar examples—but these struggles had to do with particular families and not, as was the case with the eunuchs, with the social group.

Regional or Imperial?

Significant differences of interpretation remain in evaluating the regional or state character of shi culture. To simplify the issue, Japanese scholars, particularly those associated with the Kyoto-based "local community" school of analysis (*kyōdotai*) and its precursors, have tended to emphasize the regional or communitarian character of the shi.[9] The regional school of thought has two emphases: the self-contained character of the economic life of the communities and the importance of the local recommendation system in selecting officials. This line of interpretation has also characterized a number of studies in cultural history, particularly Martin Powers's book on Han pictorial art. Those who emphasize the statist character of the shi do not form the kind of bloc that the Kyoto scholars do. Scholars in the field of intellectual history tend to see the "intellectuals" as national in scope. But the social historian Mao Hanguang also feels, contra the Kyoto scholars, that the shi can be described as a state elite.[10] Over the course of the late Latter Han there was a growing tendency toward regional concentrations of power in the great families rather than members of the emperor's family. The Han collapse in 220 C.E. has encouraged a view that the growth of regional power centers and the end of the dynasty were causally related. Imperial or dynastic collapse is among the most etiologogenic tropes in historiography. But for the Han this particular etiology of collapse might not hold: There is nothing inherently anti-statist in the existence of semiautonomous regional power centers. On the level of textual culture, in fact, regionalist differentiation exists in the Latter Han only at the level of the stereotype: The men of the Runan commandery were characterized as "impetuous" and "resolute,"[11] or the temperament of men from the region formerly known as Qi would be described as "slow and sluggish."[12] Hu Yun, in a study of "cultural regions" of the Latter Han shows convincingly that, measured in terms of numbers of shi, numbers of books, and numbers of officeholders, there were indeed changes in what could be classified as "cultural centers" between the Former and Latter Han, from the Qi-Lu centers of the Former Han westward and southward to the Henan, Nanyang, Runan, Yingchuan, and Chenliu commanderies in the Latter Han (Hu Yun 1987). Only Pei, the ancestral home of the Liu imperial family, maintained its status from the Former to the Latter Han.

Hu's standards of measurement, though, lead toward a different kind of argument. Unlike the first century of the Former Han, when the regional kings could maintain courts with a textual culture whose content diverged from court culture in Chang'an (the court of the king of Huainan is one example), the regional centers that evolved from the end of the Former Han and into the Latter Han reproduced the forms and content of imperial culture on the regional scale. I am not claiming here that there was no regional culture. At the level of popular religious practice and other areas outside of the purview of official textual culture, wide regional variance could certainly have existed. But what is striking about the regionalism expressed in the official textual culture to which Hu Yun and nearly every scholar committed to the category of Han regionalism refers is that its *content* varies little from region to region, or between region and capital. The alliances that were formed at regional levels did not produce competing versions of imperial textual culture; official textual culture was the culture of all of the regions. After the destruction of Loyang by Dong

Zhuo in 190, at the beginning of what would become consolidated as the Three Kingdoms division, it is striking how closely the textual activity at Jingzhou, for example, mirrored in form and content what existed, or what would have existed, at the center (Yoshikawa Tadao 1991). The power of the Empire of the Text was such that it knew no regional divisions.

The Affair of the Proscribed Factions (*danggu*), 167–184 C.E.

The network of personal loyalties and obligations that arose over the course of the Latter Han, in a form codified in the semiofficial terms "disciples" and "former officials," was an extension through shi culture at large of the text-system lineages in the schools of transmission of the official classics. In a bureacracy of the size of the Latter Han, which by the last half of the second century could have amounted to over 150,000 men[13] (counting the 30,000 students claimed as members of the Imperial University), the existence of lateral ties of alliance and obligation is not surprising. That one would find evidence of group interest is also not surprising, especially given the evidence of other articulations of apparently collective politics on the part of the eunuchs and the distaff clans. The monopolistic exercise of power at the court by the Liang distaff clan in the 140s has been recorded as a particular catalyst for articulations of "oppositional" shi group interest, though it should be remembered that the Liang family shared the socioeconomic background of the shi (Ebrey 1983: 540). But in the historiography of the late Latter Han, by far the most overdetermined episode in shi history was the Affair of the Proscribed Factions. This succession of prohibitions against office holding by, at most, 200 men (fewer than 10 percent of the central bureaucracy and a fraction of one percent of the entire imperial bureaucracy) is commonly held to have brought the dynasty to an end. Cho-yun Hsü writes, for example,

> Fewer than two generations after its establishment, the Eastern [Latter] Han throne once again drifted away from the influence of the literati-controlled court to form inner centers dominated by eunuchs and members of consort families. The final collision, between the eunuchs and the literati, occurred during A.D. 166–176 and brought an extensive purge of the literati. Both the dynasty and the literati were thus destroyed. (Hsü 1988: 186)

I will develop, in the following chapter, my thesis that the Proscribed Factions did not enter Latter Han shi discourse in as momentous a fashion as this. Indeed, there was general discursive support for a position *against* factionalism. The *Hou Han shu*, compiled by Fan Ye (398–446), has a chapter devoted to the collected biographies of prominent Proscribed Officials, which remains our primary source of knowledge about the affair. By Fan Ye's time, perhaps, the affair was already linked to the end of the dynasty. This has certainly been the lesson that generations of shi, not surprisingly, have drawn: Maltreatment of the shi leads to dynastic collapse. This interpretation has been repeated unquestionably throughout the current century as well, even though the need for transhistorical literati self-identification is no longer so great. Rafe de Crespigny, who has published widely on the political, social, and intellectual history of the Han dynasty, concludes an article on the Proscribed Factions:

> By the savage use of proscription against all open protest, the imperial government destroyed hopes of reform, and completed the alienation of the emperor from the very men whose goodwill and co-operation were essential to proper government. . . . Though many reasons can be found to explain the internecine conflicts of politicians at the capital and the growth of independence in the provinces, there is little question that the bitter years of proscription and persecution had weakened the bonds of loyalty between the emperor and his gentry officials, and that this erosion of trust and confidence was a major factor in the disintegration of China's first great empire. (de Crespigny 1975: 36)

Erosion of trust and confidence is difficult to measure. What is interesting is that this kind of assumption can be shared by so many with so little dissent. Such, undoubtedly, is the spell that is cast by dynastic collapse. Had the Proscribed Factions affair been followed by another hundred years of Han rule, and had dynasties, including the Han, endured worse crises, the affair would probably have been a footnote in Han institutional history.

The HHS ascribes the beginning of factionalism among court officials to the rivalry between Zhou Fu and Fang Zhi, two scholars from the Ganling commandery:

> When Emperor Huan was Marquis of Liwu, he studied under Zhou Fu of Ganling. When he ascended the throne [147 C.E.], he promoted Zhou Fu to Imperial Secretary. At that time Henan Governor Fang Zhi, also of Ganling, was famed at court. The [Ganling] locals had a ditty about them which went, "An exemplar under heaven: Fang Bowu; once a teacher; now a minister: Zhou Zhongjin." The friends and retainers of each side slandered and calumnied one another, and thus each established a coterie. The breach between them grew wider. Ganling had a northern and a southern faction, and the notion of factions arose here (HHS: 2185–6).

Whether or not we give it the etiological significance claimed by the HHS, the incident is revealing in several ways. The factions form in two ways, under a teacher and under an official. That the former teacher's faction is mocked by the official's faction precisely for being headed by a teacher suggests that "disciples" might have been less prestigious than "former officials." The seven-character panegyric (discussed further in chapter 3) is something that is included in many textual records of factional dispute, and suggests a point I will develop further: Factional disputes tend to be reducible to a simple textual formula. The geographical division of the factions suggests that regional ties, presumably from the earlier scene of pedagogy or officialdom, could also be a reference to divisions that ostensibly were being carried out at the national level. The historian's criticism of factions is also evident in the trivial nature of the conflict that supposedly gave rise to the notion of factions. This was not an ideological split, but the result of nepotism and favoritism writ large. Although the factional scholars are portrayed throughout *juan* 67 of the HHS as heroes, this initial critical position should be borne in mind.

The supporters and retainers certainly included many members of the Imperial Academy, a primary arena for character evaluation and the manifestation of factional loyalty. Although by Emperor Huan's time membership in the Imperial Academy was no longer an absolute guarantee of official appointment, it seems to have achieved the status of a discursive center, one that had assumed an importance overshadowing the function of canonical transmission associated with the Imperial University during the heyday of the Erudites. The seven-character panegyrics were the textualization of alliance patterns, and there is evidence that reputation at the discursive center was significant. Even such a powerful figure as Yuan Shao, from one of the most powerful families in the Latter Han, is recorded as having sought to remain in the good graces of the Academy members (HHS: 2217). On numerous occasions, members of the academy would line up behind an advocate on one side of a power struggle higher in the bureaucracy. Each conflict would produce the pithy seven-character panegyrics. As the primary struggle at the capital and in the regions gradually became a contest between the eunuchs and their various enemies among the scholar bureaucrats, powerful families, or the distaff clans, most of the scholars' castigatory energy became directed at the eunuchs. These criticisms or evaluations became known as "pure criticisms" (*qingyi*) and were the textual expression of the so-called "pure faction." The identification of the pure faction is taken mostly for granted. There seem to have been several ranked lists, on which the HHS bases its own lists and rankings, but whether this list consisted of a group who identified themselves as a faction or whether the label of "pure" was an identifactory label that arose in some other discursive situation is unclear. The nature of eunuch identity is physiologically based: It is a "constructed" identity in a literal and marked way. Beyond their eunuch opposition, though, it is not at all clear that the "pures" had other shi opponents. The "pures" may have been simply a subset of the shi that became central to a shi-eunuch conflict, rather than a faction of the shi.

Their political leaders were Chen Fan and Li Ying. Guo Tai, of the Imperial Academy, is described as moral exemplar and authority. As the affair unfolded, the eunuchs were the main adversaries. The power struggle in Emperor Huan's court broke out into the open in 159, when the eunuchs and the emperor crushed the power of the Liang consort clan. Three hundred officials allied to the Liangs were dismissed following this debacle. In 163 the shi officials, at the central court, led by Chen Fan, counterattacked and effected a eunuch purge. Criticism of the eunuchs by Chen Fan and his allies among the "pure faction" in government and in the Imperial Academy continued through 166. This temporary victory over the eunuchs was to be the proximate cause of the Affair of the Proscribed Factions.[14]

The charge of "forming factions" (*bu dang*) was first made in the winter of 166–167 against Li Ying and two hundred other officials by Lao Xiu, an ally of the eunuchs. The HHS report of this originary accusation casts the antifactional impulse in the worst possible light. Lao Xiu was the disciple of a Henei wind diviner named Zhang Cheng, who had used his wind divination to curry influence and favor among the eunuchs and the emperor himself. Later in Henei he had led disciples on to murder, and Li Ying, then governor of Henei, had him arrested and killed. Lao Xiu made the accusation of factionalism, reports the HHS, as revenge (HHS: 2187). Dou Wu, father of the empress dowager and then Colonel of the City Gates, secured an amnesty the following year, but anti-eunuch activity had apparently reached a fever pitch. The "pure" faction and the local elites seemed united against further eunuch power. Tensions mounted, and late in 168 Dou Wu concocted a plot to massacre the eunuchs. But the plot was leaked to the eunuchs, and they struck first. Dou Wu and his allies were defeated at court. In the winter of 168–169 the partisans arrested in the first proscription were rearrested, and the proscription was extended further. It was extended further in 172, when over a thousand students at the Imperial Academy were arrested. In 176, the scope of proscription was extended to include a more extensive list of clan members and allies of proscribed officials. The proscription was not lifted until 184, when the Han court yielded to arguments that the danger of the Yellow Turban rebellion necessitated regaining the loyalty of the dismissed officials and their supporters. Many of the proscribed officials regained office and were promoted to posts of responsibility.

Proscription nominally entailed a prohibition from officeholding and was extended to as many as five degrees of relationship to the proscribed official. It was thus an effective weapon against whole clans. The proscribed officials' declining fortunes at court, however, were reversed in the more textualized arenas of "reputation" and "moral authority," qualities that the histories report as being especially noteworthy in local society. As Wang Yao writes,

> At that time, the reputations of the proscribed officials grew in proportion to the severity of their punishment. Inclusion in the ranks of the proscribed officials was considered an honor. When Fan Pang was first released from prison and returned to Runan, the Nanyang literati came to greet him in 1000 chariots. (Wang Yao 1977: 5)

The record of a thousand chariots, which is but one of several records in the HHS of mass numbers of followers turning out for a member of the shi, is an insistent motif in the intellectual-social history of the late Latter Han. We recall that the completion of the Dongguan Stone Classics in 183 also occasioned thousands of chariots full of readers and copiers. Faced with a seeming rhetorical exaggeration, the scholar has several choices. The most common reading is to decide that the number means "many," and leave it at that. A metaphorical reading, however, may be indicative of something else: the public. In both cases of mass chariot spectatorship, what is being viewed is textual or symbolic: the reputation of Fan Pang or the authoritativeness of the Dongguan Stone Classics. "Thousands" of chariots could easily be a textual expression of circulation itself, the operation of the textual function throughout literati society.

Contemporary scholars are fairly unified in their judgment that the Proscribed Factions affair was central to the formation of the shi as a distinct social formation, and for them this means "consciousness" (Yu Yingshi 1959, Kawakatsu 1967)—the dimension that distinguishes them from the powerful families, a group constituted solely on economic grounds. For Yu Yingshi in particular, it was a group that shared a clear and conscious sense of commonality as well. Yu raises the example of Zhao Ji, who would later suffer proscription, be rehabilitated, and serve with Liu Biao in Jingzhou and Cao Cao at the capital. As a youth, he was married to a relative of the famed classicist Ma Rong. Ma Rong's family was of the eminent Ma clan, which had produced empresses in the past. Although the clan was in relative decline, it could still count as a "distaff clan." Zhao Ji resented this connection and refused to socialize with him. He wrote a letter asserting that Ma Rong "did not uphold the standards of the shi" (Yu Yingshi 1959: 26; HHS: 2121). Yu Yingshi sees further evidence of a kind of class identity formed through the Affairs of the Proscribed Factions in the currency of the phrase "comrade" (*tongzhi*), which appears for the first time in this period (Yu Yingshi 1959: 34–35).

He quotes an example from the biography of Liu Tao, one of the many "exemplary biographies" of model shi:

Liu Tao lived simply. He didn't practice petty formalities. All of his relations with friends required comradeliness. If what they valued was not congruent, he sought no union with the wealthy. If a man's feelings and dispositions were similar to his own, poverty or humbleness would not alter his intentions. (Yu Yingshi 1959: 33; HHS: 1842)

Yu Yingshi sees this as indicative of "self-consciousness," though it could also reflect the formulaic character of the exemplary biography. Indeed, a formulaic ethos seemed characteristic of the shi of the late Latter Han, whose social existence was characterized by strategies of reproduction. An extreme example is found in the biography of Guo Tai. As he was sent off by hordes of admirers, it began to rain. Guo Tai folded down a corner of his turban to cover more of his head. This became a popular fashion and was known as the "Guo Tai turban style" (HHS: 2225–6).

There is no doubt that the shi achieved at least a kind of discursive coherence in the last years of the Han dynasty. No matter how their lives actually unfolded, there had emerged a set of attributes, modes of activity, and identification/reproduction patterns that made them identifiable in texts as a common group. Within social history, though, there are only tentative answers to several questions of central concern. What was the connection between the "pures" and the Yellow Turbans? What was the extent of social division between the "pures" and their allies among the local elite in the commanderies and literati elements who either were not included in the proscription or held office in the eunuch-controlled government during the proscription? What was the political character of the "recluses" who refused both governmental office and association with factions?

The historical record offers no conclusive information on these questions. Kawakatsu Yoshio, Chi-yun Ch'en, and R. A. Stein (1963: 14–15) see evidence of "pure" faction collaboration with or tolerance of local Yellow Turban elements. For Kawakatsu, the "pures," the hermits, and the Yellow Turbans formed a broad pattern of local resistance to a corrupt and ineffective imperial regime. Our information on the Yellow Turbans is incomplete, however, and it is not even clear to what extent various local uprisings ascribed to the Yellow Turbans were part of a unified movement. It is clear that prior to 184 certain Yellow Turban elements did win literati sympathy. The fear of such an alliance was a motivating force behind the imperial amnesty. Kawakatsu and Yang Liansheng argue that divisions among local powerful families were reproduced in local divisions between the "pures" and officeholders who in one way or another served the eunuch-dominated court. Documentary evidence indicating even the existence of a "turbid" faction is lacking. There is, however, a record of criticism of factions by "pure"-minded literati, who decried the fashion of forming alliances for advantage. Masubuchi viewed this as evidence of a division among the "pures," whereas Kawakatsu sees these dissenters as forming a subfaction of the "pures" (Masubuchi 1960: 55; Kawakatsu 1967). These interpretations, which by their nature must depend on judgments of motives and psychic states, are necessarily hypothetical. What is perfectly clear from "the sources," though, is that the shi, by the end of the Latter Han, had become subjects of representation in discourse and that the "lives" of the shi took a shape that reflected their reproduction within a textual system.

In broader terms, the period from about 160 through 184 marked the first phase of a social transformation. In the Latter Han there is in the early stage of the transformation a symbiosis between the powerful local families (which were of a somewhat fluid membership) and the imperial court, with shi providing a kind of textual-symbolic recognition element and eunuchs representing a deformation of an expanded emperor faction. Toward the end of the transition we see the emergence of a locally based aristocratic elite, which was to consolidate political and cultural domination during the Northern and Southern Dynasties. The collapse of central authority was to accelerate disorder and competition at the local level among the elite, and impoverishment, displacement, and ruin among the peasantry. The emergence of an aristocracy based on kinship and clan membership later in the third century resulted in the attenuated importance of factions and local alliances less clearly based on kinship ties (Ebrey 1983: 541–2). But for the period of our study, patterns of social association that characterized the time of the affair of the Proscribed Factions were to continue in modified form throughout the remaining years of the Han.

The Shi and Dynastic Collapse

Following the 184 amnesty, consequent on the destruction wrought by the Yellow Turban rebellion and other rebellions, the political situation began to deteriorate rapidly. Military warlords like Dong Zhuo became another important factor on the political scene, competing with members of powerful families (like Yuan Shao), with remnants of the "pure" faction who had attained significant regional power (like Liu Biao), and with Cao Cao. Cao Cao, like Dong Zhuo, first gained political power through military prowess But like his rival Liu Biao, he gradually cultivated closer relationships with the shi, perhaps in an effort to consolidate political authority. After Dong Zhuo's usurpation of power in 189–90, the situation of the shi became more precarious still, and was more marked by frequent shifting of ties. In the paragraphs below I briefly trace the political careers of Wang Can and other Jian'an-era[15] shi to illustrate the character of shi familial and social connections during this period. I will not treat the subjects' involvements with the Cao court in any detail, as that is part of a later discussion of group literary activities. I have focused on Wang Can at greater length because information on him and his immediate ancestors is most complete in the historical record.

Wang Can's family, at the time of his great-grandfather Wang Gong's birth, was known as a "great family" (*haozu*) (HHS: 1819). Wang Gong achieved several high positions, one of which was governor of Runan province, a position he attained in 122 (HHS: 1820). Runan was the province of origin of many of the "pure" faction leaders, among them Chen Fan, whom Wang Gong recruited.[16] Wang Gong had a sterling reputation among the "pures." After he returned to Loyang, his brief imprisonment as a result of eunuch antagonism must have gained him further admiration. The HHS states that Wang Gong's son Wang Chang, Wang Can's grandfather, "was known in his youth for purity and straightforwardness, and didn't become the member of any faction" (HHS: 1823). The pejorative connotation applied to factional ties should be noted here. Wang Chang advanced in office largely through the networks outlined above. Within his network was Chen Fan, the "former subordinate" of his father (HHS: 1823). Wang Chang was to reach the highest local and national office, attaining in 168 the office of Minister of Works, one of the highest offices at court. When Wang was prefect of Nanyang, Liu Biao, then seventeen *sui*, became his "disciple." Notwithstanding the antifactional implications of the statement from the HHS quoted above, Wang Chang was listed as one of the "eight heroes," the second highest designation among the "pures" (HHS: 2187).

Little is known of Wang Chang's son Wang Qian, father of Wang Can. He served under He Jin during the last years of Emperor Ling's reign but became estranged from He Jin for refusing a marriage between one of his sons and He's daughter (SGZ: 598). His official accomplishments did not equal those of his father and grandfather.

When Wang Can was thirteen, he went to Chang'an, where Dong Zhuo had just relocated the capital. There he became the disciple of Cai Yong, one of the foremost literati of the time,[17] who was serving at the time in Emperor Xian's government, which was controlled by Dong Zhuo. The situation at the capital became more and more chaotic, and in 193 Wang left for Xiangyang in Jingzhou, where Liu Biao was Regional Governor.[18] Liu Biao had also been held in esteem by the "pure" faction. He was classified by the students of the Imperial Academy as one of the eight "exemplars," the third ranking in the classification of prominent "purists" (HHS: 2187). Jingzhou, under Liu Biao, had become a center of intellectual and literary activity, as many shi from throughout the country congregated there. A library was established, and the institutions of text-system transmission—schools of thought, teacher-student relationships, and so on—were put in place. The scholars who congregated there included several important members of the famed Jian'an literary circle.[19]

Despite what should have been a familial obligation, however, Liu Biao didn't favor Wang Can. The SGZ reports that he found him weak and unattractive (SGZ: 598). Wang remained in Jingzhou for fifteen years, mainly drafting letters and other memorials. Chen Shou implies that this supposed lack of favor was the reason for Wang Can's persuading Liu Biao's son Liu Cong to capitulate to Cao Cao in 208 (SGZ: 598). After Cao Cao conquered Jingzhou, Wang Can became part of the Cao court. He attained the rank of Palace Attendant, and he accompanied Cao Cao on many of his campaigns. He was the literary associate of Cao Pi and Cao Zhi, and other prominent Jian'an literati.

Chen Lin, like Wang Can's father, served under He Jin. Chen Lin had counseled He Jin against his abortive coup against the eunuchs in 189. After He Jin's death and Dong Zhuo's political ascent, Chen Lin went to seek the protection of Yuan Shao, then in Jizhou. Yuan Shao valued him for his literary talents (SGZ: 600). Among his compositions was a letter critical of Cao Cao and his family. When Cao Cao defeated Yuan Shao in 200 C.E. at the battle of Guandu, Chen shifted to Cao Cao's side. Cao Cao's magnanimity in forgiving the past slight was conspicuous.

Liu Zhen was also an important member of the Cao literati court. The biography of his grandfather Liu Liang is in the "Collected Biographies of the Literati," which concerns men throughout the dynasty whose fame came primarily from literary accomplishments. Liu Liang, although a member of the imperial clan, was of humble origin and sold books as a youth to support himself (HHS: 2635). He soon became known for his writings, which included "On Eradicating Congregation" (discussed in the next chapter). Probably because of the respect accorded his writings, he was nominated as "filially pious and uncorrupt," the highest designation in the local recommendation system and the prerequisite for most offices of any stature, whether national or local, and later he became Head of Beixincheng in Zhuo *xian*. While in Zhuo *xian* he built a school, and attracted hundreds of disciples (HHS: 2639). Nothing is known of Liu Zhen's father. Liu Liang's biography in the HHS concludes with the line "his grandson Liu Zhen also was well known for his literary talents." Liu Zhen, then, was like Chen Lin, Wang Can, and other literati attracted to the Cao court who were similarly valued for their literary talents; Cao Pi and other lords valued his company at gatherings and often commissioned compositions.[20] Although there is no direct evidence of a line of influence from Liu Liang through one of these disciples to Liu Zhen, such a connection is not at all unlikely. In addition, Liu Liang's considerable reputation undoubtedly was a factor in his grandson's literary reputation.

These brief life trajectories illustrate how patterns of relationships and family connections operated in the Jian'an era. They also provide a sense of continuity between the generation of the Proscribed Factions and the generation immediately following. We have seen clearly in Wang Can's trajectory how the aftereffects of the "pure" movement directly affected the kinds of alliances Wang made. We can also see how the patterns of relationships formed in the latter part of the second century shaped individual biographies. There is no sense of an "individual life," but an unfolding of the establishment of and consequences of alliance patterns. Even Liu Liang, who wrote on the improprieties of relationships other than familial or institutional ones, attracted hundreds of students. It is probably safe to assume that his great reputation was at least in part responsible for his grandson's advancement. But these trajectories illustrate another kind of movement: from the realm of the bureaucratic-canonical-textual to the more purely textual. The figures discussed above are among the best-known "writers" of the late Han; their importance to their contemporaries was slight, but in the Empire of the Text, especially in the version of it called "literary history," it was great. The life versions of the shi were becoming saturated with textuality.

Lifestyle, Exemplary Life, Textualized Life

Early in this chapter I quoted Patricia Ebrey's conclusion that determination of the identity of the shi is "essentially subjective." Much of this "subjective" determination is made on the basis of the individual life: One reads enough biographies in the HHS and the SGZ and a generalizable subjective sense of shi characteristics does indeed emerge. And that, I would argue, is a key function of the dynastic histories. The centrality of biography to early imperial historiography is universally recognized, but it is in the study of the shi that the ideological character of the biographical focus emerges. Shi are constructed, I have argued, through a process of self-recognition in the textual sphere. The "exemplary life" is, in early imperial historiography, precisely such a recognition device. As the culture of textual circulation expands and deepens, the recognition function itself becomes universalized. The same lives—Zhang Jian is a common example—are referred to so frequently in the secondary literature on late Latter Han shi that the secondary literature itself becomes implicated in the textual operation of reproductive exemplarity. The lives in the early imperial histories serve to shape what a textualized life is. The discursive stakes are enormous. The willingness of scholarship to accede to the early imperial historians' parameters is evidence of the reproductive power of this primary scene textualization.

We must seek this "subjective" quality not in clan registers, as we would for the later and more "objective" medieval oligarchy, but toward political, social, and cultural praxis. In discussing the lack of formal barriers to high social status in the late Han, Ebrey writes:

> Later Han society, as interpreted here, was relatively open; what gave the Ts'uis access to these higher social circles was not rank or birth, but simply their way of life. They acted as men of high status were supposed to act. With adequate economic means and social opportunities, they gained excellent educations; they knew how to act at funerals and when to defer to elders; they wrote elegant essays and prose poems; they were respected in their local community; they were asked to hold office and often accepted. . . . [T]hey normally derived much of their support from landownership, but the role of a man of local influence was also a part of their style of life; upper class men were supposed to be respected and influential in their communities. (Ebrey 1978: 38–9)

On a theoretical level, "style of life" is a very unsatisfactory formulation. The fact that many scholars who write on this period[21] have adopted it or a variant concept is due to several factors. One is, I believe, the relative richness of literati textual culture from the period and a concomitant dearth of material enabling precise descriptions of late Han socioeconomic characteristics such as wealth, landholding, commercial activity, and local adminstrative and fiscal practices.[22] A "style of life" is necessarily revealed discursively through writings, textualized "exemplary" lives,[23] and evaluations of fellow literati. All of these gave rise to a textualization of what we would call "inner" qualities.

Yu Yingshi sees in Chen Fan and Li Ying, two of the leaders of the "pures," the beginning of the "Three Kingdoms lifestyle" depicted in the *New Account of Tales of the World* (Yu Yingshi 1959). Chen Fan, in fact, is the subject of the first anecdote in the book. The portrayal of both men in the *New Accounts* emphasizes their outstanding moral character, their burning desire to right the empire, and their perspicacious and sometimes caustic judgments of other men. The "Three Kingdoms lifestyle" meant that a man's reputation had come to be based not on political or bureaucratic accomplishments but on the perceived state of his inner cultivation, as reflected in his words and writings.

Interpretation and judgment constituted much of discursive practice. In the later part of the second century, the work of judgment and interpretation took shape as the textual sphere expanded into the representation of "inner" qualities. The following anecdote is from Yu Huan's (d. c. 235) no longer completely extant *Wei Lue*, parts of which were incorporated into Pei Songzhi's commentary to the SGZ. The *Wei Lue* is a record of events contemporary with its author's life. If it is not more reliable than later sources, at least it represents the earliest stage of Han-Wei lifestyle construction. The poet Cao Zhi is perhaps the supreme representative figure of late Han pathos. The son of Cao Cao, who controlled the Han emperor during the last twenty-five years of the dynasty, he was widely believed to have been passed over for emperorship in favor of his brother Cao Pi (this is probably completely spurious; Cao Zhi appears never to have been destined to be emperor). Cao Zhi became the Ur-"poet in troubled times." The account that follows may well be completely spurious. Nevertheless, it gives a succinct early portrayal of a certain kind of historiographical determination. It concerns Handan Chun, one of the many literati who had allied themselves with Liu Biao in Jingzhou. Cao Cao sought alliance with the Jingzhou elite following his conquest of Jingzhou, and requested that Handan Chun visit his son Cao Zhi.

> Cao Zhi was very pleased when he first received Handan Chun. He invited him to sit, but at first didn't speak with him. The weather was hot then, so Cao Zhi called his attendant to get some water. After washing, he put on face powder. Then he bared his head, slapped his shoulders, performed the barbarian "Dance of the Five Hammers," juggled balls, and thrust swords. After saying over one thousand words about minstrels' anecdotes, he said to Handan Chun, "And what does Master Handan think of that?" Then he changed his clothes and put on a turban, straightened up his countenance, and had a critical discussion with Handan Chun about the extremes of primordial chaos and creation, and the meaning of evaluating things and drawing distinctions. Then he discoursed on the various merits and demerits of sages, rulers, ministers, and heroes from the days of Fu Xi and Huangdi to the present. Next he praised literature, *fu*, and elegies from ancient and contemporary times, and talked about what a government official's priorities should be. He also discussed the vagaries of military strategy. Cao Zhi then commanded his cook, and fine wine and food arrived together. He sat at his mat quietly, offering no resistance. At evening, Handan Chun returned home, and praised Cao Zhi's talent to all whom he knew, calling him "a heavenly person."[24]

What gives the anecdote a quality of near caricature is its hyper-textualization. Cao Zhi is seemingly called upon to perform a kind of "encyclopedia of the shi." The content of his discourse is the expanded content of the late shi textual sphere in its entirety, from vernacular performance to analysis of court structure. This is not an "exemplary" life, but a refiguring of life content as textual material. The anecdote also illustrates how the early Han hegemony of classical academic "textual lineages" and specialization has given way to an ethos that stresses comprehensiveness, eclecticism, and the encyclopedic. The sources' renditions of the content of literati interaction depict many instances of performances of a literati eclectic encyclopedic expertise that mirrors the contemporaneous compilation of actual encyclopedias. We can see in the shi, then, a reflection of dominant textual practice, and as a vehicle for circulation of a specific period's mode of textuality.

Re-theorizing the Shi: Sociotextual Formation

Social and economic historians are often uncomfortable with the term "shi," due largely to its subjective, idealist, indeterminate, "cultural" character, and many prefer to use terms like "aristocracy," "bureaucracy," "oligarchy," "great families," or simply "elite." Yang Liansheng, particulary in his foundational essay "Dong Han de Haozu" ("Great Families of the Latter Han") is representative of historians who hold out for a term of greater socioeconomic specificity. The categories "scholar-official," "literati," or "mandarin" too easily connote the ahistorical, unchanging China of primitive orientalism. A materialist would never posit the shi as a transhistorical category. And yet, for the analysis of textual authority, its phantasmatic, idealist, textual dimension proves it to be a very apposite category, since the shi is itself a category embedded in a regime of representation. It would be absurd for me, as a materialist, to claim that there is no social reality beyond the regime of representation. I do believe that even the Empire of the Text is determined "in the last instance" by the economic. Yet it does seem that when the object of study is the system of representation (textuality) and its strategies of authority, then a category that is so determined by representation is a useful one. I have left it untranslated not to suggest that it is a category unique to China, or that it has nothing in common with more scientific terms like "aristocracy," "oligarchy," or "elite," but to underscore the need to keep the question of representation constantly in mind, and to view the shi as a problem or a symptom rather than as an endpoint of scholarly inquiry. I also want to foreground the fact that defining this group—ascribing to it a set of characteristics of common concerns—entails a host of ideological assumptions. I am acknowledging that they are the primary subjects of Han history, as the texts have transmitted it. But another reason for my referring to them as "shi" is to emphasize my contention that they are in large part a discursive category, one that I think ultimately frustrates efforts at normative description. When talking of any social category in the pre- or noncapitalist world, though, there are substantial theoretical and ideological issues that the scholar must confront, and the stakes are significant.

For Marx, the social formation is in one sense the primary object of analysis, yet it remains undertheorized, particularly for the precapitalist period. Only with capitalism does there appear a social formation that is an objective social group that is class conscious and an agent of social transformation: the proletariat. This is because of the particular position of the economic in social relations:

> The capitalist mode of production is both the mode of production in which the economy is most easily recognized as the "motor" of history, and the mode of production in which the essence of this "economy" is unrecognized in principle (in what Marx calls "fetishism"). (Althusser and Balibar 1979: 216)

Social formations prior to capitalism are, in Marxism, of fairly limited use as categories for the analysis of political economy, since the role of the economic itself is more circumscribed. Hindess and Hirst are widely criticized and caricatured for insisting, in their Althusserian study of precapitalist modes of production (Hindess and Hirst 1975), that the investigation of concepts such as the feudal mode of production and the Asiatic mode of production must be done at a rigorous theoretical level, without any "truth" claim as to the applicability of the concepts to lived experience. This position, which would seem to obviate its utility for historical study, is actually of considerable use. It proceeds from the recognition that any *other* to the world capitalist system, such as feudal Europe, tribal exchange, or Asiatic despotism, is itself ultimately a discursive construction to the extent that this other is framed in the discursive terms set by the analysis's own location within the world capitalist system. In his own writing Marx deployed concepts such as slave society, feudal society, or Asiatic society only in terms of their relationship to capitalism: primarily as precursor or obstacle. This positing of an other to capitalism served the strategic purpose of denaturalizing capitalism itself and allowing for the imagination of its destruction. But as an other to capitalism, the precapitalist mode of production was itself always defined in terms of its own future negation.

There is an extensive literature, within various currents in Marxism and without, on precapitalist modes of production, and on feudalism in particular. In the case of the European and Japanese feudal periods, where there is a consensus that the term "feudal" can be applied with useful specificity, the problem with the rigid positioning of feudalism's status as "precapitalist" has been drawn into question. It is possible that as theoretical work on periodization and historical mode of production continues, there could be some future consensus that would hold that categories such as mode of production, social formation, or even class itself are of such limited analytical value for historical study as to be dispensed with. That would, however, have serious implications for political work in the late capitalist era that future consensus builders, one hopes, would consider. There needs, then, to be some theoretical rigor in positing classes and social formation in precapitalism.

In European historiography, issues of class and social formation before capitalism are secondary to issues of periodization and the "transition to capitalism," the latter a topic of heated debate since the 1950s. In Chinese historiography, a generation of Soviet, Chinese, and some Japanese and Euro-American historians applied mode of production stage theory in a fairly mechanical way, with the result that nearly the whole of imperial Chinese history was characterized as "feudal" in a fairly undifferentiated way.[25] This *longue durée* of undifferentiated feudalism bore a remarkable similarity to the "Asiatic mode of production" discourse, which, whether mentioned explicitly or not, was a structural principle in Marxist and some non-Marxist work in periodization of Chinese history, both in China and in the West. The Asiatic mode of production and the debates about it have been discussed exhaustively in a variety of locations, and I won't review the discussion here.[26] A formulation something like the Asiatic mode of production seems inescapable, though, when writing of non-Euro-American history prior to world capitalism. Perry Anderson traces clearly and cogently the ways in which Marx's writing on the Asiatic mode shows a direct affinity to theorists of oriental (i.e., Ottoman) despotism in sixteenth- to early eighteenth-century Europe, such as Machiavelli, Bacon, Harrington, and Montesquieu (Anderson 1974a: 397 ff). Indeed, it is in these very differentiations of an Ottoman "other" that the idea of Europe—the West—becomes coherent to Europeans. In filiating Marx and Engels's notes on the Asiatic mode to these sources, or to Hegel's appropriations of them, and in analyzing their claims logically, Anderson brilliantly dissects the theoretical inadequacy and self-contradiction of the various stages of the theory's development. Three dimensions of the theory—the prominence of the self-contained village, the absence of private property, and the powerful bureaucratic state with an ability to muster surplus labor for the construction of large-scale public works projects—are shown to be both logically inconsistent and coexisting nowhere in the world. Anderson explains the revival of interest in the theory in the 1960s to a desire for a way out of "the impasse of a quasi-universal feudalism" (Anderson 1974a: 484), while still seeking to account for the fact that European-style capitalism developed first in Europe and not elsewhere. The tautological quality to the last clause is intentional, for any phrasing of the question "why here and not there" is going to devolve on some positing of absolute difference. Janet Abu-Lughod's answer—chance—might have the benefit of accuracy, but it does not allow for the systematization that historians need to make. Anderson's conclusion is a complex and empirically convincing one: Drawing primarily on evidence from urban social formations and on specifics of property law, he sees the particular roots of the European transition from feudalism to capitalism in "the concatenation of antiquity and feudalism" (Anderson 1974a: 420). I say that his conclusion is empirically convincing, but note that he makes this conclusion in answering the question of why did the transition not take place in Japan, the only other society outside Europe that experienced a feudalism with structural features akin to Europe's. The availability of Roman institutions and legal structures could indeed have been the decisive factor in allowing the particular kind of transition that took place. But was it necessary for the resulting stage—nascent capitalism—to become world-conquering capitalism? Certainly the identification of nascent capitalism with an entity called the West, an entity whose state institutions had the propensity and will toward world domination, required, as Anderson himself reminds us, an other. And the fact that the West was posited as a place with its roots in Greece and Rome, with no intervening rôle for the Islamicate, for example, shows that even if Roman factors were decisive in the transition from feudalism to capitalism, the identification of Greece and Rome with "the West" was no less a discursive act. Without overlooking the material and human dimensions of the othering that produced the West/Orient divide, Said is not wrong to identify it as a discursive act.

The question remains, then, how to talk about premodern China in a western language in categories that allow for historical specificity but do not posit an absolute difference. There is no easy solution, and Anderson's critics, many of whom fault him for his Western exceptionalism,[27] fail to offer a language or conceptual scheme that enables difference without othering. Treating the problem of precapitalist mode of production as a wholly theoretical problem, as Hindess and Hirst do, does not solve the problem of the language and categories one should use when doing historical description of the noncapitalist world.

The shi, along with the emperor, are the personification of the Chinese state, and any determination of the character of that state in the early imperial period must analyze the elite. As I have discussed above, the shi have the particular character of being differentiable only by contrast to the eunuchs or, in some cases, the distaff relatives. Besides the minimalist definition I supplied on the first page of this chapter, which specified shi as those capable of holding bureaucratic office, other determinations of their identity are in fact "subjective." By treating the shi in terms of their function within the regime of textual authority, as the population of the

Empire of the Text, I hope to limn their theoretical status while suggesting a negative dimension to all positivist claims for their empirical or reified character. I have not attempted the final word on the shi as a subject of social history. Instead, I am claiming that the theorization of their existence must be made within a framework where such theorization is reasonable, and that framework is, in my opinion, that of textual circulation.

One common feature of precapitalist mode of production theory is the relative importance assigned to politicoideological authority as against the straightforwardly economic. As Lukács put it, "the [precapitalist] state is not a *mediation* of the economic control of society; it is that *unmediated dominance itself*" (Lukács 1971: 56). Here is one indication of the centrality of the shi, in their character as scholar-official-gentry: They were the keepers and transmitters of politicoideological authority. Another of Lukács's insights about classes in precapitalism, though, is also of use to us here. Lukács's *History and Class Consciousness* stresses the necessity, in discussion of class, of the analytical focus on social relations. The bourgeoisie and the proletariat are, for Lukács, the only pure classes under capitalism. His analysis suggests, in fact, that they are the only pure classes in history:

> [C]lass interests in pre-capitalist society never achieve full (economic) articulation. Hence the structuring of society into castes and estates means that economic elements are inextricably joined to political and religious factors. . . . This situation has its roots in the profound difference between capitalist and pre-capitalist economics. The most striking distinction, and the one that directly concerns us, is that pre-capitalist societies are much less cohesive than capitalism. The various parts are much more self-sufficient and less closely interrelated than in capitalism. (Lukács 1971: 55)

Lukács's argument for the autonomy of precapitalist social formations can lead in familiar orientalizing directions, such as "Asiatic societies," and the "never-ceasing changes of dynasty." Yet the reader will notice that the claim for autonomy resonates with my claim for a parallel history of textual authority, one that did not wholly coincide with political authority.[28]

The character of the shi as a historical social formation will remain imprecise due to both empirical and theoretical insufficiencies. What I am trying to suggest is that my analysis of textual authority as an autonomous structure in history might be evidence of a social homology: We can recognize in textual operation certain features of the social, and this is not simply a matter of coincidence. Let us assume, then, the actual sociohistorical existence of the shi. Any dominant semiautonomous group would need mechanisms for self-recognition, for group coherence.

Legal structures, complex systems of kinship and marriage ties, and performance of military, religious, and court ritual are common modes of elite self-recognition in noncapitalist societies. These elements, several of which would be more characteristic of the hereditary aristocracy of medieval China, are not as coherent for late Han and Wei shi. The textual production of the shi, however, was a primary medium through which the shi recognized itself as the shi: Shi textual production signified the shi position to other shi.

Theorizing the Relationship between the Shi and the State

In European historical literature on the transition from feudalism to capitalism, two of the great opposing social forces were the feudal elite and the state or protostate bureaucracies. As I have suggested above, the very strength attributed to the imperial state and state institutions was a major factor distinguishing the non-Western empires from the West in the early history of the othering project. In China, the presence of a developed bureaucratic system from the preimperial period, followed by its Han-era consolidation within the regime of canonical textuality, literacy, and imperial examinations, made the bureaucratic, administered character of the Chinese early imperial state all the more pronounced. This has created certain difficulties in descriptive terminology. A host of twentieth-century historians, for example, Etienne Balazs and Joseph Levenson, have classified the imperial Chinese state as a bureaucratic state. For Balazs, "the scholar-officials were the embodiment of the state" (Balazs 1964: 17). The bureaucrats' domination of peasants and the intermediate strata was absolute and unchanging throughout imperial history. The shi, being defined as actual or potential officeholders, naturally had a monopoly on officeholding, a source of power more stable than "such a risky and possibly ephemeral thing as the ownership of land" (Balazs 1964: 16). Many of the characteristics Balazs imputes to the shi are reminiscent of Max Weber's in *The Religion of China*: nonspecialization, identification with the state, strict adherence to official ideology (Confucianism) (Weber 1951: 107–52). One of the primary aims of Weber's study is to explain the absence of European-style capitalism in China, given the rationalistic potential of a bureaucracy, and Weber's identification of these particular features is structured by that aim. Many scholars would object to the identification of the shi with the bureaucrats, however. Peter Bol's study of the shi from the Tang to the Song shows that the importance of officeholding to the group he identifies as shi varied considerably. Balazs, however, is hard-pressed to identify any common interest of the officials beyond governing per se. The well-documented ambivalence toward officeholding is, for him, only explainable as dissidence.

Marx's notes on bureaucracy in his early and incomplete essay, "Contribution to the Critique of Hegel's Philosophy of Right" shows the attraction and the difficulty in identifying the shi with bureaucracy:

> The "state formalism" which bureaucracy is, is the "state as formalism." . . . Since this "state formalism" constitutes itself as an actual power and itself becomes its own material content, it goes without saying that the "bureaucracy" is a web of practical illusions, or the "illusion of the state." . . . The spirit of the bureaucracy is the "formal state spirit." The bureaucracy therefore turns the "formal state spirit" or the actual spiritlessness of the state into a categorical imperative. The bureaucracy takes itself to be the ultimate purpose of the state. Because the bureaucracy turns its "formal" objectives into its content, it comes into conflict everywhere with "real" objectives. It is therefore obliged to pass off the forms for the content and the content for the form. State objectives are transformed into objectives of the department, and department objectives into objectives of state. The bureaucracy is a circle from which no one can escape. Its hierarchy is a hierarchy of knowledge. (Tucker 1978: 23–24)

The appeal of this rather Kafkaesque formulation for this study, and for any understanding of "official" behavior for that matter, is the "formal" self-referential character of the bureaux. The bureaucracy's main aim becomes its own self-reproduction, without any structural need for external reference. This is possible under capitalism, of course, because the institutions of capitalism themselves do not coincide with the administrative structure of the state. Knowledge, as the structural principle of the bureaucratic hierarchy, is not functional or technical knowledge but is simply another expression of bureaucratic self-absorption. But it is the particular phantasmatic character of Marx's bureaux that makes the identification of the shi with the bureaucrats so problematic. Marx's phantasmatic bureaucracy is only a possible construct when the "real" structures of domination are elsewhere. The textual production of the shi can assume the self-referential structure of the bureaux, but since it is only in their textual production that the "system" exists as a system, there is ipso facto no "other" to the shi in the system of political authority. Balazs's description of the imperial bureaucratic state as "totalitarian" is only possible if one conceives of an alternative intellectual force that is suppressed by the power of the bureaucracy. This notion might be problematic as well.

Although the word "intellectuals" is not commonly used as a straight translation for shi, the intellectual ideal is behind a broad spectrum of work on the shi, particularly in the late Latter Han. Yu Yingshi is the foremost of those who would understand the greater part of shi textual work as the product of "intellectuals,"[29] which is also how he would identify the shi of the late Latter Han. One of Yu's abiding scholarly concerns, in fact, is with the transhistorical category "Chinese intellectual." The claims for the relevance of his historical work to the fate of Chinese "intellectuals" in this century, in fact, gives his work much of its rhetorical force. In the late twentieth century, most non-Marxist work on "intellectuals" has at least an indirect debt to Karl Mannheim's idea of the "free-floating" intellectual, who operates out of neither social nor personal interest, but in service of some ideal. The positing of a "free-floating" intellectual is dependent, in fact, on the separability of the intellectual from all specifiable material interests.

The model that arises most frequently in studies of early imperial China is the dissident scholar-official: the conscience of the state who mounts principled opposition to the hegemonic interests of the state. This is how Yu Yingshi would describe the late Han shi, and the idea of the dissident oppositional scholar is also central to Martin Powers's 1991 study, *Art and Political Expression in Early China*. An examination of the writings of many exemplary shi, by figures such as Wang Fu or Zhongchang Tong, makes it easy to conclude that whatever their socioeconomic origins, shi textual production was not in fact a simple articulation of privilege.[30] In the works of these and like writers, the description of the shi as dissident intellectuals seems reasonable. But before making that identification too hastily, let us examine those to whom these "dissident" works were addressed. Although they contained implicit or explicit criticism of imperial policy, they were also or even primarily addressed to other shi, even when the audience of memorials was the emperor. The fact that numerous memorials to the emperor survive in the records and that imperial memorials were a recognized literary genre suggests that their public character was at least as important as the function of mere communication. In the absence of a shi position that condemned this sort of "dissidence," one must conclude that the political autonomy of the shi could easily have allowed an articulation of certain positions that would not absolutely coincide with the emperor's positions. Here it is important, I believe, to be precise about the issue of separability. If one identifies the shi primarily as intellectuals or dissidents, the separability of the group from the state is a structural necessity. But since state power itself has various aspects, several of which take physiological or consanguinal concrete forms—the distaff families, the eunuchs, the emperor—it is possible for the shi to be equivalent to the operation of the state in one sphere (administration, textual production, etc.) while preserving the structure of separability by their differentiation from the distaff families and the eunuchs. The labels intellectual and dissident, then, rest on an assumption of a certain kind of autonomy. The idea of dissidence is not wholly inappropriate given the imperial state's punishment of writers for slander and related offenses. Yet viewed from the perspective of the Empire of the Text, even these acts of slander are not enough to substantiate a claim for the shi as an interest group distinct from the state. As I have already remarked, any sociopolitical system is by nature incomplete and its operation will be characterizable by cracks and fissures. Dissidence itself certainly does not have a transhistorical character.

A third influential figuration of the shi is found in Tanigawa Michio and the Kyoto school's theory of "local community" discussed earlier in this chapter, which has become in the postwar West and Japan the hegemonic explanation of medieval elite authority, the character of which is claimed to have been set in the late Latter Han. Tanigawa and his allies see in the local regional communities an operation of authority that derives from the local appreciation of the authority's moral qualities. Although the unverifiable psychologisms on which the Kyoto school and its adherents depend would make "community" unattractive to the materialist or positivist historian, one advantage of the Kyoto school's work is that it produces an analytical representation of elite practice that reflects the content of elite textual production. Tanigawa's sources are "exemplary biographies," funeral inscriptions, and testimonial literature, much of which indeed celebrates the shi's local beneficence. In a manner reminiscent of all scholars who protest their own independence from ideology, Tanigawa claims to have been led to his theory of "community" without preconception, guided solely by the textual evidence (Tanigawa 1987: 88). Tanigawa's formulation is a diagnostically valuable response to the real issue of the inadequacy of our theoretical and descriptive tools in the analysis of noncapitalist social and ideological structures, and he has done the field a great service by focusing attention on the affective quality of the sources. His opponents in Japan have been overly mechanistic Marxists (largely nonspecialists in the pre-Tang period) who attack him, with justification, for his defensive idealization of elite morality at the expense of any analysis of patterns of domination or relations of production. Tanigawa has made a perceptive synthesis of Kawakatsu Yoshio and Masubuchi Tatsuo, both of whom concentrate more directly on the late Han. I would not attempt to counter his idealism with materialism; that would be problematic given the nature of the sources. Where he is vulnerable to a materialist critique, though, is in taking the operation of textual culture as a transparent reflection of social reality. Were Tanigawa to pay more attention to textuality as textuality, he might see in the sources of his claims for shi moral and ideological autonomy a reflection of the autonomous sphere of the textual itself.

In general, it seems to me that the Kyoto school's analysis of the discontinuity between the Han and the Six Dynasties period underemphasizes the power of empirewide ideology that was immanent in textual practice, and, like those who would identify the shi as "intellectuals" or "dissidents," underemphasizes the statist character of the shi. The perceived autonomy of the shi class is related to the trend toward socioeconomic autonomism that began in the first century. The diffusion and decentralization of surplus extraction that resulted from this autonomism contributed to the collapse of the Han dynasty, but also laid the basis for a social formation dependent on the imperial structure for its ideological raison d'être and textual foundation, but on local, subimperial, and semiautonomous structures for its self-constitutive practices. One ideological function of the shi as a social formation within the Empire of the Text was to hold in tension the imperial on the one hand and the familial, communitarian, regional, and local on the other. The disjuncture between the Empire of the Text and imperial political authority is highlighted, naturally, in a period of imperial political collapse. The practices under the Cao court in the late Han of "garrison agriculture" (*dun tian*) and "local selection" of officials (*xiangju lixuan*) were symptomatic of this disjuncture, being related and failed attempts to acknowledge the consolidation of the imperial-local nexus within the operation of the Empire of the Text (the flourishing of "literature" in the Cao court is not unrelated), while attempting to make extraction of agricultural surplus purely imperial and no longer subject to the mediation of powerful local families and landholders. What followed the Han collapse was a regional and local continuation of the imperial-local nexus of the Empire of the Text—the group of phenomena read as "community" by the Kyoto scholars—that coincided with imperial political dysfunction.

I suggest that the shi are indeed coterminous with the state but that textual culture is not a mere equivalent to state culture. Political authority was, of course, conveyed through the textual medium, but textual circulation also served, in its pure existence, to perform authority, to signify authority to the circulators of authority. We saw in the Affair of the Proscribed Factions, though, that identification mechanisms were complex. There was simultaneously a widespread shi self-recognition as shi, along fairly codified lines, and both an official and, as we shall see in the following chapter, an unofficial ideology that condemned fraternal or factional association. We have seen the theoretical and conceptual difficulties in defining the shi as a social formation and have suggested that their function within a textual regime—as circulators of texts and as subjectivities authorized by the circulation of text—was potentially a fruitful context in which to view them. In chapters 3 and 4 I will discuss some of the specific textual practices that figured the shi in social terms.

Notes

1. Johnson (1977); CHC, 631. Pilz (1991) remains the most complete study of PRC historiographical issues around the structure of Han society.

2. Tao (1954) and others comment on the dual fuction of the shi, ascribing to them one social character while in office and another while out of office. See Dirlik (1978), 114 ff.

3. The sources on which I have relied most include Mao Hanguang (1966 and 1988), Su Shaoxing (1987), Kawakatsu (1974), Kawakatsu (1967), Kawakatsu (1958), Lao Gan (1971), Tang Changru (1955), Utsunomiya (1967), Yang Liansheng (1936), Yu Yingshi (1959), Bielenstein (1976 and 1980), Ch'en Chi-yun (1975 and 1980), Crowell, (1979), de Crespigny (1969, 1966, and 1976), Ebrey (1983 and 1978), Loewe (1974 and 1968).

4. See, for example, Mao Hanguang (1966), Ebrey (1978), Johnson (1977), Su Shaoxing (1987), Kawakatsu (1974).

5. Yang Liansheng (1936), Tang Changru. "Dong Han monian de daxing mingshi" in (1955).

6. The literature on the status of dependents is extensive. See in particular Ch'u (1972), 127–35; Utsunomiya (1954), 446–7; and Yang Liansheng (1936), esp. 1023–30.

7. After the Han, these relationships became more like the feudalistic "guest" relationships. For this development, see Kawakatsu (1958), 175–6, and Ebrey (1983), 542.

8. See the discussion below of Xu Gan's *Discourse on the Central* (*Zhong lun*) for an example of the castigation of the hypocrisy found in this relationship.

9. A large collection of work in this area can be found in the seminar collection edited by Tanigawa (1983). The kyōdōtai school concentrates its work on the Southern Dynasties period, but commonly notes the emergence of the communitarian ethos in the late Han.

10. Mao Hanguang (1988), 81 ff. His primary evidence, the context of which I will discuss below, is that shi identified as partisans in the Proscribed Factions Affair (160s–180s) represented a wide geographical spectrum and that in the panegyrics that shi at the capital used to characterize each other, the discourse of the "whole nation" (*hainei* or *tianxia*) was prominent, i.e., the field of reputation was the entire state. Hsü Cho-yun (1988), however, reaches the opposite conclusion through a reading of the same source as Mao's. Both scholars use evidence collected in Jin Fagen (1963).

11. Quoted in Nylan (1982).

12. Li Shan commentary to Cao Pi's *Dian lun: lun wen.*

13. Bielenstein (1980) admits that there is no reliable figure for the Latter Han, but his data suggest this number as a minimum figure.

14. The standard accounts derive from HHS *juan* 67. Secondary studies include Yang Liansheng (1936); Kawakatsu (1967); Ch'en (1975); 10–39, CHC, chap. 5; and de Crespigny (1975).

15. 196–220 are the precise dates of the Jian'an, but the term is generally used to refer to the last period of the Latter Han.

16. The HHS records that when Chen Fan was initially appointed, he missed a meeting with Wang Gong, who subsequently revoked the appointment. A subordinate interceded on Chen Fan's behalf, citing Chen Fan's outstanding character. Wang Gong admitted his mistake and reinstated him. For this act of admitting his faults he is said to have won the loyalty of all the local shi. HHS: 1821.

17. Cai Yong was not prominent among the "pures." Kawakatsu Yoshio is of the opinion that although he was known as a strict Confucian, he was in fact antipure on the local level. In Kawakatsu (1974), 399–401.

18. Liu Biao had been appointed to the position of Regional Inspector in 190 by Sun Jian, Prefect of Changsha, after Sun had assassinated the previous Inspector. By 193, the office of Regional Governor was virtually an independent warlord.

19. For the "Jingzhou coterie," see the discussion below on literati groups. Also, HHS, 2421. Matsumoto (1961), 1335–8.

20. From the *Dian lue* in the Pei Songzhi commentary to the SGZ: 601.

21. Chiefly those scholars who underemphasize the economic characteristics of the ruling elite, like Kawakatsu Yoshio, Tanigawa Michio, and Yu Yingshi.

22. The CHC, among other texts, points out that the last part of the second century is the period in the Han about which our information is most spotty.

23. The term is Ebrey's. CHC, 632.

24. SGZ: 603. The *Wei lue* goes on to claim that at that time the succession had not yet been decided and that both Cao Zhi and Cao Pi wanted to gain Handan Chun to their causes. The *Wei lue* certainly construed Cao Zhi's performance as a tactic to gain him an ally and the concomitant political advantage. This is of course beyond our knowledge.

25. See Dirlik (1978), 186–90, for a chart outlining Chinese historians' positions on the periodization question.

26. For a sample of the literature, see Brook (1989), Krader (1975), O'Leary (1989), Tökei (1979), Godelier (1978).

27. See, for example, Vali (1993), 24–27, 60–68. In "The Uniqueness of the West," Paul Hirst, predictably, faults Anderson for his empiricism. Other methodological criticism includes Heller (1977), Millband (1975), and Thomas (1975).

28. Ferenc Tökei, a Hungarian sinologist, theorist, and former student of Lukács's, is best known for his writings on the Asiatic mode of production. His earlier work, however, was on pre-Qin and Six Dynasties Chinese literature. Tökei's theory is that at the heart of both the "elegiac mode" that characterizes lyric production since Qu Yuan and the "aetheticism" that characterizes the medieval literary scene is the particular social character of the shi: to be near political power (the court) but not to possess any (due to insufficiently developed systems of private property and commerce). Tökei (1967, 1971).

29. He uses the term in his collection of essays *Zhongguo zhishi jieceng shi lun: gudai pian* (1980). Yu is also author of one of the most widely cited, widely anthologized, and influential articles on the shi of the late Han and early medieval period: "Han-Jin zhi ji shi zhi xin zijue yu xin sichao" (New Self-consciousness and new currents of thought among the shi of the late-Han-Wei-Jin period).

30. See Balazs (1964), 187–225.

3

Social Texts

In 1595 Matteo Ricci published his *Jiao you lun*, a collection of translated excerpts from Greek and Latin writings on friendship—by Plato, Aristotle, Cicero, and others—and it quickly became the most widely copied, widely published, and widely read Western text in China.[1] It appeared during a time of a proliferating discourse on homosocial life among Ming dynasty shi, a discourse broad enough to allow the position that loyalty to friends was more important than loyalty to the state.

The Specter of Asociality

Ricci's collection was in most respects a representative collection of classical thought on the subject. The explicit problematics of homoeroticism in Greek writings were not represented in the sixteenth century in China or in Europe, but the Ming reader could gain from the collection a confirmation of a prior belief in the higher calling of the homosocial relation:[2] its disaffinity with personal advantage and profit and its affinity with moral principle and thought itself. In one sense, with the introduction of Ricci's text, shi discourse of self-representation enters its world-historical stage. That homosocial relations among late Ming shi could be imagined as taking moral precedence over service to the state is certainly a consequence of developments in late Ming political and intellectual history, but it is also no accident that a vision of extrastatist social universalism could take shape alongside a nascent Sino-European discourse on homosociality. The complex social structure of the late Ming, however, was characterized by a wide and competing variety of social discourses—the commercial, the aesthetic, and the religious, not to mention a developed urban performative-cultural scene—that made inadequate a simple equivalency between the public (or the social in any of its concrete forms) and the state. Many literate men were not able to serve in the state even if they wished to, and "literati" culture was able to take shape with some genuine autonomy from the state. And just as the state could be figured in the abstract rather than in the concrete sociality of government service, so was Ming asociality—reclusion—even more assimilable into a socially signifying "style of life." Even the ideal of "self-containment" unfolded in an at least minimally social sphere.

A perceived cultural and "literary" emphasis on friendship as opposed to love is a "Chinese characteristic" in the view of many twentieth-century interpreters of shi cultural production in the imperial period. The perceived discursive centrality of homosociality is related to the more generalized representation of the shi ideal: a moral uprightness born of self-cultivation in service of the higher ideals of the state. The friendship relationship, being more "philosophical" than the erotic or amatory one, is structurally the only relationship that can at once convey the multiple aspects of self-recognition, sociality, and morality that structure the idealized sense of the elite "public" in political philosophy in China and elsewhere.

Ming dynasty shi not only lived in a society of greater structural complexity than the Han, but Ming theorization of the state and society had the perspective of a long and varied history. In the Han, the empire did not have the perspective of the *longue durée* of previous dynasties, and theorization of the state had less an historical character than a prescriptive or administrative character: Han state discourse was performative in a way that later imperial discourse did not need to be. Just as we saw in the earlier discussion of canon formation, Han discourses of the social and of the social character of both the state and the individual life were in the process of being determined. The Affair of the Proscribed Factions has loomed large in sociointellectual history because historians have seen it as a crucial moment in defining relations between shi and state, especially with regard to shi autonomy. In the Affair, it has been argued, one can witness a conception of shi "class" interest that was not coterminous with the state. In chapter 2 I suggested that the Affair had been overdetermined in historiography. Although it certainly involved some form of articulation of group activity, it would be exaggerating matters to suggest that it had produced a shi "class consciousness." There is no class consciousness without class, of course, and another point of chapter 2 was to suggest that the concept of class itself has distorted our view of early imperial society. The concept of community, too, is limited in its applicability to the case of the Han shi. In discussing Foucault's historicization of textuality and its various functions, Brian Stock suggests that

> Foucault's plea on behalf of the hidden plasticity of discourse occasionally sounds like an echo from another age: from antiquity perhaps, when the supremacy of the verbal arts was established; or more aptly, from the later Middle Ages, when it was first successfully challenged by the rise of literacy

and textuality; or if the notion is not too far-fetched, from the moment when ahistorical sociology was born from empirical historical research, since his idea of discourse, at least in its productive side, reminds one of the nostalgia for Gemeinschaft, the small community of speakers, hearers, and face-to-face relationships obscured and obliterated by the internalization of texts, methods, orders, disciplines, and prejudices. (Stock 1990: 111)

Stock's notion here is an intriguing one, but it also admits of infinite regression. Perhaps to posit the medieval textual community is to admit of a nostalgia for the pretextual, a scene of immediate revelation of spoken and heard. And before language itself, what?

As community is one specter behind modernity's discursive constructs (Foucault), I would posit asociality as the spectral presence behind shi social life—a life of textual circulation within a nexus that combined aspects of elite and bureaucratic-administrative socialities. But, and this is a crucial caveat, it is the formalized and functionalized asociality of the state itself. Consider the following passage from the late Han shi, Zhu Mu (99–163):

> Someone asked, "You have cut off visits and inquiries. You refuse guests. You also don't respond [to anyone]. Why?" I said, "In ancient times people came and went about their business. There were no private [i.e., nonprofessional] relationships. People met at public court, and gathered together according to propriety and rules. Otherwise friendship would just become customary practice." (HHS: 1467)

This is an idealized vision of the shi state: There were no private—i.e., nonofficial—homosocial relationships. The "public" was official life, the life of the court. "Life" is not compartmentalized into "work" and "social life": Life is performed according to precise codes.

In chapter 2 I discussed the inadequacy of the term "bureaucracy" in characterizing the Han shi, despite the fact that I believe it is accurate to define them in terms of their ability to function as government office-holders. In quoting from Marx on Hegel I meant to draw attention to the particular autonomous character of the bureaucracy as Marx theorized it. We must remember, though, that central to Marx's theorization of the bureaucracy is its parasitical structure:[3] The self-absorbed, self-referential character of bureaucratic life is only possible because the "real" system of domination and extraction is elsewhere. The irrational dimension of bureaucratic life (contra Weber)—the play of personal contacts, favoritism, and arbitrary authority—is only possible given this sense of bureaucracy as parasitical, with little at stake or at reference beyond its own reproduction.[4] Early imperial officialdom has in common with Weber's bureaucracy several features which I also discuss in chapter 2. But it diverges in significant ways. It is not, in the Han at least, structured as parasitical: the government is the primary agent of extraction, and is not a phantasmatic doppelganger of rentier, commercial, or capitalist extractive bodies. Early imperial officialdom is, as I have stressed, fundamentally coterminous with textual culture: the creation, circulation and transmission of texts. This means that unlike capitalist social structure, with its well-developed and semiautonomous cultural, ideological, pedagogical, and intellectual spheres, the early imperial shi were also the social articulation of the work of the state: *to be a shi was to work.* Zhu Mu was able to see in "socializing" a decadent sphere of activity that represented a debased alternative to the work of the state. To see how that formulation was possible, we turn now to preimperial and early imperial theorization of the nature and social character of the work of the state.

Work, Family, State, and Homosociality

The distinction made between commoners and nobility on the basis of noble monopoly of performance of authorized ancestor ritual, noted in many pre-Qin texts and confirmed by lists of ritual attributes (Lewis 1990: 31), is also reflected in early usage of two of the most common words for officeholding, both pronounced *shi*,[5] the latter word certainly derived from the sinograph for the shi. Both of these words can have the sense of sacrificial ritual, which was, in common etymology, the originary official function of the early state. In its originary sense, officeholding would be hereditary and would consist of communication with the souls of clan members, according to the dictates of clan law. This could be Zhu Mu's utopian past: a fusion of "public" and "private"; of the state and of life itself. Zhu Mu's utopia recalls the teachings of the Confucian texts, which developed within the aristocratic discourse of clan law at just the period when the system of clan law was being transformed.[6] Hsiao Kung-ch'üan argues that at the heart of the Confucian texts is the elevation of *ren* ("benevolence") to the "one all-pervading concept," which brought into discursive alignment the spheres of self, family, and state. More important than the content of the concept is the alignment brought between these various spheres and the structural impossibility of an antithesis between individual and state at the broadest conceptual level. The correct fulfillment of familial duties, then, is not private but is an affair of the state. This is not, of course, unique to China. Most entries of the familial into normativizing discourse function to reinforce statist authority. Hsiao Kung-ch'üan suggests that the merging of clan law with the "all-pervading concept" is a prescriptive measure, with an implicit criticism of the impartiality and arbitrariness that inhere in the administration of clan law.[7]

The possibility that the family could be a private sphere is thus elimi-
nated in Confucian texts. There remains, however, the somewhat ambiguous sphere of the homosocial. The five relationships, codified in Zhou
times, consisted of sovereign and minister, father and son, husband and
wife, elder brother and younger brother, and friends (*pengyou zhi jiao*).
Of all of the terms, only friendship is not expressed as a hierarchical dyad,
with the superior figure in the first position. This is the source of the first
ambiguity: Although much of the discussion of the actual homosocial
dyads in pre-Qin texts concerns hierarchical relationships, the structure
of hierarchy is not implicit: There is, in friendship, a possibility of pure
reflexivity. If we are to follow Hsiao in seeing Confucian texts as effecting
an adequation between clan law and the state, then social life in general,
and friendship in particular, would be one form of relationship most re-
sistant to that adequation. Not surprisingly, then, there is considerable
attention devoted to friendship in the *Analects* and the *Mencius*. In the
Analects, virtues central to friendship are predictable: honesty, respect,
loyalty, and self-respect.[8] Confucius describes three kinds of advanta-
geous friendships and three kinds of disadvantageous friendships:

> Friendship with the upright, friendship with the sincere, and friendship with
> the man of much observation—these are advantageous. Friendship with the
> man of specious air; friendship with the insinuatingly soft, and friendship
> with the glib tongued—these are injurious. (Legge 1893: 311; *Lun yu* 16.4)

The placement of friendship within the larger context of moral teaching
is articulated more clearly in Mencius, who devotes much of book 5, part
B, chapter 3 to friendship, particularly the question of friendship with
social inferiors or superiors.

> Wan Chang asked, "May I ask about friendship?" "In making friends with
> others, do not rely on the advantage of age, position, or powerful relations.
> In making friends with someone you do so because of his virtue, and you
> must not rely on any advantages you possess.
> "The reverence of the inferior to the superior is called honoring what is
> honorable. The respect of the superior to the inferior is called respecting
> sageliness. The two are fundamentally one in meaning." (*Mengzi* 10.3: 237)

The classical philosophers' location of friendship within the general rubric of virtuous behavior may seem rather simplistic and obvious, yet two
dimensions of the discourse stand out. The first is that friendship is a
potential site of "advantage," and the second is that "true" friendship
can posit a kind of homological equivalence. Included in the "way of the
superior man" in the *Doctrine of the Mean* is the following precept: "To

set an example in behaving to a friend as I would require him to behave to me" (Legge 1893: 394; *Zhong yong* 13.4).

Confucius expresses the self-reflective equation more succinctly in the *Analects*: "Have no friends not [equal to] yourself" (*Lun yu*, 1.8). The self-reflective character of friendship expresses further ambiguities within the concept. If friendship is a reflective structuring of self-cultivation and self-knowledge, why is there any *need* for friendship at all? And further, friendship is the only one of the five relationships that is structurally open to the vice of "advantage" in a way that the hierarchical dyads are not. Friendship has contained within it the potential for individualist deviation. The concern for friendship in these early Confucian texts may simply reflect an acknowledgment of the actual content of social life and its dangers.

A related contextual parameter of the rhetoric of friendship is that of knowing and being known by others. "Knowing" is normally operative in the downward direction of the hierarchy and has as its basis the ruler-minister relationship, as well as the necessity for the ruler to discern able ministers. Although it is common in shi texts to stress imperial dependence on the ministers, we should also bear in mind that this form of recognition is also an expression of control: To know the minister is to employ him appropriately. Knowledge and recognition are exercises of power. When homosocial discourse reaches its apogee, in the late Han and Wei-Jin period, a related but transformed dimension of homosociality would emerge paramount—the ideal friend as "he who understands me." The *Shi ji* provided a stock of examples of this kind of "knowing," and it served as a metaphor for a ruler's recognition of the worth of a shi, and as a figure of "knowability" in general. A commonly referenced archetype from the *Shi ji* is the story of Guan Zhong and Bao Shuya (also known as Bao Shu). Guan Zhong was constantly with Bao Shuya when he was young, and Bao Shuya "understood the sageliness of his friend" (*Shi ji*: 2131). Later they served separate masters. Bao Shuya's master became Duke Huan of Qi, and Guan Zhong's protector, the duke's enemy, was killed. Guan Zhong was imprisoned. Bao Shuya arranged for his release and found him employment with Duke Huan, under whom he became a wise and famous minister. Upon his release from prison, Guan Zhong praised his friend:

> Earlier when I was poor, I did business with Bao Shuya. I would keep the greater share of riches and profits for myself. Bao Shuya did not think me greedy; he knew I was poor. I would devise [business] strategies for Bao Shuya and we would end up poorer still. Bao Shuya didn't think me stupid; he knew that there were lucky and unlucky times. . . . My parents gave birth to me; Bao Shuya understands me. (*Shi ji*: 2131–2)

Most often cited from the *Shi ji* in the writing on homosociality in the late Latter Han are the stories of Zhang Er and Chen Yu (*juan* 89), and the story of Ji An and Zheng Dangshi (*juan* 120). The first story tells of the destructive effects of power and ambition on a lifelong friendship, the second of the transient nature of friendship based on association with the rich and powerful. In these archetypal stories, homosociality has its limitations. The Guan Zhong–Bao Shuya story has a happy ending only because Guan Zhong goes on to become a virtuous and capable minister. The "knowledge" ends up being bureaucratic knowledge: knowledge in the service of employment. It is only in official service that the arbitrariness associated with homosociality is obviated.

In the "five relationship" formula, we assume that the friendship relationship is a dyad, since all of the other relationships are dyadic. But that need not be the case: friends can include any number of men. Friendship is a category that is expandable in a way that the others are not. With emperor-minister, there is always only one emperor. Therein lies another source of the ambiguity in the homosocial: its expandability. Here we enter the sphere of the faction. "Faction" (*dang*) has several related senses. It appears as a Zhou administrative distinction, corresponding to five hundred families, and continued to be used in this neutral, descriptive way. In the compound *pengdang*, often but not exclusively pejorative, it can refer to a nonofficial, nonlineage association. But from a very early date it can also convey the pejorative sense of the private. There is a poem in the *Book of Documents* that begins:

> No partiality; no inconstancy
> Is to follow the sense of the kingly.
> To be without selfish attraction
> Is to follow the way of the kingly.
> To be without selfish aversion
> Is to follow the road of the kingly.
> No partiality; no factionalism;
> Then the kingly way is vast and broad.
> No factionalism; no partiality
> Then the kingly way is level and plain
> (*Shu jing*, Hongfan, 4.2).

The greatest danger in the homosocial, then, is that it provides a social sphere for the exercise of partiality and selfishness: It is the opposite of the "public."

In the Former Han codification of classical canonicity and the establishment of state Confucianism associated with Dong Zhongshu, homosociality is no longer problematized. In fact, it disappears. The Five Relationships (in the pre-Qin texts the phrasing is "five constants" [*wuchang*] or "five relationships" [*wulun*]) have become, in Dong Zhongshu and in later texts, the *"three* warp-skeins" *(sangang)*: ruler and subject; father and son; husband and wife, all of which are structured in a hierarchical dyad.[9] The "three warp-skeins" also figure in the *Records of the White Tiger Hall,* which is evidence that it had become normativized by that time. In Dong Zhongshu's totalizing system of correspondences, each element occupies its position by virtue of its function. There is no structural need for the sphere of the social, as distinct from "work." Work, by which I mean administrative work only, had its putative origin in ritual sacrifice, the performance of a family/state duty structured as a communicative act. The actual content of administrative work was textual circulation.

Late Han Philosophical Writing on Homosocial Relationships

In the latter half of the second century, the period that witnessed the Affair of the Proscribed Factions, the Yellow Turban revolt, Dong Zhuo's sack of the capital, and the rise of Cao Cao, writings against factionalism were widespread among the shi. Their authors included shi who were involved in the Affair and shi who were not, as well as those who have been identified as sympathetic to the "pure" factionalist cause. These writings did not represent a partisan point of view that formed one half of a debate. There was no dissent from the view that partisanship and "unofficial" relationships were dangerous and were to be avoided. Zhu Mu's rejection of private social relationships, quoted earlier in this chapter, is typical in tone and content. Although most of the texts I will discuss in this section use the word "faction" as the primary object of criticism, most suggested that *all* homosocial activity was worthy of censure. The writings I discuss in this section have no unified generic character. Several are from "discourses" *(lun),* the most common vehicle for general observations of a philosophical or moral type, and miscellaneous in character.[10] Others are from miscellaneous essays or letters. One of the lengthiest pieces on the subject is a chapter in Xu Gan's *Discourse on the Central,* singled out in writings by Xu's contemporaries as being one of the major textual accomplishments of the late Latter Han.

Writing on friendship appears in Latter Han writings after a relative silence on the subject after the age of the pre-Qin philosophers and extending throughout the Former Han. It is overwhelmingly negative in tone, condemning the relationships of the time. Although a certain amount of this criticism is directed at improper *kinds* of homosocial association, we can also see in the late Han discourse of homosociality a sense of its inherent ambiguity. It is possible, as well, that homosociality allowed a discourse to function that could treat certain issues of concern. Differentiation between the genuine and the opportunistic, as well as many other qualities that we associate with the "inner life," were explored within the context of homosocial discourse. The *Hou Han shu* writes of Liu Liang (?-181) that

> he had always detested the current abundance of relationships for personal advantage and the devious and immoral formation of factions. He thus wrote his *On Breaking Congregation.* Perceptive contemporaries felt that "just as Confucius had struck terror in the hearts of the degenerate officials of his day in writing the *Spring and Autumn Annals,* how could the common scholar of the day fail to feel ashamed with the appearance of this text?" The work has not survived. (HHS: 2635)

Fan Ye's description could apply to most of the late Han discourse on friendship and faction, which was almost uniform in its condemnation of "utilitarian" personal relationships. Wang Fu (c. 67–158) was a friend of Ma Rong, Zhang Heng, and Cui Yuan, all prominent literati of the genera-tion immediately preceding that of the proscribed officials. His *Eremetic Discourses,* a work in ten *juan,* is an extended critique of the government and morals of his time that has been called the most trenchant work of social criticism in the Eastern Han.[11] Wang Fu's writing illustrates a man-ner of dichotomizing individual and state that characterizes much of later Han thought. Public (*gong*) and private (*si*) are recognized as two distinct realms. Wang Fu's work gave further ideological justification to the in-creasingly common pattern of refusing office on moral grounds. Chapter Thirty of the *Eremetic Discourses* is entitled, "Forming Relationships" (*jiao ji*).[12] It begins:

> It is said that "in men it is the old [which is valued]; in utensils it is the new."[13] As brothers grow apart, friends grow closer. This is the pattern of relations between friends and feelings among men. Today, however, it is not so. Many long for the distant and forget what is close. They turn their backs on the old and look toward the new. Some grow more distant with every passing year, some harm each other in mid-passage. They disobey the rules of the ancient sages and break the bonds of ancient oaths. Why is this? When we reflect upon it, this too can be known. Power and position have constant attraction; patterns have their determined nature. Men will struggle to cleave to wealth and high rank; this is the constant attraction of power and position. Men will struggle to escape from poverty and low rank; this is the certainty of pattern.[14]

The great disparity between rich and poor and the ostentatious lives of certain sectors of the elite were the targets for several late Han social crit-ics.[15] These writers do not advocate anything like redistribution of wealth. They attack what they perceive as wasteful and excessive. Excess in a variety of contexts is a theme to which we will return in the discussion of homosocial discourse. Wealth and poverty form the parameters for Wang Fu's discourse on friendship, just as they do for his discussion of most topics in the *Qian fu lun*. People befriend the wealthy for real or imagined advantage, and it becomes difficult to differentiate the opportunists from the sincere. Material wealth, for Wang Fu and like-minded critics, is excessive and exterior: It is too directly a signifier of itself. Wang Fu's figuration of an interior coherence shaped by morality and sincerity shifts representational power away from material display and toward textual standards, from ostentatious wealth to a reconfirmation of the all-pervading concepts of the canonical texts. In the *Eremetic Discourses*, the social disintegration and corruption occasioned by the pursuit of material wealth break the cosmological bond between inner qualities and outer behavior that would inhere in a just society. Human relations in this postlapsarian state become complicated by the pull of the external. His blanket condemnation of friendship is the result of the relationship's perceived subsumption into the realm of the functional and instrumental. This denunciation of opportunistic friendship characterizes the Confucian critique of social relations in the latter half of the second century. Zhu Mu's[16] "Exaltation of Liberality,"[17] and especially his "On Breaking Relations" (quoted above), expand on this theme. Zhu Mu's discussion highlights another side of homosociality's threat to semiotic and hermeneutic order: It is an anarchic threat, a realm where the textual logic of universal order of humans no longer applies.[18]

Cao Cao's famous critique of factionalism is similar to Zhu Mu's in that it finds relationships not bound by sanctioned ties of family or government hierarchy to be dangerous to the well-being of the state. His "decree" known as the "Correction and Regulation of Customs" (*zhengqi fengsu ling*), given in the winter of 206, reads:

> The banding together of deviant factions is something that the former sages all detested. I have heard that the customs of Jizhou[19] are such that father and son are in different groups, and even calumniate each other. In the past Zhi Buyi had no elder brother, but people of the time said that he had seduced his sister-in-law.[20] Diwu Lun married orphan girls three times, but it was said that he had beaten his fathers-in-law.[21] Wang Feng had usurped power, but Gu Yong compared him to Shen Bo.[22] Wang Shang was loyal and righteous, but Zhang Kuang said that he was corrupt.[23] These are all examples of calling black white, deceiving heaven, and slandering honorable lords. I want to correct and regulate customs. If I don't eradicate these kinds of things, it will be my great shame. (SGZ: 27)

The danger noted here in factionalism is the obvious one: It threatens principled government. An interesting subtext to his piece, however, is the prominence given to familial relationships, likewise seen as part of the problematic of interrelationships. Zhi Boyu must deny that he has a brother; Diwu Lun must deny that his wives had fathers; Wang Feng uses his family connection to the throne to advance his corrupt power. Cao Cao's piece captures the tension between the personal and the governmental and between conflicting structures of hierarchy and loyalty.

Xu Gan held several positions in the Cao-dominated Han court but is known to have refused appointment on various occasions. His *Discourse on the Central*, twenty chapters in two *juan*,[24] is described in Cao Pi's letter to Wu Zhi as having "a classical elegance in style and sense sufficient to insure its place in history"(QSGW 7:6a: 1089). It parallels in many ways the topical concerns of the *Analects*. Chapter 12, "A Denunciation of Homosociality" (*Qian jiao*), brings together most features of antihomosocial discourse. I translate it in its entirety:

A Denunciation of Homosociality

People today are fond of cultivating social friendships, and in this respect follow customs inferior to those in the days of the sage-kings. Those of the ancient times did not make social friendships, but rather sought sustenance in themselves.[25] The ancient way of governing the people was thus:

People were employed according to the nine occupations.
People were regulated according to the eight punishments;
Led according to the five rituals;
Corrected according to the six musics;
Taught according to the three things;
Practiced according to the six etiquettes.[26]

This makes the people well-labored,[27] but not to the point of pain and exhaustion; relaxed, but not to the point of depravity.

At a time like this, within the four seas virtue will be promoted and occupations will be followed,[28] and matters will be pursued diligently and without idleness. How could one dare to indulge the heart and cast aside one's efforts and do what was not one's task, thus harming the great accomplishments? From kings and dukes to the knights (*lie shi*), all were complete in their rectitude, reverential toward the chief ministers, and reverential toward their occupations;[29] none dared let themselves into idleness or abandon.

Thus the *Chunqiu waizhuan* says, "The son of heaven does the Sunrise Ritual in ritual dress;[30] and then with the Three Dukes and the Nine Ministers learns the nature of the Earth. When dealing with governance at midday, the ruler, with the administrative officials, leaders, protectors, ministers, and officials, would order and set out the people's affairs. When ritually dressed for the autumn moon ceremony, he would come together with the Historian and Astrologer to a reverence for the way of the heavens. At sunset, he would observe the Nine Concubines cleaning and preparing the sacrificial grains for the Imperial Sacrifice. And only after this would he sleep. The feudal lords would follow the Son of Heaven's orders in the morning, in the day would deal with governmental affairs, in the evening reflect on eternal principles [laws] and at night admonish the collected officialdom not to fall into laxity or depravity, and only after this would they sleep. The Ministers and the Lords in the morning would reflect upon their duties, in the day would carry out governmental affairs, in the evening arrange their affairs, and in the night take care of family matters and only after that go to sleep. The shi would in the morning receive their orders, in the day carry them out, in the evening review, and in the night reflect on errors or shamefulnesses, and only after that go to sleep."

On the first month (of the Xia calendar), officials with responsibilities were so ordered:

Each of you should do your job; reflect upon your methods, accomplish your tasks, and listen to the king's orders. Wherever there is disrespect, there will be punishment in the feudatories.[31]

Considering the matter in this light, it is clear that refraining from social intercourse is not something to be detested in governance. When minds are devoted to tasks, there is no relaxation. Furthermore, the teachings of the former kings say that officials should not lead the people through [the practice of the promotion of] social intercourse. So in the recommendation of worthy candidates from the localities, officials should not rely on social connections. Thus the people are not prohibited [from conducting social intercourse] but they reject it on their own accord.

Social intercourse flourished with the decline of the Zhou dynasty.

A questioner asks, "You have written in your book that when the gentleman (*junzi*) sought social intercourse, he sought it among the sages. Now you say that social intercourse is not part of the way of antiquity. So the gentlemen of antiquity could have had no sagely social intercourse."

I say, "Strange, the way you have missed the basic doctrine. Now, if one remained sitting inside an empty room, not venturing ouside, although one wouldn't see a mountain elf or water sprite [i.e., evil people], one also wouldn't see any sagely ones. Now you haven't truly examined the substance of what I mean by social intercourse, yet you raise questions about the terminology. Terminology can be the same while the substance can be different, just as terminology can differ while the substance is the same. Therefore, the gentleman, where this principle is concerned, acts according to the substance of the issue and does not trifle with terminology."

When I proclaimed that the ancient ones did not make social friendships I did not mean that they were living in a corner of their homes, facing the walls. And to speak of the current fashion for forming social friendships is not to say that people take a bath in the rain in the middle of the road. The *junzi* of ancient period used time not needed for administrative business to pay respectful visits to their fellow officials or to sages within the kingdom. At banquets they spoke of humanity and righteousness, and did not occupy themselves with fame or personal advantage. Likewise, those whom the lord had not yet commanded used time not used for farming to pay respectful visits to those like them in their districts and neighborhoods. When the sages of old were like this, then there is no reason not to say that they had sagely social intercourse. There were none, though, who over the course of many years abandoned their royal duties, cast off their jobs, or traveled to distant districts. Thus, social intercourse in ancient times was done over small distances; today it is over large distances. Of old it was practiced rarely, but today it is abundant. Social intercourse in ancient times was to cultivate sageliness; today it is to cultivate nothing more than fame and profit.

Of old, in the establishment of a kingdom, there were four categories of people. Those who upheld contractual obligations, regulated the royal and official residential charts, upheld the king's laws, and governed the institutions of sacrifices and rituals were called the shi. Those who exerted all their strength and took full advantage of the soil's potential were called agriculturalists.[32] "Those who discern curved from straight shapes, and who make the five materials into the various implements for the people were called miscellaneous artisans."[33] Those who get the rare and the precious from far and wide and sell them are called the merchant clans. Each passed on his occupation to the succeeding generation; no one changed occupations. "Mastering it when young, the heart was content."[34] When the character is fixed in this way, the achievements will not cease, and the position will be fixed. Everyone followed his customary way, and there was no conflict. Thus, those who possessed all their capacities but did not perform one of the Four Roles were called Error People, and were put in prison. When people exited, entered, moved, or stopped; gathered together, ate, or drank, all of these were regulated, and could not be done casually. To hinder an occupation was punishable. So how could one possibly find the type of person who files off in a herd "beyond the square" [i.e., in an unorthodox style of life] and makes a profession out of cultivating relationships?

For these reasons: five families constituted a Neighborhood; this was made responsible for mutual security. A Neighborhood had a Head. Five Neighborhoods constituted a Village, which was made responsible for mutual management. A Village had a Village Assistant. Four Villages constituted a Precinct, which was made responsible for burials. A Precinct had a Mentor. Five Precincts constituted a Ward, which was made responsible for mutual relief [from disasters, etc.]. A Ward had a Head. Five Wards constituted a Township, which was made responsible for mutual alms and charity. A Township had a Township Head. Five Townships constituted a District, which was made responsible for selection. A District had a District Grand Master.[35] There had to be an intelligent, kind, and compassionate person for this position of officials. Each was responsible for being in charge of orders and instruction in his District.

On the first day of the New Year, the Grand Master would receive the Law from the Minister of Education. Upon returning he would promulgate it to the officials of the townships, wards, precincts, villages, and neighborhoods. Each used it to instruct the people he governed, to evaluate their morality, and to discern those who had knowledge and abilities. At the proper times and seasons they would record the adult members of their populations, registering their number. Regarding those who had kindness and compassion, knowledge and ability, the Neighborhoods would report them to the villages, the villages to the precincts, the precincts to the wards, the wards to the townships, the townships to the districts; and the districts would also report.[36] If there were people with serious or unusual crimes, this must be reported as such too. If there is good conduct that is unreported, this is considered concealment of worthiness, and there is punishment for this. If there is evil that is unreported, this is considered cover-up of treachery, and this also carries a punishment. Thus there can be no virtue in reclusion, nor can there be any hidden evil.

The District Grand Master holds a Major Enlistment every five years to promote the talented and the virtuous. The elders of the District and the District Grand Master and all the officials of the district proffer the document with the talented and the virtuous to the king. The king respectfully receives it and registers it in the central government. This is the way of investiture and recruitment. Determination of official duties was done according to what one's talent was best suited to. The greater were not made to serve the lesser; the slight were not allowed to employ the weighty. Thus the Book says, "If all officials treat each other as teacher/models, then all of the work will be done in a timely way" (*Shang shu*, "Gao Taomo"). This is the way the former kings chose knights and made men into officials. Thus their subjects all returned to the basics and sought fulfillment in themselves. They paid careful attention to virtue and built up to greatness from a small beginning, knowing that fortune and prosperity do not come from [the acts of] men. Thus there were no social relations. There was no mixing of private concerns into public life. Their minds were pure and their bodies were in repose. They were at peace, and self-content. They led each other according to orthodox ways, and they were stern and serious toward each other with straightforward sincerity. Crafty speech does not occur, and depravity ceases of its own.

Times go bad when there is no brilliant son of heaven above, and when below there are no worthy feudal lords. The lords do not know the difference between right and wrong, and the ministers cannot differentiate black and white. Seeking knights was done through the districts and wards, and evaluation of service was not done on the basis of achievement and experience. Those with many allies were considered worthy talents. Those without allies were considered abnormal. In evaluating officials, unsubstantiated talk was considered. In deciding privileges and emoluments, they collected rumors from all corners of the land.

When the people saw that it was like this, they knew that they should follow the rich and powerful and that empty reputations would be protected. So they left their families, abandoned their neighborhoods and villages, ceased cultivating knowledge and virtue, and did not work on virtuous action. They spoke in ways fashionable at the time and formed partisan factions. They followed these customs in a nattering frenzy, day in and day out, but they still praised each other unrelentingly, filling in where each other was remiss. [The original is unclear here.] The lowly people, due to those who cheated the masters, benighted the ministers, stole the selection process, and kidnapped the ruler's favor, could do nothing. So those who were protected considered themselves as worthy and went on repeating the errors of their pasts, and the flatterers rushed together in a mass to follow them. Gradually they all became like this. Who could avoid becoming like them?

Under Emperors Huan and Ling, this situation became most pronounced. From the high ministers at court to the officials of the provinces and the commanderies, all neglected royal business and considered their task the maintenance of Guests and Retainers. Officials filled the gates and blocked the roads. When hungry they didn't take time to eat; when tired, they didn't take care of themselves. In a flurry and a flutter, they turned night into day. Down to the small official and the enfeoffed lower officials, none didn't debase themselves in order to attract people. Self-promotion and arrogance extend to even the lower shi. "By starlight, in the morning, they would yoke their carriages" (*Shi jing*, "Ding zhi fang zhong") and send off travelers, and welcome arrivals. The roadside inns were always full, attendants waited at every gate, fires burned through the night, and palace gates were never closed. In holding up shoulders and clasping wrists, piercing the sky with their oaths of loyalty, they make no distinction between light or weighty in their desire to attract and depend on kindness and generosity.

Documents were foisted off on the officials; convicts filled the prisons; yet no time was taken for reflection. Examining their actions carefully, there was no concern for the country or the people, or to ponder over the Dao or to discourse on virtue. Their own selves are their only projects and concerns, and all they do is jockey for position and self-benefit. There are even those who have official appointments at court but call themselves disciples of the rich and powerful families. They are everywhere. There are those who call themselves teachers but don't teach, and students who don't study. As for their conduct in affairs, there are those who even embrace a husband's countenance while putting on the appearance of a concubine or a wife. Others proffer goods in bribery, all in order to strengthen themselves. They devote their wills to currying favor, and scheme over advancement and promotion. So there are those who give piercing stares as they hit their palms, speaking great words in lofty language. This kind of people . . . speaking of them gives one shame. But those who act thus know no shame. Alas . . . The kingly teaching comes to ruin with this.

Moreover, when those who cultivate social relations go out in the world, some end up being buried in another region, and some grow up and never return home. Parents are left with lonely yearnings, and wives know only the sorrow of the empty room. They are cut off from their relatives and separated from their families. This is a pattern of going into exile "without crime or offense of any kind" (*Shi jing*, "Shiyue zhi jiao."). When the ancient ones went off on a government assignment, and the time had passed and they had not returned home, they made poetry to make their plaint. Thus there is, in "The Fourth Month," "Were not my forefathers men?/How can they endure that I should be thus?"[37]

Now how much worse are those who do this on their own, without the lord's orders? Considering the argument like this, then those who cultivate social relationships outside and go off for a long while without returning . . . they do not show the feelings of a man of humanity/compassion.

I want to stress at the outset that the Lentenesque utopia described here is neither a political program nor an historical document. I don't take Xu Gan as an "advocate" for constant work, but I am interested in the articulation of shi temporality. If Xu Gan is making an argument, I would say that his implicit argument could be phrased as follows: Nonofficial time does not submit to the regime of textualization and representation and should be avoided for that reason. Homosociality is for "free" or surplus time only, and ideally there would be precious little of that. Following the line in the *Analects*, "When the job is done, study; when the studies are done, work," leisure-time homosociality should be subsumable under "study." One should seek out the company of sages for education. I will discuss "free time" at greater length in chapter 4, but note here the difficulty in representing time other than work. The regulation of the state and the execution of official duties could be adumbrated and categorized with textual ease, since the content of social relations does not lend itself as easily to categorical description. Although "former official" and "disciple" had acquired semiofficial status by the time Xu Gan composed this text, we can see in his criticism of these relationships the difficulties posed by their irregularity. It would be easy to dismiss this text as the Lentenesque rant of a Confucian puritan. We should recognize, though, that discursively the stakes were high: The imperial textual order depended on the same hierarchies that the political order depended on. Homosociality threatened order.

Xu Gan's complaints would find more Daoist echoes in the writings and anecdotes about friendship in the *New Account of Tales of the World*. Xi Kang's famous letter breaking relations with Shan Tao[38] is an impassioned rejection of the world of patronage, duty, and influence in favor of self-cultivation and adherence to "natural" principles. The *New Account of Tales of the World* abounds with anecdotes of friendships rejected in favor of self-cultivation or out of fear of personal ruin through inappropriate association. In 7.3 Fu Jia rejects overtures of friendship by three contemporaries. He finds them "externally . . . addicted to profit and internally [lacking] the restraints of bolt and key. . . . Even keeping my distance from them I'm still afraid of becoming involved in their downfall. How much worse would it be if I were intimate with them."[39] Friendship in the context of self-cultivation is expressed in 9.26: "Chancellor Wang Tao said, 'Whenever I meet Hsieh Shang, he always enables me to reach a higher level of existence, but when I converse with Ho Ch'ung' . . . Wang simply raised his hand and pointed to the ground, . . . 'it's exactly like this.' "[40]

In these anecdotes from the centuries following the end of the Han, we can see that they are in part simply bold, dramatic statements of the concerns expressed at the end of the Han. Yet there is a subtle discursive shift in emphasis between the era of the Proscribed Factions and the Jin dynasty anecdotes preserved in the *New Accounts*. What begins in the Han as an emphasis on reputation (*ming*) turns by Jin times into a greater concentration on eccentricity and extraordinariness (*yi*), which is a reified version of an "extreme" subjectivity: a more wholly textualized selfhood. This shift has been discussed in another context as the shift from "pure criticism" to "pure talk" (*qingtan*).[41] Comparing documents preserved from the era of the Proscribed Factions with the *New Accounts* shows that the comprehensive nature of character evaluation in the latter book, which extended to all realms of human behavior and "lifestyle," had given priority to odd, eccentric types.

The characterology of the *New Accounts* reflected a developed version of late Latter Han tendencies in other ways. Character analysis had its discursive roots in the technology of "knowing" that was necessary for bureaucratic recruitment. Already in the seven-character panegyrics of the Proscribed Factions Affair, one can witness the textual formulaic character of that knowing. In the rise of the language and practice of character evaluation, we see the extension of the textual-regularization function to patterns of behavior and speech. The resultant social scene could be interpreted, as most cultural historians have indeed interpreted it, as a rise of "individuality." It could also, as I have suggested, represent an extension of the textual field.

Evaluation and Recommendation

In chapter 1 I suggested that in Han China there was no "reading" in the
sense that reading came to acquire in the printing era, where the quantity
of texts, their manner of circulation, and the nature of their ownership
and accessibility created a fundamentally different conception of reading.
We saw that the function of "understanding" a text could be associated
with textual production and circulation, in the practices of pedagogy or
commentary. Character evaluation was, in some respects, analogous to
the practice of reading within the text-circulation system. A "character"
acquired a reading, which then circulated and formed a "reputation." But
character analysis had, in some ways, a more directly functional role in
official life. In the context of the performance of duty, "knowing" became
important because it was the means of recognition by which duty was
assigned. "Knowing" took a codified, textualized form, and that was the
discourse of character evaluation. Character evaluation was not complex.
One cannot discern, from the Han texts, a multifaceted science of personality. The standard virtues and vices are the ones praised in any culture,
and the exemplary lives would be exemplary in any culture. Character
evaluation was formed within the textual regime in two ways: as a subject
of discourse and as a means by which subjectivity—personality—became
codified discursively. The evaluated character was the textualized character.

The self-recognition factor was evident in the character evaluation system, which had unofficial and official dimensions. During the Affair of
the Proscribed Factions, the "pures" claimed that their loyalties were to
moral ideals rather than power or position. Visible in their character ranking system, though, is a quasi-bureaucratic codified "moral" hierarchy,
in which virtuous shi were ranked and graded in terms of reputation
alone. De Crespigny translates this ranking system as the "three lords,"
"eight heroes," "eight exemplars," "eight guides," and "eight treasures"
(de Crespigny 1975). The "Collected Biographies of the Proscribed Factions Affair" in the HHS explains the categories as follows:

> A lord is venerated by the age . . . the hero is the flower of humanity . . . an
> exemplar can lead men by virtuous action . . . a guide can guide men in their
> pursuit of the venerated . . . a treasure can use great wealth to rescue people.
> (HHS: 2187–88).

We see in this version of homosocial discourse an abstraction that is striking in its lack of clear functional character. The lords, heros, and exemplars are . . . good. This discourse, along with the exemplary biographies,
which I would argue are related phenomena, is largely responsible for the

ability of later scholars to characterize late Latter Han shi as moral dissidents who valued principle more highly than position or profit. My position, as I have outlined it above, is that although this may indeed have been the case, we do not have sufficient access to late Han psyches to make any conclusions about how the moral stance and public position determined each other. What needs to be underscored is that codification itself—the adoption of a regular vocabulary for evaluation and classification—must also be understood as a discursive shift into purely textual terms. Position and prestige had become tied to their codified and textualized representations. Social and intellectual historians would generally accept the proposition that the late Latter Han was characterized by a vogue in character evaluation. From the point of view of textual authority, however, we can claim that rather than a new focus on "individual" characters, what we instead witness in the discourse of character evaluation is the rise of a systemized vocabulary of shi self-identificatory representation, a development that one could as easily argue implied *less*, not more, "individualism."

Character evaluation's various formal functions and discursive characteristics were acquired over a long period. Throughout most of the Han, at least until the Affair of the Proscribed Factions, it must always be understood in the context of official recruitment. The structure of the Han recruitment system has been succinctly outlined in Bielenstein (Bielenstein 1980: 130–2), on whose work my summary is based. The two paths to office that accounted for the vast majority of officeholders were (1) local and regional recommendation, primarily via the "filially pious and incorrupt" system and (2) direct appointment by designated higher officials in the central, regional, and local government. Additional paths to office included hereditary office, purchase of office, direct imperial appointment, and appointment directly from the Imperial Academy.[42] The direct appointment system was, most scholars argue, open to a number of abuses and was also a major factor in determining filiation within the system of "former officials" discussed in the previous chapter. The local and regional recommendation system, however, played a direct and central role in shaping the discourse of character evaluation.

In one dimension of the "regional promotion and village selection," central and local officials would recommend candidates who were characterized by moral formulas such as "capable and good," "sincere and upright," or "flourishing talent." This system accounted, according to Bielenstein, for at most a few thousand officials over the course of the Former and Latter Han. Far more important was the "filially pious and incorrupt" system, which was instituted under Emperor Wu in the Former Han and continued through the Latter Han. "Filially pious and incorrupt" was a formulaic term that was not limited to the two virtues mentioned; it designated "outstanding" individuals from the localities. The system began with an annual recommendation of two candidates per commandery or kingdom but was altered to one of modified proportional representation around the turn of the first century C.E. The "filially pious and incorrupt" system, hereafter occasionally referred to as *xiaolian*, accounted for 250–300 recommendees per year. Unfortunately, the large number of officials chosen thereby so greatly overwhelms the number of officials about whom we have documentary evidence that it is difficult to make solid empirical conclusions about how the system worked.

Among recent scholars, Martin Powers has taken the moral-evaluative character of the regional recommendation system most literally. According to Powers's study, the system worked to enforce attention to moral reputation at the local level, and contributed to the fostering of a shi class identity, especially when contrasted to the "noveaux riches," i.e., the eunuch and distaff relative officials. Donald Holzman's view is that the regional selection system began in relative fairness and deteriorated, over the course of the Latter Han, to a system of favoritism and nepotism:

> Cet équilibre entre le gouvernement et les communautés rurales était en vérité délicat et ne pouvait être maintenu qu'avec un gouvernement sain et fort. Cependant, dès le début des Han Postérieurs, on peut voir le système s'effondrer . . . A la fin des Han, les richards régionaux commencèrent a rompre le *modus vivendi* qu'ils avaient établi avec le gouvernement central, alors que de leur coopération dépendaient le système d'examens et les méthodes de sélection alors en vigeur.[43]

Xing Yitian, in a comprehensive demographic study of Latter Han *xiaolian*, has identified over three hundred individuals in the Latter Han, the largest number identified to date, though still a relatively small sample of the total (Xing Yitian 1983). Still, Xing's figures strongly indicate that the system overwhelmingly favored sons of officeholders and powerful local families. Xing's work also suggests that the proportional representation system worked less than perfectly in practice. Candidates from the commanderies of Runan, Nanyang, Yingchuan, Henan, and Chenliu are greatly overrepresented in the total numbers of *xiaolian*, of Confucian scholars mentioned in the "Collected Biographies of the Confucian Scholars" of the HHS, and of officials mentioned by name in the Affair of the Proscribed Factions.[44] This area represented the richest part of China in the last century of the Han, in terms of agricultural, artisanal, and commercial activity, which could be one explanation for their numerical prominence.

Holzman and others argue that the practice of "pure criticism" was an outgrowth of the regional recommendation system and that "pure criticism" was the basis for the later "nine categories of the impartial and just" (*jiu pin zhong zheng*), the blatant consolidation of the power of regional elites over national officeholding in the Wei-Jin period.[45] Character evaluation from the time of the "pure criticism" during the Affair of the Proscribed Factions until the time of the institution of the "nine categories" system in 220 played dual roles. On the one hand it continued to serve as the discursive field for bureaucratic recruitment. But it also served the nonimperial function, which, as I have suggested, was basically one of shi self-recognition. The regional character of shi discourse in the late Han suggests yet another dimension to character evaluation. All of the spheres of late Latter Han textual culture we have been discussing thus far—*xiaolian* recommendation, text-system transmission, and "pure criticism"—were concentrated geographically in the five commanderies mentioned above. It is not impossible that geographical concentration of this kind and the material circulation of texts were related phenomena. In a manuscript culture, physical ease of circulation could easily be a cultural determinant.

Yu Yingshi notices in the unofficial evaluative system of the "pures" a movement from a system whose emphasis was on fate (*ming*) to one whose discursive center was talent or ability (*cai*).[46] He sees this as evidence of a "new individualism," an attention paid to the way a person's internal capabilities shape his presence in the world. The *New Acounts of Tales of the World*, so many of whose anecdotes concern character evaluation, suggests the importance of this activity in literati life.[47] Utsunomiya Kiyoyoshi has described this activity as reflecting a dominant ideology of "humanism," which he sees as characterizing literati activity in the Han-Jin era (Utsunomiya 1954: 508–12). This discourse of moral and character evaluation, so popular in the seven-word panegyrics of the Imperial University, would see echoes one hundred years later in Liu Shao's *Study of Human Abilities*, which provided the most codified and comprehensive discussion of character evaluation up to that time.[48] When Yu and Utsunomiya note a turn to the "inner," they are of course referring to a discursive phenomenon whereby the content of the "inner" acquires a vocabulary in which it can be circulated among the shi. A codified set of "inner qualities" becomes a kind of currency that expresses the social reality of career trajectories and alliance patterns. Character evaluation as practice is analogous to bureaucratic recruitment even when it is not functioning overtly as recruitment. In character evaluation and bureaucratic recruitment, a "type" is recognized and assigned a role within a system composed of other homologous types. Reading a character is simultaneously writing a character into the system.

Reading the Person

When we consider reading, interpreting, and evaluating in the context of their roles in system maintenance, we need to be careful of our spatialities. Where are we placing the inner and the outer, the hidden and the visible? A model hermeneutics can be found in physiognomy, which was a common Han practice. The anecdote in chapter 2 about the Guo Tai turban style showed that the connection between reputation and physical appearance was easily made.[49] Much of the terminology of character evaluation, in fact, overlaps with physiognomy: the focus on bone, on *qi*, on uprightness, on clarity.[50] Physiognomic analysis as a hermeneutic act is one of entextualization: One begins with a signifying object that is nontextual (the face, the voice, the body, and the head were all possible objects of physiognomy) and produces a textualized version of it. A certain ear lobe shape, for example, means "intelligence." The physiognomic "reading" is thus an occasion for textual production.

Records of physiognomic practice begin in pre-Qin times, and are found with increasing frequency throughout the Han dynasty (Wang Meng'ou 1984: 75–6). From at least the time of the composition of the *Lu shi chunqiu* in the Qin, physiognomy had come to include a wide variety of hermeneutic practices, including analysis of an individual's speech.[51] There are many records of physiognomic practice in the late Latter Han. For example, Cao Pi's designation as heir apparent to his father Cao Cao was made after consulting a physiognomist. In vocabulary and style, physiognomic practice had much in common with the vogue for character evaluation discussed above. There are several areas of overlap. The judgments of physiognomists and character analysts were written in similar ways, generally in pithy, two-sentence epigrams. Several famous practitioners of character analysis practiced physiognomy as well. Xu Shao, known for his characterization of Cao Cao as a "hero of a rebellious age, villain of an orderly one" and for his "first of the month" character critiques, was a well-known physiognomist.[52] Terms for physiognomic analysis and character or stylistic analysis overlap. It is not merely coincidental, I believe, that *ti*, or "style" as I translate it, means physical body or that *gu*, "bone," should so often be applied to human or literary characteristics.[53]

A physiognomic dimension can be seen in one of the first important texts of "literary criticism," Cao Pi's *Authoritative Discourses: On Literature*.

> Literature (*wen*) is ruled by temperament (*qi*) and if a writer's temperament is clear or turbid, his style (*ti*) will be so too: this is not something that can be achieved by force. To take an example from music: if you asked two musi-

cians to play exactly the same melodic line and to follow exactly the same rhythm, they would not be able to do so. Not even a father or an elder brother would be able to explain the way of playing in exactly the same way to his son or younger brother, because each one has his own way of controlling his breath (*qi*), and each one has his own technique that is innate within him. (Holzman 1974: 130–131)

Most discussions of the use of the term *qi* in the *Lun wen* involve an attempt to provide a normative definition of *qi* along physiological and cosmological lines.[54] Of particular significance in this filiation is Mencius's well-known notion of the importance of cultivating his floodlike *qi*. Before Mencius, *qi* had primarily been conceived cosmologically as "primordial matter-energy" and physiologically as "physical vitality" or "inherited constitution" (Pollard 1978: 45). The importance of the Mencian reformulation is that *qi* came to be associable with the object of character analysis, with what some scholars identify as an individual's moral character or personality. Xu Fuguan, who has been a major influence on contemporary scholarship on Han Wei-Jin writing, sees Cao Pi's writing on *qi* as representing the crude, inchoate formation that would reach maturity in Liu Xie's *Wenxin diaolong*. This is because, according to Xu, Liu Xie's "Style and Nature" (*Tixing*) chapter defines "personality" (*xingqing*) as being the essence of literary writing. Cao Pi fails, in Xu's view, to sufficiently identify *qi* with individual personality.

It is difficult to determine exactly what is meant by *qi* in Cao Pi's short text. We know that it refers to something that can be expressed. It is not inheritable, perhaps not even teachable, and may have something to do with an individual's "character." But whether Cao Pi views it as acquired or innate, cultivatable or not, we cannot know. The various discussions concerning the normative definition of *qi* have probably exhausted that line of speculation. I would like here to refer to a recent line of inquiry into the nature of *qi* in the *Lun wen*, one that concentrates on its functional character.

Wang Meng'ou's speculative essay on Cao Pi's discovery of *qi* in literature (Wang Meng'ou 1984: 69–83), in an implicit attack on Xu Fuguan's position, attempts to remove the *Lun wen*'s notion of *qi* from the line that supposedly reaches from Mencius to the *Wenxin diaolong*. His argument calls attention to the way *qi* functions in an evaluative system, which is indeed the clear import of the *Lun wen* and is more important for my purposes here. He refers to the following passage from the text to show that Cao Pi is not talking about *qi* as an interior element of a writer's "character" or "personality," but rather as a quality that inheres specifically in the words of a text.

The character [*qi*] of Kong Rong's writing is extraordinary, and in some ways surpasses other men's, but he cannot hold an argument: his reasoning is too weak to support the beauty of his words, and he even [falls prey to the errors of] ridicule and jest. In what he excels, he is the equal of Yang Xiong and Ban Gu.[55]

This passage suggests a clear separation of *qi*, or *ti qi*, from "content" elements like argumentation and reasoning. The fact that Kong Rong's writing can be found deficient in content does not seem to have had a concomitant effect on Cao Pi's evaluation of his literary style. Wang's conclusion, and a central part of his argument, is that *qi* in the *Lun wen* functions in the reader or critic's response to a piece of writing (Wang Meng'ou 1984: 73). *Qi* serves as the category that allows for the operation of interpretation.

Locating *qi* in the evaluative function refigures it as part of a textually productive hermeneutic activity. There are important conceptual reasons for doing so. We can refigure the focus, evident since pre-Qin times, on the externality of words, that is, on the separability of an "inner," motivational or emotive state from an "outer" manifestation. The commonsense tendency in face of such a dichotomy would be to value the inner. But a focus on the capacity of the "outer" to generate interpretive discourse and textual circulation suggests that the "inner" is not the absolute value. The manifestation is more important than the referent. The notion of words as manifestations is a very ancient one. As external manifestations, they are the primary generative site of the interpretive activity. The "Appended Judgments" of the *Yi jing* concludes:

> The words of a man who plans revolt are confused. The words of a man who entertains doubt in his innermost heart are ramified. The words of men of good fortune are few. Excited men use many words. Slanderers of good men are roundabout in their words. The words of a man who has lost his standing are twisted.[56]

This passage is referred to frequently in physiognomic texts. Physiognomy is, of course, the most comprehensive "reading" of outer manifestations of "inner" qualities or potentialities. The notion of *qi* occurs with great frequency in physiognomic texts as well. Wang Meng'ou believes that it is the physiognomic model that most clearly informs the use of *qi* in the *Lun wen*.

The significance of Wang's argument is not, however, in the uncovering of a secret signification system in the *Lun wen*. Rather, by invoking the physiognomic model, we are able to read the *Lun wen* as emphasizing the interpretive project over the creative one, as a text whose import is not as an adumbration of the expressive function of literary writing but of the interpretive and reading functions. The first line of the *Lun wen* argues against the tendency of literati to "denigrate one another," and the text offers a hermeneutical system as its corrective.

Cao Pi's text says, "a superior man examines himself so that he can judge others" (Holzman 1974: 129)· But this self-knowledge seems to be largely a matter of knowing that one's own skills are not absolute, but are part of a generically and stylistically determined system. Cao Pi suggests that, like physiognomy, interpreting texts requires specific skills, a system of categorizing outer manifestations. With texts, the system depends on a clear conception of the style or genre of a piece of writing, its function within the text system in its totality. In this chapter I have considered antifactional discourse and character analysis as social texts: practices that brought into textuality the organization of social life, in its official and unofficial forms. We have seen that official life, though wholly textualized, was designed to preclude excess and indulgence, or any deviation into the "private," commonly deemed the province of belletristic writing. Although the *Authoritative Discourses: On Literature* is acclaimed in histories of Chinese literary theory as an early and foundational text of "literary criticism," late Han writers assigned a relatively low importance to belletristic writing. There is no indication that writers of poetry in the Jian'an era (196–220 C.E.) thought of themselves as poets or valued their poetry above their official memorials. If our own emphases were to match the generic priorities assigned in the Han, a study of late Han writing would have little to say about belletristic literature. Our reading of the belletristic writing of the period has been overdetermined by the era's post facto designation as the time of the birth of "individualistic" lyric writing, and I would not want to perpetuate that. But as long as we acknowledge the low esteem in which belletristic writing was held, the scene of belletristic writing can deepen our understanding of textual culture in general. To "literature," then, we now turn.

Notes

1. It was also called the *You lun*. Li Madou [Matteo Ricci] (1965 rpt.). Joseph McDermott (1992), 67–96

2. I use this term following Eve Kosofsky Sedgwick in *Between Men: English Literature and Male Homosocial Desire*. My use of the term is meant neither to suggest an erotic character to male-male ties nor to deny it, but to allow for some critical distance from the term "friendship" and the affective associations that the term carries.

3. Marx uses the term in *The Eighteenth Brumaire of Napoleon Bonaparte*. In Marx and Engels, *Collected Works*, 11: 185.

4. For critiques of Weber and Marx on bureaucracy, I have been influenced

by Claude Lefort, "Qu'est-ce que la bureaucratie," in Lefort (1971), 288–314. An English translation is in Lefort (1986), 89–121.

5. Shi 1 and shi 2 in the glossary.

6. This interpretation, and much of what follows on the public-private divide, owes much to Hsiao-Kung Ch'üan (1979), *A History of Chinese Political Thought*.

7. Hsiao (1979), 103–4. It is not, we must add, "the family" as a universal category that is the object of discourse, but official families.

8. The primary locus is *Lun yu* 5.16; 12.23.

9. *Chunqiu fanlu*, j 35. See also Wu Hung (1989), 169–72; Anne Cheng (1985), 48–9.

10. Liu Xie makes this point in the WXDL, 326.

11. For a discussion of Wang Fu's thought, see Balazs (1964), 198–205. My citations of this text refer to Peng Duo, *Qian fu lun jian*, which contains the annotations of Wang Xupei.

12. The chapter is all about friendship. This accords with my contention that unspecified, nonfamilial "human relations" generally refer to friendship. The title of the chapter is probably taken from Mencius 10.4 (239).

13. The reference is to the *Shang shu* 18:1a.

14. My translation follows the annotations in Wang Fu, *Qian fu lun jian*, 333.

15. See Balazs (1964), chapter 13.

16. Zhu Mu was a contemporary of Cai Yong's. His biography is in the HHS: 1461–1476.

17. "Hou" has many senses in this text. "Liberality" is Chi-yun Ch'en's translation (CHC, 787–788).

18. Chi-yun Ch'en (CHC, 787–8) characterizes Zhu Mu's thought as Daoist. Although there is certainly something Daoist-like about Zhu's indictment of the adverse effects of strict Confucian teaching, especially with regard to its corruption of a good and pure "original nature," neither the Confucian nor the Daoist labels conveniently apply. As his biography in the HHS shows, Zhu Mu was certainly not known to his contemporaries as a Daoist thinker.

19. By 206 the Cao court was firmly established in Ye, which was in Jizhou.

20. Zhi Buyi's biography in the *Han shu* reports that Zhi Buyi was slandered by people at court for having had relations with his older brother's wife. Zhi Buyi answered "But I have no elder brother." HS: 2202.

21. Diwu Lun was a minister under Emperor Guangwu known for his uprightness and virtue. In 53 the emperor made this accusation as a joke, and Diwu responded that the women he had married were fatherless. HHS: 1396–97.

22. Wang Feng was the maternal uncle of Emperor Cheng in the Former Han. He and his relatives monopolized power at court. Although there was much criticism of this, the minister Gu Yong sought favor with Wang Feng and memorialized to the emperor comparing him to Shen Bo, the maternal uncle of King Xuan of the Zhou dynasty, known as a loyal supporter to the king. From Gu Yong's biography, HS: 3451 ff.

23. Wang Shang's biography says that Wang Shang was a loyal and able minister under Emperor Cheng, but was dismissed by Wang Feng (see previous note).

Zhang Kuang was known as a crafty and cunning politician who sought to curry Wang Feng's favor. HS: 3370–5.

24. Liang Rongmao (1979) is a minimally annotated, textual study. Ikeda Shuzo (1984–1986) has a redacted an annotated version and translation (Chinese text; Japanese annotations). For an analysis of Xu Gan's philosophy, see Luo Jian-ren (1973) and Makeham (1994). See Ikeda, Makeham and Loewe, ed. *Early Chinese Texts: A Bibliographic Guide* for the textual issues. Makeham sees the *ming/ shi* ("name and actuality") dichotomy as the central concern of the *Zhong lun*. This reading locates Makeham's work within a certain school of interpretation of "Confucian" thought, whose concerns I do not share. My translation is from the *Sibu congkan* edition, and I have followed Ikeda, for the most part, in his sugges-tions for annotations.

25. A reference to the *Yi jing*. "Pay heed to the providing of nourishment and to what a man seeks to fill his own mouth with." Wilhelm and Baynes (1967), 107.

26. The reference is to lists in the *Zhou Li* in the *Tian Guan Da Zai* section and the *Di Guan* section: "Employ the myriad people in the 9 occupations: first, farming, to grow nine grains; second is orchard keeping, to get the herbs and trees; third is mountains and rivers, to get the products from there, fourth is aviary and husbandry, to get the birds and animals, fifth is the hundred trades, to transform the eight elements; sixth is commerce and selling, to deal with exchange; etc. The first punishment is for unfiliality, etc.

27. *Analects* 19.10. Legge (1893), 342, "The superior man, having obtained their confidence, may then impose labours on his people."

28. Quoted from the *Wenyan* on the *Qian* hexagram.

29. The *Shang shu* 10.9. Legge (1893), 406–407, "Jiu Gao" chapter, has "From Him, Tang the successful, down to the emperor Yi, the sovereigns all completed their royal virtues and revered their chief ministers, so that their managers of affairs respectfully discharged their helping duties, and dared not to allow them-selves in idleness and pleasure." Pi Xirui (1925) thinks that Xu Gan's variant derives from his use of the Jinwen version. Liang Rongmao does not see this kind of variance in the *gu* and *jinwen* texts. Liang (1979), 84.

30. This long section is quoted from the *Guo yu: Lu yu*, j. 5, 2056.

31. This and following is a reference to the *Zhou li*, "Tian guan."

32. There are many references to the four categories. This is a paraphrase from *Zhou li*.

33. Another *Zhou li* paraphrase, clearly meaning "artisan" and not "official."

34. From the *Guo Yu*, 226. The following phrase underscores the fact that changing occupations is discouraged.

35. The reference is to *Di Guan Da Situ* in the *Zhou Li*. This is a direct quote from the *Zhou Li*, although the expression about the administrators was interpo-lated.

36. There is certainly an object to this verb, but it is unclear. The text is corrupt. Wang suggests the district reports to the *situ*.

37. *Shi jing*, "Xiaoya" bk 5 ode 10. "Si yue." The Lu reading has it that this poem is composed on the plight of someone sent off for a long time without returning. Note that Xu is following the Lu reading.

38. QSGW, 1321–22. See the translation in Birch (1965), 162–68.

39. Mather, trans. (1976), 197. Liu Yiqing, *Shishuo xinyu*, 293.

40. Mather, trans. (1976), 256. Liu Yiqing, *Shishuo xinyu*, 390.

41. See, among others, Yu Yingshi (1959); Zhou Shaoxian (1972); He Qimin (1976); Mou Zongsan (1975).

42. Many students at the Imperial Academy were already officeholders who were required to study at the Academy. Bielenstein points out that the number who went directly into office from the Academy was very small.

43. "The equilibrium between the government and rural communities was indeed very delicate, and could only be maintained under a strong and healthy government. However, from the beginning of the Eastern Han, one can see the system deteriorating. At the end of the Han, the local elites began to rupture the modus vivendi that they had established with the central government, whereas the system of examinations and the means of selection depended even more on their cooperation." Donald Holzman (1957), 389–90.

44. Xing Yitian (1983), 28. Figures on the *xiaolian* and the Confucianists are from Xing; figures from the Proscribed Faction chapter are taken from Jin Fagen (1963), using Xing's numbers for total population figures.

45. Johnson (1977), Yang Liansheng (1936), Ebrey (1978), Tang Changru (1955), "Jiupin zhongzheng zhidu shi shi," 85–126.

46. Yu Yingshi (1959), 50 ff. Tang Yongtong, however, does not make such a distinction. He sees the evolution of character evaluation as being one dimension of the influence of the "school of names" branch of philosophical thinking, codified in Liu Shao's *Ren wu zhi*. In Tang Yongtong (1957), 5–11.

47. Probably the most extensive study of character evaluation is in Okamura Shigeru (1976). Drawing from the HHS, the SGZ, and commentary to the *Shishuo xinyu*, Okamura identifies over thirty people whose biographies mention a specific talent for character evaluation, with supporting evidence to show that such talent was widely valued. Okamura's classification system of the various kinds of evaluative practice is perhaps too rigorous, but he does make a case that literary criticism as practiced in the late Han was an outgrowth of these practices.

48. See Liu Shao, Shryock (trans.), 1937. See also Tang Yongtong (1957), 5–25.

49. Guo Tai's connection to physiognomic practice is strengthened in his identification, probably spurious, as the author of the *Xiang wude pei wuxing disan*. The identification is made in the early physiognomic compilation: *Shenxiang quan pian*. Chen Tuan, comp. Yunjing Tang ed. 1793 (Gest Library).

50. See Liu Shao, *Ren wu zhi*, chap. 1.

51. Lu Buwei (Chen Qiyou, ed.) (1984) "Lun ren pian," 159–60.

52. HHS, j. 98. *Shishuo xinyu*, j. 8. Mather, trans. (1976), 531.

53. Okamura Shigeru (1976), 35–42, shows clearly the relationship between literary evaluation and larger patterns of character evaluation present in the Latter Han.

54. See David Pollard (1978), 43–46. Pollard's analysis generally follows that of Xu Fuguan in "Zhongguo wenxue zhong de qi de wenti—*Wenxin diaolong* fenggu pian shubu" in Xu Fuguan (1974), 297–304.

55. This translation differs from Holzman's (1974), 130 in some significant

ways. For *ti qi*, Holzman has "the temperament of his style," which I find somewhat illogical. I use "character" rather than "temperament" to accord with the evaluatory emphasis. Another difference is in the last line. I follow Wang Meng'ou in reading "ridicule and jest" as a criticism of Kong Rong, perhaps based on Kong Rong's memorial against Cao Cao's taking of Yuan Shao's daughter-in-law as a wife, for which he earned Cao Cao's undying enmity. SGZ: 371.

56. The translation is from Wilhelm and Baynes (1967), 355. *Zhou yi zheng yi* 8:79a.

4

Literature

What Is Chinese Literature?

This question leads first to an interrogation of its basic terms. Victor Mair, recent anthologist of translations from Chinese literature, asks the question as a way of questioning several commonplace assumptions about the nature of literature in the imperial period. In arguing that an English-language anthology of "Chinese literature" should include works translated from the nonstandard vernaculars that have not passed through the intermediary stage of Literary Sinitic or Modern Standard Mandarin, the question that Mair forces us to ask is, What is Chinese? (Mair 1995). Mair's essay reveals the failure to interrogate the assumptions whereby Literary Sinitic or Modern Standard Mandarin was made coterminous with "Chinese" as the internalization of elite textual ideology. Application of "international" rather than elite Chinese standards for inclusion into the "literary" creates a very different kind of anthology. Mair's work of inclusion is an important and necessary step in demystifying the constructs of imperial textual culture. But Mair's anthological principles still accord with "international" consensus views of what constitutes the literary itself. In both Cao Pi's *Authoritative Discourses: On Literature* (early third century C.E.) and Liu Xie's *The Literary Mind and the Carving of Dragons* (sixth century C.E.), two of the earliest works of "literary criticism," one finds within the purview of the "literary" alongside various "poetic" genres the following forms: contract-oaths (*meng*), memorials (*biao*), edicts (*zhao*), war proclamations (*xi*), disquisitions (*yi*), tomb inscriptions (*ming*), eulogies (*lei*), and petitions (*zou*). Few if any examples of these literary forms ever appear in translated anthologies of imperial literature. What we have received in most of our anthologies to date is the elite Chinese determination of what constitutes "Chinese" but a more limited version of what constitutes "literature." Mair's worry is that by excluding literary production not in Literary Sinitic or Modern Standard Mandarin, we risk allowing our view of Chinese literature to be dominated by "the culture of bureaucrats" (Mair 1995). But by excluding the various official subgenres from anthologies of translations, we risk a view of elite literary production that is not bureaucratic enough.

By "belletristic literature" in this chapter, I mean to underscore the purportedly "nonfunctional" character of this kind of composition, though it was often used in official contexts. The primary belletristic genres I will treat here are the poetic genres of *shi, yuefu,* and *fu.* To avoid confusion with shi (in the sense of "literati") I will refer to *shi* compositions as *gushi. Gushi* are short, rhymed poems in regular line length (pentameter is the most common but tetrameter is not rare, and there are examples of septameter). *Yuefu* are short rhymed poems grouped according to song title. Although pentameter predominates, they are more irregular in line length. *Yuefu* compositions that share a title need share no thematic or content elements. *Fu,* sometimes translated as rhyme prose or rhapsody, can refer to poetic composition in general, but more commonly refers to longer pieces that have more irregularity in rhyme and line length.

It is common knowledge that the widespread term for "literature" in Modern Standard Mandarin, *wenxue,* is a late nineteenth-century borrowing from the Japanese appropriation of the nineteenth-century European consensus. Han and pre-Han texts refer frequently to "writing" (*wen*) as a whole, but conceptions of suprageneric categories such as "belletristic" are only vaguely operative in critical texts. The terms in which this category is described reveal much about the social and temporal character of textual authority. In chapter 1 I discussed the broad capacity of signification attributable to textuality in general. This capacity of writing in general, though, raises the question of writing in the generic or subgeneric particular. The classics, and those works that constitute a "school of thought," can certainly claim a place in the lineage of immanent cosmic signification. Contemporary critics such as Francois Cheng would ascribe the same capacity to classical poetry. But, as in any textual culture, some forms of textual production in early imperial China are less valued than others. Textual authority is meaningless, after all, unless the content of textual production can be regularized and hierarchized. The last sentence of the *Analects* of Confucius, 1.6., reads:

> The master said, "The youths should be obedient within the home; respectful of authority without; assiduous and honest; magnanimous in their love for all, but seek intimacy with those of benevolence/humanity. If after doing these things they have extra energy, they can use it to study writing ("essay writing"). (*Lun Yu* 1.6).

The admonition, echoed in texts such as the *Family Instructions of the Yan Clan* (Teng 1968: 85), parallels the discussion in chapter 3 about social life. "Essay writing" is here consigned to the same realm of nonofficial temporal excess that was the location of social intercourse in the earlier admonition. The senses of *wen* are so many, though, that the nature of the prescription is ambiguous. *Wen*, as we saw in an earlier discussion, can have the sense of "natural" patterning, as in the veins on a rock or the skin of an animal. In its meanings of "decoration," "adornment," or "elaboration," usages it acquired at an early stage, it already conveys a sense of "unnatural" excess. The teachings of Confucius on government in the *Great Learning* and the *Doctrine of the Mean* sought to center rulership on the "human" (*renzhi*) or "humane" (*rennzhi*), as embodied in the person of the ruler, to avoid the decay that can befall a government that, like the Zhou, relied too heavily on Institutions (*wen* texts) (Hsiao 1979: 116 ff). Recall the quotation that begins chapter 1: "The government of Kings Wen and Wu [of the Zhou] is laid out on the wood and bamboo tablets." There are two sides to this formulation. The government is immanent in the material textual form, and this underscores the importance of "study," the authority of textuality, and the central work of the scholars' transmission. But the textual form is always already in excess of the "human." Much of the philosophical writing that has been labeled "Confucian" has concerned the adequation of the human and the textual: The "name and actuality" (*ming-shi*) question is one version of this. The difficulty is that the effort to specify and codify the "human" has unfolded within a textual logic. I am not making the obvious point that all criticism of writing by necessity takes the form of writing and therefore perpetuates the regime of writing but that textual authority in early China is a practice with a distinctive logic, and that the "human" in its textual incarnation is a figure with attributes determined by its textual environment. The delineation of the Confucian "human" is the primary content of the "Confucian" texts, most of which illustrate or analyze "human" attributes. Hsiao Kung-ch'üan underlined the explicitly political stakes in elevating humanity/benevolence (*ren*) to the "one all-pervading concept": the possibility of a universalist moral/behavioral code. The work of the Confucian texts is to render the "human" delineable through various textual formulae, while positing the category of the human as the permanent *Aufheben*[1] of the term's determinant textual structuration. The *practice* of "humanity" becomes equivalent to textual practice, and the history of Han textual authority, including the official establishment of Confucian teachings in the second century B.C.E., is also the history of the adequation of the "human" with the textual so that, first, there is nothing "human" that is outside the textual purview and, second, the category of the "human" is still the implied critique of the textual. The "excess" of "essay writing" becomes the figure for the excess in all writing that is hidden at the center of textuality.

The HS *Yiwen zhi* posited six categories of writing: (1) the classical canon and commentaries; (2) philosophical works; (3) poetry and *fu;* (4) military texts; (5) astronomy, calendrics, and divination; and (6) medical formulas and cures. The compilation of works in the first three categories was said to have been supervised by Liu Xiang himself. That, and their order of listing, indicate their importance. The poetry and *fu* category lists Han and pre-Han works, including works by Liu Xiang and his contemporaries. The "Summary on the Poetry and Fu Category" reads (in its entirety):

> To recite without singing is called fu. The *Commentary* says, "Those who can compose fu upon climbing a height can serve as a Grand Master."[2] This means that the ability to be moved by external things and make words and phrases from this is a sign of deep and wonderful talent and wisdom. This kind of person can be placed in charge of things, and so can be included as a Grand Master. In ancient times, when Marquises, Chief Ministers, and Grand Masters had interaction with those from neighboring states, they used formulaic language to influence each other. When performing greeting rituals, they had to quote from the *Book of Songs* to express their intentions. It was probably in this way that the ministers' talents could be gauged, and, by extension, the fortunes of a state could be predicted. This is why Confucius said, "If you don't study the Book of Songs, you will have nothing to say."

> After the Spring and Autumn period, the way of the Zhou dynasty declined. Since the formulaic use of poetry and song in diplomacy was no longer practiced, those shi who specialized in the *Book of Songs* could find no employment, and thus was occasioned the rise of fu by worthies who could not realize their desire to serve in office. The great Confucian Xun Qing [Xunzi] and the Chu minister Qu Yuan were calumnied and attacked at their courts. They both composed fu to express their frustrations, and in these fu can be seen the spirit of remonstrance of the *Book of Songs*. Later came Song Yu and Tang Le, and, in the early Han dynasty, Mei Sheng and Sima Xiangru, and still later, Yang Xiong. They outdid each other with florid verbal excess, abandoning the original spirit of remonstrance in fu. This is why Yang Xiong lamented "the compositions of the *Book of Songs*'s authors were beautiful yet regulatory; the compositions of the belletristic writers [of today] are beautiful but depraved. If Confucius's disciples had composed in fu, then Jia Yi and Sima Xiangru would be considered among the inner circle of the elite. But his disciples didn't, so what are Jia and Sima worth in the end?"[3]

> Since the Emperor Wu established the Music Bureau to collect songs and ditties from around the empire, there have been the songs of Dai and Zhao, and the airs of Qin and Chu. These were all responses to joy or sadness, to events. From reading them one can observe customs and know what is superficial and what is genuine. I have divided the "poetry and fu" section into five sub-categories.[4]

Because the *Yiwen zhi* attaches such great importance to canonical filiation, the filiation to the *Book of Songs* is no surprise. The particular narrative of decline, from the "beautiful yet regulatory" to the "depraved," from the worthy to the worthless, is instructive. The opening section specifies the connection between poetry composition or recitation and officeholding. Later, the *Book of Songs* is used by courtiers specialized in its use. When the Way of the Zhou is practiced, no new songs are composed, but experts in the classic recite its formulae on prescribed occasions. Only when the way declines do we witness the figure of the disaffected minister who carries on the moral spirit of the *Book of Songs* in original composition but without occupying official position. This we must realize also represents a decline: the move out of court signifies moral/political/institutional failure. The further decline, in the Han dynasty, is into total artifice. Sima Xiangru and Jia Yi have neither the official function nor the spirit of remonstrance that characterize the "frustrated officials." The story of poetry's decline is the story of its growing separation from official function.

In chapter 1 I quoted from a letter that Cao Zhi wrote to Yang Xiu, a letter that denigrated belletristic composition:

> Belletristic writing is a minor path, certainly insufficient for proclaiming and championing the Great Content in order to make it a shining example for generations to come. Yang Xiong was only a court attendant in the Han, but he still said that "a grown man does not compose literary pieces."[5]

Contemporary scholars generally take this and similar pronouncements as formulaic self-deprecation, often adding that it is ironic or shortsighted that the masters of literature could disparage literature so. The parallel with the antisocial discourse discussed in the previous chapter, though, suggests another way of viewing the question. Most of the literary genres mentioned at the beginning of this section were practiced on official occasions or in an official capacity. Writing memorials or other documents, as I have stressed throughout, defined the occupation of the shi. The *Yiwen zhi* passage suggests that *fu* writing, too, has its originary roots in the performance of official duty. In later times, however, poetry and *fu* were "leisure" activities and were relegated to the potentially dangerous sphere of excess, elaboration, ornamentation, and self-indulgence.

In the late Han polemical writing on homosociality that dichotomizes work and social life (leisure time), work has an atemporal aspect: As ritual, as repetition, it acquires, in its ideal performance, a formalized timelessness. Like most utopias everywhere, all early imperial utopianism is marked by a timeless structural stasis. When official work is being done well, it is repetition: Its content is regular and predictable. "Leisure time" is problematic. The prescription offered in the antihomosocial essays—that people should "work" all the time—makes human time disjunctive: There is a contradiction between the atemporality of repetition and the temporality of a life span. Belletristic writing works through numerous modalities on the temporal problem. "Occasional" *gushi* and *fu* composition, which accounted for so much belletristic composition for centuries to come, appears for the first time in significant quantity around the end of the Han. *Gushi* or *fu* were written at specific events such as banquets and outings or on specified occasions such as parting or gift presentation. The sources suggest that these feasts, parties, or colloquia were also scenes of group composition, primarily on themes of temporality itself: carpe diem, old age, passing of youth, and so on. These concerns, which are often taken as evidence of the individualistic, subjective character of belletristic composition, could just as easily be viewed as the textual organization of the temporality of the nonofficial, of "temporal life" itself.

The *Yiwen zhi* passage, and all similar disparagement of literary production, suggest, in ways similar to the discourses on homosociality, a fundamental ambiguity to belletristic production. Its very existence is often symptomatic of the decline of the kingly way and of the pathology of social excess. And it is indeed in the social that we must locate belletristic textual production, just as the social is also the site of canonical transmission and "schools of thought." I am arguing here for a deaestheticizing view of Han belletristic production,[6] not with a view toward relegating the poetic arts to some kind of bureaucratic functionalism but simply in an effort to take seriously a large body of writing about and contemporary with Han belletrism. It is by no means certain that anything like the aesthetic existed as a category in the Late Han. The social work of textual culture was, as Han writings recognized, performed in other genres to far greater effect than it was in *gushi* and *fu* poetry. But it is the belletristic production of late Han writers that has attracted the inordinate attention of scholars who write from regimes like the present, where the discourses of aestheticism are much better established. Central to their arguments is a particular figuration of subjectivity, as well as the centrality of subjectivity to early imperial literary production.

Late Han Poetry and the Subjectivity Question

There is almost no useable evidence to establish the self-consciousness of concrete historical secular individuals in the high Middle Ages. Where there are declarations of purpose and theoretical elaborations in medieval literary texts, they are almost invariably identifiable as part of a medieval convention, and hence represent a typical repetition rather than an authentic indication of authorial or even textual intentionality. It is the characteristic of conventionality as consciousness that makes it awkward to use as a principle of analysis in the case of medieval literature, even though it is generally agreed that medieval literature is the most conventional produced in Europe. Hence my choice of the word "repetition": its meaning here is the same as the meaning of "conventionality," except for the semantic component of "consciousness": "repetition" refers to the phenomenon of conventions without the presence and presuppositions of any consciousness. (Haidu 1977: 876)

Scholarly consensus would have it that in China, where the "medieval" period is ushered in with the collapse of the Han, a new subject is claimed to have been born: the poet. The Seven Masters of the Jian'an era (196–220 C.E.) are the poets of a generation who bear witness to tragic, dislocating times. In the judgment of later poets and literary historians, lyric poetry is the privileged vehicle for that witnessing. The end of the Han has all the ingredients for lyrical melodrama—dynastic collapse, a land divided, and an epidemic that carries away the leading literary lights at court. The twenty-second year of the Jian'an era, the year of the epidemic, is Year One of the Dead Poets, a year which saw the deaths of Wang Can, Xu Gan, Chen Lin, Ying Yang, and Liu Zhen—five of the seven masters of the Jian'an era. Their deaths are mourned in three of Cao Pi's writings on literature that are included in nearly every twentieth-century anthology of classical Chinese "literary criticism"—the letters to Wang Lang and Wu Zhi, and the *Authoritative Discourses: On Literature*.

A group of friends die in the Jian'an and a "literary society," if indeed it ever existed as such, is broken up. For later critics, this was the era when the individual poet was born, when poetry left behind both bureaucratic functionalism and the supposed formal constrictions of tetrameters in the style of the *Book of Songs*.[7] In the consensually accepted version of literary history, the age is marked by a new attention to poetic form, a more "personal," more "emotional," more "self-conscious" poetry. Qian Mu's evaluation is typical. He locates the beginnings of a new conception of literature in the inclusion of literati biographies in the HHS and the SGZ:

> This marks the appearance of so-called literati. With literati, there is literati literature. The distinctive feature of this kind of literature is its disregard of functional value. It takes the individual self as its center and daily life as its subject, writes of character and soul, and sings of the feelings and emotions.[8]

Yu Guanying, in his introduction to the *San Cao shi xuan*, contrasts Jian'an literature with that of the rest of the Han dynasty, which was

> represented by Wang Bao, Yang Xiong, Mei Sheng, and Sima Xiangru, whose works took as their main purpose the celebration of the rulers' virtue, under

a pretense of censure or admonition. [Jian'an literature] was expressive of emotions and personality. (Yu Guanying 1956: 2)

This description of Jian'an literature as expressive of emotions and "personality" is a formation with particular roots in nineteenth- and twentieth-century figurations of the (bourgeois) individual. The linking of late Han literary expression and something like "personality" has roots, though, in the earliest literary histories of belletristic writing, which were all composed in the late fourth and fifth centuries in the great Qi-Liang dynasty flourishing of canon-formation and literary history whose most renowned product was the compilation of the *Wen xuan* (*Literary Selections*). Near contemporary pieces such as Shen Yue's "Postcript to the Life of Xie Lingyun," Zhong Rong's *Poetry Systematically Graded*, and Liu Xie's *Literary Mind and the Carving of Dragons* make similar linkages of literary production and some figuration of the "inner." As I suggested earlier in this chapter, though, much of this later exaltation of the "literary" referred to a generic scope that extended far beyond the belletristic genres. What had happened by the Song-Qi-Liang period was a consolidation of court literary practice. In the southern courts the symbolic capital of "adornment" counted for more than it did in the Han, and "leisure" frequently had more of the character of "work."

The Song-Qi-Liang critics wrote within the parameters of dichotomies like substance and adornment, essential and excessive. There was a general consensus that feeling (*qing*) was a primary component of substance and that the literature produced at the Cao court was strong and substantial, genuine, full of feeling, and vigorous. Zhong Rong, for example, sees in the Jian'an "wind and strength" (*feng li*) the purest and most vigorous expression of a classical essence, one that declines in the "doctrinal" (*xuanyan*) poetry of the Western Jin. Shen Yue's brief literary history in the "Postscript to the Life of Xie Lingyun" accords even greater centrality to the Jian'an in literary history, judging it a time when feeling (*qing*) was the framework for style and when style was subordinated to being a bearer of substance. As we saw in the judgment in the *Yiwen zhi*, a literary response to a troubled time was preferable to empty indulgence in verbal excess. By the southern dynasties, the iconic status and significance of the fall of the Han had been consolidated, and it could be articulated as a time appropriate to the "heroic" or "strong" response. The Jian'an writers, then, did what was expected of them. The question of "individuality," however, was not an issue for the Song-Qi-Liang critics.

Most modern critics see the emotional and personal expressivity whose origins they locate in the Jian'an as characteristic of the entire later history of classical poetry. The Jian'an era's foundational significance in literary history is generally attributable to (1) the sudden great rise in the number of poems positively attributable to known authors and currently extant (over three hundred in the Jian'an, which exceeds the number for the rest of the Han dynasty); (2) the great number of poems with identifiable occasions or circumstances of composition; and (3) the new attention to "literary criticism," which many later critics have seen as evidence of both a new valorization of literature and a growing literary "self-consciousness." All of these evaluations of the era's significance, like those in the brief passages quoted above, rest ultimately on some determination of lyric subjectivity, on the kind of "consciousness" that Peter Haidu claimed was inaccessible for medieval European literary production. Modern critics who are uncomfortable with the overdetermined interpretative tradition attached to the *Book of Songs* because of its status as canonical classic, the mytho-historical contexts of the *Chu ci*, or the often questionable attribution of Han *yuefu* and the *Nineteen Old Poems* to specific authors with specific compositional circumstances, could find in the Jian'an era a body of poetry with various seemingly concrete connections to individual lives. They could approach it with a firmer conviction that poetry arose out of individual consciousnesses in particular situations and that it was aimed at certain ends.

In fact, the prominence accorded to subjectivity in Jian'an poetry is problematic on nearly all counts, starting with the prominence given to the poetic genre itself. Why, despite many Jian'an documents that testify to its low position in the hierarchy of letters, is poetry overwhelmingly the most studied Jian'an genre? The antibelletristic rhetoric referred to above continues throughout imperial history as a cothematic element, but nowhere is it as untempered as in the Jian'an writings. In later discourse (the Ming-Qing critic Gu Yanwu's "The Wind and Bone of the Two Han Dynasties" from the *Ri zhi lu* is a foundational example) the literary flourish of the Jian'an is an important symptom of decline. But even in Gu's stern formulation, this characterization of the Jian'an as the "literary era" remains.

I attempted, in my exposition of the "text system" in chapter 1, to give a sense of the social, circulatory character of texts and to suggest that the generalized intertextual character of textual production makes problematic a focus on a discrete individual text. The critical focus in literary history, though, is nearly exclusively on the unified, individual poem. This is equally inappropriate, since a variety of textual evidence from the late Han suggests that the individual poem had little ontological weight. The individual instantiation of a given poem seemed to be overshadowed by its membership within a group of poems, such as in a collected anthology[9] or as part of a group composition. Individual lines or couplets easily became separable from their "source" texts—to be quoted, excerpted, or recombined into other compositions. The ontological assumptions that govern our notions about the individual poem could derive from the same ideological formation that focuses attention on the individual poet. But why do we think of the Seven Masters of the Jian'an as poets? No doubt this is due to a teleologizing of early literary history, wherein all poetic genres point toward the hegemony of Tang and Song lyrics, as well as to the privileging of poetry as the hegemonic literary genre in Qing and Western sinology. I have left my own discussion of poetry for the last part of this book, but the Jian'an figures supreme in most histories of Chinese poetry, and I think it is worth questioning the ideological character of histories of poetry. If histories of a single genre concentrated on the genre's formal and generic features, that would be understandable. But histories of poetry are more commonly histories of the expanding referential capacity of the poem, particularly when practiced by a specific poetic genius.

One explanation for the preeminence of poetry study, I think, is that the very hegemonic status of the poetic genre, accumulated through years of examinations, accumulated *shi hua*, various canonization practices, and the work of twentieth-century giants in literary scholarship in the West and in China, has made work on poetry the highest form of literary connoisseurship. And it is precisely through connoisseurship that a "high" or canonical tradition reproduces itself. Readers and critics in a canonical tradition such as classical *gushi* poetry, through their appreciative or critical commentary on the poetry in lectures, books, essays, *shi hua*, or textual editions, or in their own poetry based on or commenting on other poems in the canonical tradition, are positioning themselves to an extent as "ideal readers"—(*zhi yin*)—as dead poets' friends and compatriots. This evaluative function, expressed in formulations like the appreciation and/or ranking of the degree of beauty, greatness, or skill found in a given poetic work, is rarely absent from discussions of classical Chinese poetry, particularly in the United States,[10] whatever the author's theoretical orientation. Proper connoisseurship conveys membership in the tradition, validating simultaneously both the critic and the canon. The subject position offered by the practice of connoisseurship, however, is always ideologically determined. A consideration of connoisseurship over the last three hundred years reveals much about that ideological character.

Putting "subjectivity" at the center of analysis of late Latter Han poetry raises questions that its proponents rarely address. What do we really mean when we refer to subjectivity or the "self" in Jian'an literature and beyond? What are the means by which this impression of greater subjectivity is created? What is subjectivity's historical character? What political and social formations influence the presentation of subjectivity? Why is poetry such a privileged vehicle for the presentation of subjectivity? If we take a look at representative recent critics of classical Chinese poetry in

the West, we find that although their critical approaches differ considerably, they make similar assumptions regarding the basic nature of lyric
subjectivity. Contrasting the classical Chinese lyric with all of Western
poetry (although like most critics writing in English, his choices for comparisons are the English Romantics, those other Ur-dead poets), Stephen
Owen argues for a reformulation of our notion of meaning and for a
reorientation of our reading practice along "Chinese" lines. For Owen
this involves discarding the Western assumption of "fictionality" (Owen
1985: 73). What the poet seeks in a reader and what the reader aspires to
in reading, according to Owen, is the relationship of the "true friend,"
the *zhi yin* (Owen 1985: 73). A poem is a means to know the poet, hence
the use of poetry in examinations to evaluate a candidate's fitness to hold
a bureaucratic position.

In this formulation, "reading" takes place along a linear continuum.
We begin as readers. Anterior to the reader is the poem. Anterior to the
poem is the author, and anterior to the author is the world. Subjectivity
is thus ontologically prior to and anterior to the poem. The poem is the
product of a subjective consciousness and the producer of an ideal reader,
who, like the "true friend" (*zhi yin*, or "knower of the tune") is a mirror
of that subjectivity. The "knower of the tune" formulation contributes to
a construction of a monadic chain, from individual to individual, wherein
writing and reading are always solo activities. Contemporary critics of
classical Chinese poetry, whether modeling their work on New Criticism,
Jakobsonian structuralism or semiotics, rarely deviate from some version
of the communicative model, with ontological priority assigned to the
creating consciousness (Owen 1985, Francois Cheng 1982, Kao and Mei
1978, and Francois Cheng 1982).

It would be absurd to deny the communicative function of literary or
any other discourse. In questioning this model, I want to suggest that we
take the communicative function as *one* aspect of discourse, rather than
the totality of it, and that we remain aware of the paradigmatic limitations
that the communicative model imposes. The philosophers and critics who
are generally labeled "post-Saussurian" insist that we accord ontological
primacy to the signifier. This does not mean that we cannot talk about
intentionality or an author. Rather, we are given new contexts in which
to discuss these features as textual products or effects. Here are some
suggestive formulations for those of us working on Classical Chinese
writing:

1. Poetry is ideology. The precedence of the signifier, which is agreed
   to be especially significant for poetry, "makes visible as ideological
   what otherwise is disregarded as merely the means of representation" (Easthope 1983: 23). The post-Saussurian dissolution of the

distinction between form and content also allows us to see ideology inscribed at the level of the signifier. Thus the critic Antony East-hope is able to analyze iambic pentameter ideologically and suggests other possibilities of analyzing the historically determined, ideological content of "form" (Easthope 1983).

2. The ideological nature of form, or signifying practices, does not rest solely in its being historically determined. Discourse is a *social* fact (vide Saussure); discourses "produce" readers. This perspective allows us to analyze the ideological effects of a given discourse. Many critics in the West, for example, have shown how "bourgeois forms of discourse will aim to provide an absolute position for the subject, others a relative position" (Easthope 1983: 29).

3. Another alternative to the communicative model is M. A. K. Halli-day's notion of "antilanguages" and related notions from social se-miotics, which study the various "reality-generating" mechanisms of discourse. An antilanguage, in Halliday's usage, is a set of particular usages among a given subculture. Like ordinary language, anti-languages are always part of conversation. Yet even more than ordinary language, antilanguages foreground the social dimension of discourse (Halliday 1978: 164–182). As Halliday says,

> A work of literature is its author's contribution to the reality-generat-ing conversation of society—irrespective of whether it offers an alterna-tive reality or reinforces the received model—and its language reflects this status that it has in the sociosemiotic scheme. (Halliday 1978: 182)

Halliday would lead us to see in conventions, codes, and shared techniques signs not necessarily of a literary *self*-consciousness, but of a social semiotic.

If Jian'an poetry, compared with the poetry of earlier times, indeed appears to offer a greater weight to the subject position, how and why does this occur? To answer *how*, we can look for "signs of person" in syntactic features like pronouns, demonstratives, relative adverbs and ad-jectives, temporalizers, and modalizing terms and particles.[11] If we accept the proposition that an elaborated and codified set of techniques indicates a distinct set of authorial intentions, we can turn attention to those formal elements by which a poem calls attention to the materiality of its signifi-ers, in sound elements such as rhyme, alliteration, and other structures of repetition. At the discursive level, we can look at elements like the line, the couplet, the parallel couplet, beginnings, endings, and other formal or semiformal divisions of the poem, as well as allusion, quotation, and the various means by which the poem is situated in larger discursive structures such as genre and "the tradition" (Connery 1991).

I am more interested here, however, in exploring the more intractable question *why*? This returns us to the particular problematics of textual authority. What was the "work" of poetry, and what, in sociotextual terms, did that work produce? I have argued above that the self-recognition function was a central component in shi textual culture. Is there a separate work for poetry, and, if not, does poetry accomplish the self-recognition function in a different way? For the Han, at least, our expectations must at this stage be more modest than those that operate in the study of early modern English literature, for example. Easthope is able to refer to "bourgeois" poetic discourse in his discussion of English poetry, and he can be confident that the notion of an historical bourgeoisie is well understood and accepted. In the Empire of the Text, which exists in a history parallel to and contingent with the sociohistorical empire, the category of social formation is more difficult of access. But first it is important to establish the textual character of late Latter Han poetry. This is not the obvious point that it seems. In the consensus version of early imperial literary history, late Latter Han poetic writing was a consequence of a fusion. On the one side was, as we have seen, shi "subjectivity" or "self consciousness." But on the other side was the oral: the folk. In the consensus version, the marriage that produced Jian'an poetry, and, by extension, the mainstream of the lyric tradition, was between shi subjectivity and "oral," "folk" language and themes. First we must lay to rest the specter of orality.

Orality

There is no reason to think that the poetry of the Jian'an period has anything to do with oral poetry, if by "oral poetry" we mean poetry both composed and circulated in oral form. For the Han and pre-Han periods, in fact, there exists no contemporary record that would allow a description of what an oral poetry would have been like or how such a poetry would have been transformed when written down. This situation is unlikely to change. We will continue to learn more about the spoken language in Han times as our tools of linguistic analysis become more refined and as prestandardization or protosyllabary sinographs continue to come to light through archaeological investigation. But there is no reason to think that even new documentary evidence could allow a conceptualization of an oral poetry that would meet minimum standards of evidence. Even without the requirements of evidence, claims to support the oral origin analysis are generally theoretically weak as well. The most common "evidence" for a prior orality—the use of verbal formulas—has been shown to be equally prevalent in written compositions.[12] Questions of diction and decorum, where one word in a paradigmatic set would be the less formal and hence more "oral" choice for insertion into a line, can just as easily be conceived as thoroughly embedded within a textual logic. The arguments for the wholly textual character of late Han poetry are more convincing: the prevalence of explicit authorial identification and the phenomenon of regular line length. Four-, five-, six-, or seven-character lines do not suggest the vocal flexibility of an oral composition.

The matter of oral composition is not raised in Han sources. In fact, the status of the oral is ambiguous. Many of the canonical classics have extensive passages that take the form of quoted conversations or interrogations; frequent exclamatory particles contribute to a textualized effect of orality. In texts attributed to Confucius, though, as I have indicated earlier, the objects of study are texts. There is no added authenticity or special efficacy to oral teaching. Several Han and pre-Han sources refer to the oral, and there are some explicit descriptions of what must be called a scene of pure orality, the most developed of which must be Yang Xiong's (attr.) *Fang yan*. Yet there is nothing like the Greek debate about writing's deleterious effects on civic and moral life, nor are there texts that allow, as late Roman and early medieval European texts do, a reconstruction of the continuities and differences between the world of the text and the worlds of oral rhetoric, recitation, or public speech. The ambiguity of the relationship of the purely oral to the written can be seen in the following well-known passage from the "Great Preface" to the *Book of Songs*, which alleges the linear continuity between feeling, text, and sound:

> Poetry is the path of feeling. In the heart it is feeling; expressed in speech, it is poetry. Feelings are stimulated within, and formed into words. When words do not suffice, there are sighs and exclamations; when sighs and exclamations do not suffice, therefore there are extended plaints and songs. When plaints and songs don't suffice, without realizing it the hands dance and the feet stamp. Emotions are expressed in sound. When sound becomes regularized it is called tone. The tones of a well-governed age are peaceful and happy, and its government is harmonious. The tones of a chaotic age are angry and resentful; its government is decadent. A fallen kingdom's tones are sad and pensive; its people are forlorn. So in regulating achievements and failures, in influencing heaven and earth, and in moving the spirits, nothing is better than Poetry.[13]

There is a double movement here, hastened by the stimulus of insufficiency. The immediate production of feeling is words; the insufficiency of words leads to plaints, songs, dance, and stamping. That is one trajectory: The words are indicative, in one direction, of the "feeling" and, in the other, of the excess. Another trajectory goes from emotions to sound to tone—the pure emanation of the political state. The first trajectory is a compositional logic, the second is the diagnostic logic. Nowhere in what has been judged to be the earliest sustained piece of "literary criticism" is an ontological priority assigned to the oral. What would be, in a claim for orality, the crucial transition—from spoken word to written word—is not mentioned. Words are written words. Critics often give insufficient emphasis to the fact that this text refers to the *Book of Songs*, the poetry classic, and not to poetry in general. The lesson of the classic's official exegeses is that the *Book of Songs* expresses the character of an age. No claim is made for its oral composition. The claim is made instead to a "popular" referent—that the songs indicate the mood of the times. The same claim can be made and indeed was frequently made for textual compositions: We see at work again here the force of adequation between the "human" and the "textual." In general, the claim for orality is itself a strategy for delineating the human and the textual. The pioneering work on "oral literature"[14] commonly had a defensive polemical tone. Proponents of oral literature were indeed proponents in that they were trying to rescue from logocentric scholarly and aesthetic neglect a body of extra-textual cultural production. In China, the championing of the oral and the popular in the May Fourth era of this century was related to a new cultural politics among the intelligentsia, as well as to their definition of their sphere of authority in the postimperial scene.[15] Yet the easy acceptance of the "oral origin" hypothesis for the belletristic poem suggests that the issue has not received sufficient theoretical elaboration.

There are frequent references in Han-Wei texts to poetic composition based on songs from an oral repertoire. These are songs that were sung on specific occasions: the cymbal songs of the Han or the dirges. But oral performance and oral circulation of poetic material need not interfere with a prior and dominant textuality. These songs could easily have originally been written compositions. We know that much of the material in the classical canon circulated in oral form, but the propensity for a poem to circulate orally says nothing about its circumstances of composition, or about its language or diction. Archaic, "literary" locutions are as amenable to oral circulation as is simple, conversational diction.[16]

Claims for orality have been made primarily in this century and were related, as I suggest above, to claims for an authentic "folk" culture. For the Han, "folk" culture is a more complicated matter than orality. It is undeniable that a significant quantity of Han poetry, particularly in *gushi* and *yuefu* forms, treats subjects that have more to do with commoners' lives than with the lives of the shi. Agricultural life, village life, singing-girl experiences, orphans, and footsoldiers represent a range of the thematic content available. The language of many of these poems is from a more restricted set of sinographs and has fewer textual allusions than does poetry judged to be more "literary," so there is some justification for the stylistic-thematic category of the "folk." But there is a great risk in carrying the category of the folk too far. Conjurations of the "folk" can too easily suggest a Bakhtinian dialogism in which the "folk" element is a remnant of a parodic and travestying "outside" to a dominant agelast culture.[17] The "thematic" is a weak analytical category to begin with. And it is quite possible that the thematics of the "folk" spring from a discourse of containment. We see no dialogic voice struggling to emerge.

Many scholars and critics claim that a central feature of Jian'an poetry is its incorporation of "folk" themes and language into new "literati" forms, including both *gushi* and "literati" *yuefu*. Such an analysis makes assumptions that merit closer attention. First is the assumption that the Jian'an literati adapters, at least, saw a clear demarcation between the "folk" and the literati writing community. Second is the assumption that "folk" pieces and literati compositions differ in intention, if not in content. Related to this is the assumption that "folk" compositions have their roots in oral performance, whereas literati compositions are "originally" textual. This assumption has been widespread in the twentieth century, influenced by German romantic conceptions of "folk" literature, and, in the Chinese case, by "new historians" like Gu Jiegang, whose aims included the liberation of "folk" materials from the oppressive strictures of perceived historically and situationally determined authorship.[18] Contemporary theorists of popular culture have attacked the notion of any clear demarcation between "low" and "high" culture, and I have suggested above some reasons why the oral/written dichotomy is untenable.[19] *Yuefu* poetry offers a clear area for examination of this putative binarism in the Chinese context, since *yuefu* supposedly divides into "literati" and "folk" compositions. The distinction between "literati" and "folk" *yuefu* is made generally on the following grounds (I will dispense with quotation marks around the words "literati" and "folk," but the reader should keep in mind that the distinction is problematic):

1. Literati *yuefu* are more often regular in line length, with pentameter predominating.
2. Literati *yuefu* use allusions, to classical texts and other literati texts, to a far greater extent than do folk *yuefu*.
3. Literati *yuefu* are less often narrative than are folk *yuefu*.
4. Literati *yuefu* show greater attention to compositional principles like parallelism than do folk *yuefu*.
5. Literati *yuefu* use "nonsense syllables" or exclamations less than do folk *yuefu*.

6. In literati *yuefu*, a single voice is more common than the dialogic voices of folk *yuefu*.[20]

I must note that these distinctions are also of little meaning when differentiating anonymous *yuefu* from *yuefu* with an ascribed author. Many anonymous *yuefu* meet the criteria for literati composition, and some literati compositions, like Cao Pi's "Shang liu tian," show pronounced use of features normally associated with orality, such as the use of nonsense syllables as a refrain. There is no indication, in fact, that the distinction *gushi-yuefu* meant anything in the Jian'an. Even in the Qi-Liang era, it is a distinction marked by Liu Xie but not by the *Wen xuan*. It might be significant, though, that beginning roughly in Jian'an times, the "author function" (cf. Foucault) is extended to many literati compositions in the *yuefu* genre. Following Foucault, we might surmise that this shift has a generalized ideological character with social roots, rather than a strictly formal or generic character. Joseph R. Allen has suggested that *yuefu* is distinguished by its "non-occasional" character, and that *yuefu* poems have an "intratextual" relationship to other poems of the same title. As I have argued elsewhere, the intertextual referents in fact range well beyond poems that share a particular title (Connery 1993). But Allen may be correct in positing, in *yuefu* composition, evidence of a purely textual occasionality. Unbound by formal or generic occasions, *yuefu* compositions may have had no referents beyond the textual scene at large. This must remain a matter of speculation. We do, however, have substantial records about the social, collective character of poetry, which includes anthological practice and group composition. These records allow another challenge to the myth of the individual subject.

Social Poetic Practice

A well-known letter from Cao Pi to Wu Zhi, a foundational document in the figuration of the Jian'an era as the era of the Dead Poets, includes these lines:

So many of our friends and family were carried off in last year's epidemics. Xu Gan, Chen Lin, Ying Yang, and Liu Zhen all passed away at the same time: what unspeakable sadness it has caused me! In days gone by, we would ride out in our chariots one after the other and sit together with our mats touching: not for an instant could we be separated! We would fill our wine cups and pass them to one another and then, when the strings and winds played together and our ears were hot from the wine, we would raise our heads and chant poetry. How unconscious we were then, not knowing our happiness! We thought that we would each live for a hundred years, and stay together forever! It pains me to talk of it. I recently gathered together their remaining works and assembled them in a single collection. Their names look like a list of the dead. Our old parties, when I think back on them, still seem to be in front of my eyes, but those who accompanied us on them have turned to dust.[21]

We have what may be the first reference in history to the compilation of the collected writings of the compiler's contemporaries.[22] It is significant that this collection is a multiauthored collection—the collected works of Cao Pi's dead friends, who are mentioned collectively and individually in the *Authoritative Discourses: On Literature* as well. In chapter 1 I suggested the anthology as a normative model that described material and social circulation of texts better than the model of the individual work. The history of preimperial and early imperial textual culture is the history of the anthology. Many pre-Qin texts are anthologies. The *Book of Songs* and the *Stratagems of the Warring States* (*Zhanguo ce*) are prominent examples. Cao Pi's letter also shows an anthological practice that diverges from Liu Xiang's. Cao Pi's claims to have its basis in social life, whereas there seems to be a greater sense of thematic or generic unity in Liu Xiang's principles of compilation.

The sources indicate that the Jian'an witnessed a renewed attention to compilation and collectanea after decades of neglect. At the court level, Ying Shao, for example, wrote a memorial advocating increased attention to collectanea in the first year of the Jian'an era (QHHW 33, 9-b, 657). The few sources we have suggest that Jian'an belletristic compilation seems to have been without any overt connection to court bibliography, nor indeed to official purposes of any kind. Wu Zhi's reply to Cao Pi is indicative of the status of the belletristic compilation. While expressing sympathy for Cao Pi's loss at the death of his friends, he suggests that Cao Pi get back to the Cao capital at Ye and devote himself to government, instead of remaining too involved in writing (QSGW 30, 8a-b, 1221). Belletristic collectanea seems, however, to have been a common albeit informal practice. The correspondence between Cao Zhi and Yang Xiu, for example, mentions Cao Zhi's collection of juvenilia, which seems to have enjoyed at least limited circulation. The multiauthored compilation that Cao Pi mentions in his letter has not survived. I do want to stress, though, its multiple authorship. Although the bibliography section in the (Liu) *Song shu* and later bibliographies mention poets' collected works organized according to individual authors, we cannot deduce from Cao Pi's own writing any sense that individual literary output marked any kind of interpretive horizon.

When individual authors' particular traits are discussed in the letter to Wu Zhi and in the *Authoritative Discourses: On Literature*, the extent to which individual talents divide along generic lines is striking: Wang Can as master of *fu*, Chen Lin of memorials (*biao*), Liu Zhen of *gushi* poetry, Ruan Yu of letters. It is as if belletristic writing itself is only constituted in parts by individual authors—only in the collective is there writing as a whole. Of all Jian'an writers, only Xu Gan is praised as a whole and outstanding individual talent (Cao Zhi concurred in this judgment) for his authorship of the *Discourse on the Central*, a work discussed in chapter 3. We may find evidence here of a fundamental generic division that would become more pronounced in Xiao Tong's *Wen xuan*, the division between the anthologizable and the nonanthologizable.

Guo Shaoyu has suggested that Xiao Tong excluded genres from the *Wen xuan* that did not consist of isolatable "single pieces" (*dan pian*).[23] This principle would explain the absence in the *Wen xuan* of chronologically based records of events, histories, and longer works such as Xu Gan's. But Guo Shaoyu is operating on the principle—which evidence suggests was more operative in Xiao Tong's time than in the Jian'an—of the ontological primacy of the individual and isolatable single literary composition. It might not be too far-fetched to classify Han and even later belletristic writing in general as anthologogenic. When compilations or collectanea are mentioned in the Jian'an, they are predominantly of *gushi* and *fu*, which are precisely the two genres that are most represented in the *Wen xuan*. I would suggest that this is no accident, but I would also suggest that the prominence of these genres in anthologies is not simply a function of the "independence of belletristic literature" that so many critics have seen operative in *Wen xuan* aesthetics. I would rather suggest that belletristic writing *demanded* anthologizing and that its composition and reception practices militated against the isolability of the individual lyric. This assignment of ontological priority to the anthology or collection rather than to the individual poem, of course, further militates against an overreliance on the communicative model discussed above.

When Jian'an writers are mentioned collectively as a group, as in Cao Pi's letter to Wu Zhi, there is always reference to group activity, to parties, play, and group composition. We know from many sources that group activity was the setting for much compositional activity and that much literary production, particularly poetry, depended not on solitary inspiration but on the imitations, responses, variations on themes, and other activities that were part of the public character of literati life.

Shen Yue's discussion of the poets Lu Ji and Pan Yue in his "Postscript to the Life of Xie Lingyun" mentions two archetypal locations of past literati group activities. He refers to Lu Ji's and Pan Yue's practice of adorning their works with the "sublime resonances of Level Terrace and the lofty tones of Nanpi" (*Song shu*: 1778). Nanpi was a hunting ground near Ye and site of the literati outings referred to in Cao Pi's "Letter to

Wu Zhi." Level Terrace was constructed in 153 B.C.E. under King Xiao of
Liang in the Western Han, who was also known as a book collector. On
one occasion, illustrious worthies from all over the country came to cele-
brate the completion of a road linking the terrace to the king's palace (HS:
2207–8).

The *Miscellaneous Records of the Western Capital* records that

> King Xiao of Liang went on an outing to the Hall of Forgetting Sorrow,
> and asked each of the assembled scholars there to compose a *fu*. Mei Sheng
> composed his "Willow *fu*" [text follows in the original]; Lu Qiaoru com-
> posed a "Crane *fu*" [text follows]; Gongsun Gui composed a "Spotted Deer
> *fu*" [text follows]; Zou Yang composed a "Wine *fu*" [text follows]; Gongsun
> Sheng composed a "Moon *fu*" [text follows]; Yang Sheng composed a "Wind
> Break *fu*" [text follows]; Han Anguo could not complete his "Table *fu*," so
> Zou Yang completed it for him. Zou Yang and Han Anguo were punished
> by being made to drink three *sheng* of wine; Mei Sheng and Lu Qiaoru were
> each rewarded with five *pi* of silk. (*Xi Jing zaji* 4, 3a–5a)

There is little doubt that court belletristic composition in group form
existed for hundreds of years prior to the Jian'an, and probably antedated
the Level Terrace period as well. Suzuki Shūji identifies nearly all early *fu*
as a court genre practiced under royal patronage, which probably involved group composition activities (Suzuki 1967: 505–8). Although *fu*
continued to occupy a central place in group compositional activities in
the Jian'an, historical and textual evidence is insufficient for any precise
characterization of such activity for earlier periods. The *Miscellaneous
Records of the Western Capital* was probably not composed before the
third century C.E., and recently Wang Meng'ou has pointed out the similarities between the description in the *Miscellaneous Records* and descriptions by Jian'an authors of the character of literati group activities in their
own era.[24] Thus the primary text on which Suzuki bases his conclusions
about the social nature of Former Han *fu* could easily have been influenced by what was then known about the clearly social character of later
Han *fu*. What I believe to be more significant about Shen Yue's discussion
than the simple facts of the history of literati group activity, though, is
the manner in which he closely identifies the literary style of a particular
time with a particular group's practice. This was a common discursive
feature in Shen Yue's day. In Jian'an literary and historical texts, though,
we have the first significant body of documentary evidence of the social
character of literati production.

The literati group activities described or referred to in Jian'an writings
take place over a fairly short period of time, roughly from 204 to 217.[25]
The nature of these activities was affected by the changing character of
interpersonal life over the course of the latter half of the second century.

Although courtly literature in the Former Han, centering on *fu*, seems also to have been characterized by patronage and group compositional activities, these activities took place under the aegis of a fairly stable imperial or provincial court at a time when there was no serious challenge to either the stability of the empire or the solidity of hierarchical organization. The sociopolitical character of the Jian'an era gave their literati groupings a different character. From the time Dong Zhuo ascended to power in 190 to the time Cao Cao gained control of Emperor Xian in 196, the central regions of China were in a state of near total anarchy, particularly in the latter half of that period, which was marked by rivalries between armies controlled by more than seven different generals. Chang'an itself became more and more dangerous as the period progressed. Massive depopulation and migration had, we must imagine, profound effects on the social order and the nature of local allegiances and dependencies. The historical record is scanty with regard to commoner migration, but we are able to trace the broad outlines of literati migration and the consequent new alliances.

Although literati migrated in all directions from the Chang'an-Loyang region and other dangerous areas,[26] the main tendency was southward, to Yangzhou, and, more importantly, to Liu Biao's power base at Xiangyang in Jingzhou. Liu Biao, named as one of the "eight exemplars" among the "pure" faction, had been made Regional Inspector of Jingzhou immediately after the death of Emperor Ling (HHS: 2419, SGZ: 210). Shortly after that, he became Regional Commander, an office that by the Late Han was roughly equivalent in status to independent warlord (Hucker 1985: 336). Xiangyang was reasonably safe from a military standpoint, transportation to it was relatively easy, and Liu Biao's status among capital literati indicated an ability to reproduce court culture in his region. One measure of the extent of the migration to Jingzhou is the biography of Ying Rong, a prominent scholar in the north, who the sources report was joined in his Jingzhou exile by over one thousand disciples (HHS: 2584). We can probably assume that migration by other prominent literati also included disciples and/or dependents.[27] The SGZ uses similar language to describe many of their migrations to Jingzhou. Wang Can's biography states that he "entered into dependence" (*yi*) on Liu Biao (SGZ: 598). In the biographies of Du Ji (SGZ: 493–4) and Handan Chun (SGZ: 603) the verb is "to guest" (*ke*) with Liu Biao, a usage that certainly suggests the kind of relationship implied in the categories of "guests and dependents" mentioned above. The biographies of Du Xi and Pei Qian contain identical phrases describing their reception by Liu Biao: "Liu Biao treated [each] according to etiquette befitting an honored guest" (SGZ: 664–665, 671). That migration itself had a social determinant is evident in Zhao Yan's biography, which records that, "going to Jingzhou to escape the chaos, Zhao Ji, Po Qin and Du Xi pooled their resources and planned together, becoming as if one family" (SGZ: 668).

There is a teleological quality to the SGZ's descriptions of most literati reactions to their exile in Jingzhou, one that points inexorably toward their move to Cao Cao's court. The following are some typical examples:

[Wang Can to Cao Cao] The literati that sought refuge from chaos in Jing-zhou were all the outstanding heroes of the entire country. Liu Biao didn't know how to use them. Thus the country was endangered, with no one to aid it. (SGZ: 598)

[Du Xi to Po Qin] The only reason I came with you here was to be as a dragon curled up in a dark swamp, waiting for the opportune time to soar like a phoenix. How can you say that Commander Liu is the ruler to sweep away the disorder? (SGZ: 665)

[Pei Qian to Wang Can and Sima Zhi] Liu Biao does not possess the talent of a hegemon or king, yet he compares himself to the Duke of Zhou. His end will come soon. (SGZ: 671)

Many of the relationships formed in Jingzhou among the literati, such as those between Wang Can, Pei Qian, and Sima Zhi, would continue into their days in the Cao court.

The kind of evidence we have of this social activity is, perhaps, an indication of the colonization of the sphere of the social by the textual. The era records a great increase in the number of "letters" (*shu*) written. Since these letters survived, and were circulated and anthologized during their authors' lifetimes in many cases, we can assume that the "personal letter" was also a public genre. One of its functions may have been the codification of alliance patterns. Zhang Hong's biography states:

Zhang Hong saw a carved cedar pillow, admired its patterns, and composed a *fu* about it. Chen Lin was in the north [with Yuan Shao], and seeing it, showed it to people saying, "This was done by my fellow countryperson Zhang Hong." Later Zhang Hong saw Chen Lin's "Arsenal *fu*" and his "Discourse on Responding to Opportunity" and wrote a letter to Chen Lin, highly praising them.[28]

There are similar epistolary relations between Kong Rong and Wang Lang and between Wang Can and Shisun Meng during the period immediately prior to the establishment of the Jian'an literary group. The new modes of shi self-identification that would come to fruition in the Jian'an were in evidence all over the country at this earlier period.

The nucleus of the Jian'an literary group began to be formed in 205, when Cao Cao began recruiting scholars from all over the country to serve as clerical officers and thus, the sources suggest, add to his prestige among the literati generally.[29] Chen Lin, Liu Fang, and Ruan Yu were among the better known literati to arrive in that wave. Ding Yi, Ding Yì, Ying Yang, and Ying Qu had arrived by 207. By the end of 209, many more had arrived, primarily those who had been with Liu Biao at Xiangyang in Jingzhou but also including Liu Zhen and Xu Gan. Most of them, at first, had largely ceremonial positions. Wang Can, Ruan Yu, and Chen Lin, for example, were all Military Planning Libationers. We know little about their actual political functions, if any; the records are mostly of their literary activity.

These activities were centered in Ye, which had been Cao Cao's capital from about 205. Many of the places mentioned in group literary activity were there: the Nanpi hunting ground, the Xuanwu Pool, constructed in in 208, and, most importantly, the Bronze Magpie Terrace, constructed in the winter of 210 (SGZ: 32). The Bronze Magpie Terrace was the scene of Cao Zhi's oft-mentioned literary triumph:

> When the Bronze Magpie Terrace was newly completed, Cao Cao climbed it with his sons and ordered each of them to compose a *fu*. Cao Zhi took up his brush and completed his in an instant. Cao Cao found him extraordinarily talented.[30]

Bronze Magpie Terrace and the adjacent Western Garden were probably the site of most literary gatherings, as they are referred to in many *fu*, poems, and their prefaces. The southern Qi literatus Wang Sengqian has a document that states:

> The tunes [lit. *qing shang*] of today all actually come from the Bronze Magpie Terrace. It is filled with the inspirational echoes of the three Caos.[31]

Cao Cao's "Will" shows the importance attached to the Terrace:

> My concubines and music attendants have all had a hard lot. Put them in the Bronze Magpie Terrace, and treat them very well. In its Main Hall put a bed six *chi* in length, surrounded by a Spirit Curtain. At morning and night offer sacrificial foods. On the first and fifteenth of every month perform dances and songs in front of the curtain. You can often climb to the top of the Bronze Magpie Terrace and view my grave in the Western Tombs. (QSGW 3: 6A, 1068)

The activities at Western Garden and the Bronze Magpie Terrace coincided with the composition of texts extolling the beauty of specific sites. Yu Yingshi has claimed that shi were at this time inaugurating the custom

of constructing scenic dwelling spots for the appreciation of natural sur-
roundings; this does seem to be the era of the villa, the pavilion, the retreat
(Yu Yingshi 1980: 72–3). Whether or not this construction was unprecedented, the textual work that surrounded it conveys an expression of a
growing "aestheticization" or textualization of "leisure" life. This could
be looked at in two ways—as decadent indulgence in excess or as the
extension of the "work" of the textual to social "leisure" activity.

Before the activities at the Bronze Magpie Terrace, there is some evidence of group composition on military campaigns. Matsumoto Yukio,
in fact, characterizes the first half of the group's activities, up until 212,
as being largely conducted in relation to military campaigns (Matsumoto
1960: 1339). Chen Lin and Ruan Yu each have *fu* on "Stopping Desire"
that concern pre-Red Cliff military campaigns, and there are other *fu* on
military campaigns written by nearly all the important members of the
group, including Cao Zhi, Ruan Yu, Wang Can, Yang Xiu, Cao Pi, Xu
Gan, and Po Qin. Cao Pi and Wang Can each have a *fu* on "Sailing the
Huai River," that refers to a military campaign against Sun Quan in Hefei
in 209. Matsumoto dates many other compositions from this period, but
his evidence is often based on a literal reading of scenic descriptions that
would match physical or geographical conditions of known campaigns.
This line of interpretation may not be tenable, given the generic or formulaic quality of many landscape descriptions in *fu* and in poetry.

Most group compositions consisted of *fu* or *gushi* poetry on shared
themes. Many prefaces to *fu* include specific records of group composition, such as "I ordered [someone] to write a *fu* on it," or "Cao Pi commanded me to write a *fu* on." In the Appendix I have included a list of *fu*
titles with a list of authors who wrote *fu* with those titles or minor variants about the same occasions or events.[32] I have added translated material
on the circumstances of composition where relevant. Several of these
comments indicate there could very well have been other compositions
on the same titles that no longer survive. Numerous other prefaces to *fu*
mention similar occasions of command composition. We can assume that
the practice was fairly common.

That Cao Pi was at the center of group activities is well attested. Many
of these date from 211, when he was made Leader of Court Gentlemen
for Miscellaneous Uses (*wuguan zhonglang jiang*), a position that had
military and civil authority. Cao Pi's attention to literary affairs and his
active role in collecting the works of his contemporaries is well attested.
Bing Yuan's biography gives a sample of the extent and flavor of the gatherings under his sponsorship:

When Cao Pi was Leader of Court Gentlemen for Miscellaneous Uses, all
under heaven revered him, and his guests and retainers swarmed around him

like clouds. . . . At one of Cao Pi's banquets, with guests numbering well over one hundred, Cao Pi began a discussion, saying, "Your lord and your father each have a serious illness. There is one pill that can save one person. Should you save your father or your lord?" The crowd's opinions were divided; some said the lord and some said the father.[33]

The frivolity of these exercises should not be underestimated. This sort of evidence is reason to take seriously the claims by contemporaries that the life of a literatus could include many activities, including production of poetry and other belletristic writing, which were viewed as less weighty or essential than writings in other genres or for other uses.

Cao Pi served as Leader of Court Gentlemen for Miscellaneous Uses until his designation as Heir Apparent in 217, the year of the fatal epidemic. The designation of Cao Pi as Heir Apparent had the additional effect of polarizing the supporters of Cao Pi and Cao Zhi. It took two more years, and several disgraces, for Cao Zhi to fall definitively from favor. This fall is marked by the execution in 219 of Yang Xiu, one of Cao Zhi's most powerful supporters. The atmosphere at court must have been further poisoned by events surrounding Cao Pi's discovery of Wei Feng's aborted coup, after which hundreds of the alleged conspirators were executed (SGZ: 52). Cao Pi's rise to greater power thus marked the end of the Jian'an literary group. It is possible that what was mourned in Cao Pi's letter to Wu Zhi was not the passing of a particular poet but of the collectivity.

Intertextual Composition

The tenuous boundaries between works, which is reflected both in their compositional circumstances and in what we can infer from contemporary accounts of the reception practices, weakens the ontological primacy of the individual work, which is the basis for the construction of the Jian'an as a fountain of individual expression. This tenuousness is further reflected in Jian'an intertextual practices, which I will describe as they appear in the poetry of Cao Pi. Cao Pi's reputation as a poet has not matched his father's and brother's. Readings of both Cao Cao's and Cao Zhi's work, though, have been determined by a mythologizing of the lived context of their poems: Cao Cao as ruler and (anti-) hero and Cao Zhi as victim and witness of traumatic times. Cao Pi's historical persona is implicated in readings of his poetry in only limited ways. A reading of Cao Pi's poetry, unimpeded as it is by the extratextual figuration of a mythic persona, offers us a clearer picture of the nature of Jian'an lyric production than the conventional readings of Cao Cao and Cao Zhi.

Cao Cao's compositions are all in *yuefu*, and they have few "folk" elements in them. Even those songs on typical folk themes, like the hardships of the traveling soldier in "Ku han xing," have very little intertextual use of folk material. Much of Cao Pi's poetry, however, is laden with intertextuality. His tetrameter borrows heavily from the *Shi jing*, and his poems on *Chu ci*-like themes borrow words and images from the source texts (though not phrases and lines as in the poems derived from the *Shi jing*). In several of Cao Pi's poems, intertextual use of elements from anonymous poems abounds. "Lin gao tai" is an example. Very little of the poem seems to be original to Cao Pi. Cao Pi's text, the first of the translations below, is followed first by the two "source" texts of "Lin gao tai" in the *Yuefu jie ti* (quoted in YFSJ)[34] and in the *Yuefu shiji*,[35] and then by the first three stanzas of "Yan ge he chang xing," an intertextual source text, but with a different title. Phrases in the source texts that Cao Pi's poem quotes directly are italicized.

Lin gao tai[36]

Looking down from the terrace—tall!
Tall and soaring.
Below is a river—clear and cold.
In the midst are yellow geese—flying back and forth.
To act as a minister—requires utmost loyalty.[37]
Wishing the emperor three thousand years!
It is good to live in this palace.

The gander wants to fly south;
The goose can't follow.
I want to carry you in my beak;
My mouth is sealed—I can't open it.
I want to bear you on my back;
My feathers are crushed and wrecked.
Five *li*—a look back;
Six *li*—circling aimlessly.

Source Text (*Yuefu jie ti*):

Looking down from the tall terrace
Below I see the clear river
In the midst yellow geese fly and *circle.*
I bend my bow to shoot them
And wish my lord ten thousand *years.*

Source Text (*Yuefu shiji*):

Looking down from the tall terrace—soaring.
Below is a clear *river—clear and cold.*

The stream has fragrant plants—I see them as orchids.
A *yellow goose* flies high—leaving! *returning*!
I stretch my bow to shoot the goose,
To wish my lord ten thousand long *years.*

"Yan ge he chang xing"

Flying come a pair of white geese;
So they come from the northwest
In tens and fives
Lining up in scattered formation.

The wife dies from sickness
And in the travels *cannot follow* them.
Five li—a backward *look.*
Six li—circling aimlessly.

I want to carry you in my beak;
My mouth is sealed—I can't open it.
I want to bear you on my back;
My feathers are crushed and wrecked.

The first stanza of Cao Pi's poem appears to be a conflation of earlier sources, omitting the act of shooting the goose to present to the ruler. The rest of the poem is from the "source" text of the "Yan ge he chang xing." Guo Maoqian lists the above version of "Yan ge he chang xing" as the anonymous original words to that tune (Cao Pi has an authored *yuefu* to that tune as well). I have translated only the first three stanzas. The rest of the poem (fourteen more lines) is in the voice of an abandoned wife and speaks in a fairly standard way about the sorrows of "parting while alive." This poem is in regular pentameter lines, with the exception of the three tetrameter lines.

It is curious that Cao Pi's poem shows less verbal regularity than does the purported source poem for his second stanza. It is also curious that the sentence order of this source is rearranged in Cao Pi's version. The two sources have two different themes: praise for the ruler and sorrow of separation. The Qing critic Zhu Qian suggests a way of combining these themes on an intentional level:

> This poem divides into two stanzas. The first copies "Lin gao tai" in the *Han Nao ge*; the second copies "Yan ge he chang xing" of the *se diao* mode. I suspect that at the time [Cao Pi] was ordered on a distant mission; therefore he uses the yellow goose as a simile. The first part praises the ruler; the second part is a lament for himself. The subtle intent is in the line "To act as a minister—requires utmost loyalty." The poem says that the minister

should be wholly loyal, but that the ruler should also be compassionate toward his minister.[38]

The impulse to create an intentional unity for disparate verbal elements is a common one in traditional Chinese criticism. Thus in a curious but common twist, it is precisely in those features that threaten subjective unity that a greater and deeper subjectivity is alleged by the critic. The intentional unity of this poem, if indeed it exists, is of course no longer accessible to us. The combination of the source material reveals no clear intent to me. The poem does seem to divide in the middle and the ending seems abrupt—untypical of Cao Pi's and other literati conventions of endings. In general, Cao Pi's composition shows *less* verbal artifice than even his sources. The only kind of subjectivity clearly presented here is Cao Pi as a reader/anthologizer/compiler/circulator of *yuefu* poetry.

This is not one of Cao Pi's better-known poems. I bring it up to illustrate an extreme example of intertextual composition, with which his work is replete, and to suggest that this intertextual principle can serve to lead us far away from the "individualistic" expressions said to be so typical of Jian'an poetry. My analysis of recent critical assumptions about subjectivity in classical Chinese poetry suggests a need for a rehistoricization of certain basic conceptual categories and a rethinking of the unquestioned primacy accorded to the individualized subject in Jian'an writing. Political and social history can continue to inform our understanding of late Han writing, but not necessarily by positing political and social transformations as triggers of the individualized pathos that most critics find so central to Jian'an lyrics. What I see as a more significant historical "context" is the historical character of the value accorded to belletristic writing. One consequence of the chaos and dislocation that marked the end of the Han, from the Affair of the Proscribed Factions through the Yellow Turban revolt and into the partitioning of the empire, was the general devaluation of the currencies of land, family, and official position. The lives of most Jian'an shi were marked by frequent shifts in alliances and locale, and their associations took place within a complex system of patronage and protection. In this situation, the Empire of the Text remained, while the structures of the political empire were losing their coherence. The sources suggest, perhaps not accidentally, that shi had acquired both administrative value and symbolic value for their patrons. Textual production as currency, as means of exchange, could have acquired an ontic weight that exceeded its function in earlier periods, when it could be said to form a kind of formal or expressive parallel to the requisites of political administration. Shi textual production was always, as I have argued, a means of self-recognition and social existence. In the Jian'an, there was perhaps a higher premium on the capacity to generate mutual recognition and some form of "community." Twentieth-century readers who see an individualized subject as the distinctive product of Jian'an writing might consider the remarkable *fluidity* of subjective identity reflected in Jian'an textual practice. The interpretive move from the social to the individual might have an ideological character worthy of analysis.

In Conclusion: A Humanist Fantasy

When I read contemporary scholarship on early imperial writing that describes what a given writer thought, felt, must have thought, or might have thought, my critical exasperation is sometimes tempered with sympathy for the desire to commune with the souls of the long dead. I confess that I have delineated, in this book, something of an iron cage: a power in suprahuman textual authority that was at least the equal of imperial political and military authority. This power was neither unchanging nor timeless, but its legacies, I think, remain alive today. I'd like to end this book, which is itself an analytical experiment, with a humanist experiment. The following passage from Cao Pi's *Authoritative Discourses: On Writing* is one of the most widely quoted apologies for poetry from the early imperial era:

> For Writing is the Great Work in the ordering of the state; it is an accomplishment that does not pass away. A life span ends with its allotted time; and when the body goes, so do honor and glory. Life and body must reach their temporal limits, unlike Writing, which is eternal. Therefore the writers in antiquity delivered their bodies unto ink and brush, and materialized their thoughts in tablets and collections. With neither the encomia of the historians nor the patronage of the powerful, their names and reputations transmitted themselves unto posterity. (text in glossary under "gai wenzhang")

The verb that I translated above as "ordering" has many senses, and by the Han dynasty was the common word for "canonical classic." In preimperial times it referred to the principal north-south thoroughfares, a sense from which would derive the current term for longitudinal meridians. To order the state with writing, geographically: the Empire of the Text.

Beyond this first sentence, the passage is a fairly conventional formula whose equivalents can be found in apologia for writing in many languages and across many centuries. We should bear that first phrase in mind, though, as we consider what follows it. Writing *is* the work of the state and it would appear, indeed, to endure. Those who made their successful bids for immortality were those who were already privileged citizens of the textual empire; they had crossed over in life. What is more human, though, than mortality itself? We are humans, after all, because we die.[39] Contemporary versions of those who have crossed over into the nonmortal—media celebrities—bring with their images a frisson of horror, a horror born of the uncanny encounter with the flesh made word or image.

The consciousness conjurers, those who intuit the dead's thoughts or motives, those who grant textual immortality its due, are, in their contract with the nonmortal, rendering unto the great work of the state order the fullness of its power. For it is not, after all, the human that lives forever, but the name, the word, or the text that endures. In my humanist, deauraticizing fantasy I read Cao Pi's text against the grain. The human in my reading resents textuality for its alienating immortality, for its power over and beyond the corporeally human. In this imagined scenario of a resented textuality, the human yearns for the real humanity of its particular death-bound temporality, free from the transcendent negating power of the undead and the deathless.

Notes

1. There is no precise equivalent to the Hegelian term *Aufheben/Aufhebung*. In popular German it has two antonymous senses: to cancel, to abolish; and to supersede or to transcend. Hegel used it to describe a process by which a higher form of thought or nature supersedes a lower form, while at the same time "preserving" its "moments of truth." It is used enough in English to merit adoption.

2. Refers to the Mao commentary to the *Shi jing* "Ding zhi fang zhong" 4.6.

3. A slightly modified quotation from the "Wuzi" chapter of Yang Xiong's *Fa Yan*.

4. HS: 1755–56. There is some question about the number of subcategories.

5. SGZ: p 559. The quotation is from Yang Xiong's *Fa yan*, "Wu zi" chapter, 3a (same reference made in the *Yiwen zhi* piece.)

6. Cai (1996) is the latest exponent of the aestheticist view.

7. I use "tetrameter" for the four-character line, "pentameter" for the five-character line, etc.

8. Qian Mu (1977), 100. The point about the collected biographies of the literati is an interesting one. In the HHS, the "Collected Biographies of the Literati" follow the "Collected Biographies of the Confucian Scholars" and precede the "Collected Biographies of the Eccentrics." As a group, their main distinguishing feature seems to have been compositional facility and recognition of their abilities by others. But it is in fact difficult to discern a strong underlying logic for inclusion in this chapter. The trope of the "discovery of the individual" is common to the descriptions of many traditions beyond the Chinese. In fact, determination of the date of the discovery of the individual seems to be one of twentieth-century literary history's central tasks.

9. Pauline Yu's "Poems in Their Place: Collections and Canons in Early Chinese Literature" (1990) is a pioneering theoretical study of anthology making and canon formation in Chinese poetry.

10. For example, David McCraw's article "A New Look at the Regulated Verse of Chen Yuyi" (1987) concludes: "Still, his best work weathers comparison with creations by the Titans of Chinese poetry, a claim that can be made by very few mortals. Chen Yuyi is a splendid poet of the second rank, a step below and a world away from the gods of the Chinese poetic pantheon" (21). Or Stephen Owen's first line in his chapter on Du Fu, "Tu Fu *is* [italics original] the greatest Chinese poet" (Owen 1981: 183).

11. Based in part on a list in Tzvetan Todorov, "Enunciation," in Durot and Todorov (1981), 324.

12. Ruth Finnegan (1977). The formulaic argument is made in Hans Frankel (1974), 69–107. See also Hans Frankel (1976), 97–106.

13. *Shi jing*; *Da xu* (Mao).

14. In Lord (1960); Eric Havelock (1986); Walter Ong (1982), and even Paul Zumthor (1990), for example.

15. See Mary Scott, *The Invention of Chinese Popular Culture* (forthcoming).

16. U.S. orally circulated material like the "Pledge of Allegiance" or "The Star-Spangled Banner" is one example of that.

17. "But of the rich heritage of laughter that was part of the written tradition of Rome only a minuscule quantity has survived: those upon whom the transmission of this heritage depended were agelasts who elected the serious word and rejected its comic reflections as a profanation (as happened, for example, with the numerous parodies of Virgil)." M. Bakhtin, "From the Prehistory of Novelistic Discourse," in Bakhtin (1981), 58.

18. Gu Jiegang (1926–41). For a discussion of the ideological character of Gu's work, see Laurence A. Schneider (1971), 164–87.

19. For the popular/high culture distinction, see Peter Burke (1978). For a re-thinking of the oral/written distinction, see Ruth Finnegan (1977).

20. For all of these points, see, for example, Hans Frankel (1974, 1976, and 1986); Suzuki (1967), 90–257; Xiao Difei (1976 rpt); Wang Yunxi, "Yuefu minge yu zuojia zuopin de guanxi," in Wang Yunxi (1981), 12–17. For some useful de-mystifying of the *yuefu*, see Joseph R. Allen (1992). But see Connery (1993).

21. The translation is from Holzman (1974), 123.

22. Not including state-sponsored projects like the bibliographic work of Liu Xiang, Liu Xin, and Ban Gu.

23. Quoted in the translator's introduction to Xiao Tong (1982), 18.

24. Wang Meng'ou. "Guiyou wenxue yu liu chao wenti de yanbian." In Wang Meng'ou (1984), 125.

25. These are the dates given in Matsumoto Yukio (1960–61). Scholars posit various other beginning dates, the most common being 205, when the Cao court was firmly established at Ye. The ending date is widely recognized as 217, for it was both the year of Cao Pi's designation as heir apparent and of the epidemic that killed several of the "Seven Masters."

26. He Qia's biography states that his refusal to take refuge with Yuan Shao in Yizhou, choosing instead to join Liu Biao in Xiangyang, was based on his feeling that "In Yizhou the land is flat and the population has a limbic character. It would be of strategic advantage to the heroic warriors, and is thus a land well disposed to war." SGZ: 655.

27. Among other prominent literati who migrated to Jingzhou were (1) from the capital region, Wang Can, Sima Zhi, Du Ji, Handan Chun, Mi Heng, and Pei Qian; (2) from Yuzhou, He Qia, Du Xi, Zhao Yan, and Po Qin; (3) from Yanzhou, Mao Jie, who intended to go to Liu Biao but may not have arrived, and Zhuge Liang. SGZ: 374. This list is based partially on Matsumoto Yukio (1961), 1144.

28. *Wu shu*, quoted in Pei Songzhi commentary to SGZ: 1246.

29. From *Fuzi*, quoted in the SGZ: 434.

30. SGZ (Wei) 19, 557. Cao Pi's "Fu on Ascending the Tower" refers to the same occasion. The preface says, "In the spring of 212 we made an excursion to the West Garden and climbed Bronze Magpie Terrace. My brothers and I composed together on [my father's] command." QSGW 4: 5a (1074).

31. Quoted in Morihasa Yokosuka (1977), 299.

32. This list is based on a chart in Suzuki Shūji (1967), 511–13.

33. From the *Yuan Bie zhuan*, in Pei Songzhi's commentary to SGZ: 353.

34. In a note to the main text in YFSJ, 231.

35. YFSJ, 232. Wang Xianqian (1978 rpt,), 66–70

36. For punctuation I have basically followed Ding Fubao (1979 rpt.). Huang Jie's punctuation differs considerably. Huang Jie (1962), 51–52.

37. Other punctuations include putting the character *xing* as a separate line (Huang Jie).

38. Quoted in Hebei Shifan xueyuan Zhongwen xi gudian wenxue jiaoyan zu (1980), 82

39. These thoughts were stimulated by a reading of Bauman (1992).

Appendix

Group Composition of *Fu*

Title	Authors
Sailing the Huai (*Fu Huai fu*)	Cao Pi, Wang Can
Curtailing Excursions (*Jie you fu*)	Cao Zhi, Yang Xiu
The Hunt (*Jiao lei fu*)	Cao Pi, Wang Can

In the Jian'an, Cao Pi went hunting with Cao Cao. He wrote a *fu* and commanded Chen Lin, Wang Can, Ying Yang, and Liu Zhen to also compose one. Chen Lin wrote a "Martial Hunt." Wang Can did his "Bird Hunt." Ying Yang wrote a "Western Hunt." Liu Zhen wrote a "Great Hall." All had their good points, but Wang Can's was judged best.[1]

Title	Authors
Climbing the Terrace (*Deng tai fu*)	Cao Cao, Cao Pi, Cao Zhi[2]
Summer (*Da shu fu*)	Cao Zhi, Wang Can, Chen Lin, Liu Zhen, Po Qin

Yang Xiu's "Letter to the Marquis of Linzu [Cao Zhi]" says, "I left after responding to the 'Fighting Cock' (see below). I worked on 'Summer' all day but did not proffer it" (QHHW: 51: 11a, 758).

Title	Authors
Grieving Over Rain (*Chou lin fu*)	Cao Pi, Cao Zhi, Ying Yang
Joy at the Clearing Rain (*Xi qi fu*)	Cao Pi, Cao Zhi, Miao Xi
On the Campaign (*Shu zheng fu*)	Cao Zhi, Ruan Yu, Wang Can, Yang Xiu, Cao Pi, Xu Gan, Po Qin[3]
The Divorced Wife (*Chu fu fu*)	Cao Pi, Cao Zhi, Wang Can
The Widow (*Gua fu fu*)	Cao Pi, Cao Zhi,[4] Wang Can, Ding Yi's wife

Ruan Yu and I were good friends. He was ill-fated and died too young . . . I have written this *fu* to describe the suffering of his widow and orphaned child. I also have asked Wang Can to compose one. (Cao Pi's preface in (QSGW, 4: 4a, 1073)

Arresting Desires (*Zhi yu fu*)	Chen Lin, Ruan Yu
The Goddess (*Shen nu fu*)	Cao Zhi ("Goddess of the Luo River"), Wang Can, Chen Lin, Ying Yang, Yang Xiu
Pellet Chess (*Danqi fu*)	Cao Pi, Wang Can, Ding Yì
Rosemary (*Midie fu*)	Cao Pi, Cao Zhi, Wang Can, Chen Lin
The Agate Bridle (*Manao le fu*)	Cao Pi, Wang Can, Chen Lin

Agate is a type of jade. It comes from the Western Regions. Its decussated veins resemble a horse's brains, so that's what the locals call it. It can be worn around the neck, or used to adorn bridles. I have that kind of bridle. Admiring it, I composed a *fu* on it. I ordered Wang Can and Chen Lin to do likewise. (Cao Pi's preface in QSGW 4: 6b–7a , 1074–5)

Cao Pi obtained some agate. He had it made into a jeweled bridle. He admired the brilliant shine of its flowery appearance. He ordered me to make this *fu*. (Chen Lin's preface in QSGW 4:6b–7a , 1074–5)

The Jasper Bowl (*Juqumu wan fu*)	Cao Pi, Cao Zhi, Wang Can, Ying Yang, Xu Gan
The Scholartree (*Huai fu*)	Cao Pi, Cao Zhi, Wang Can
	Cao Pi, Wang Can, Chen Lin, Ying
The Willow (*Liu fu*)	Yang, Po Qin
The Oriole (*Ying fu*)	Cao Pi, Wang Can
The White Crane (*Bai he fu*)	Cao Zhi, Wang Can
The Fighting Cock (*He fu*)	Cao Cao, Cao Zhi, Wang Can
The Parrot (*Yingwu fu*)	Cao Zhi, Wang Can, Chen Lin, Ying Yang, Ruan Yu[5]
The Fan (*Shan fu*)	Cao Zhi, Xu Gan
On Wine (*Jiu fu*)	Cao Zhi, Wang Can
Toss Bowl (*Tou hu fu*)	Wang Can, Handan Chun

Notes

1. From Zhi Yu's *Wenzhang liubie lun*, quoted in Zhang Qiao's annotation to the *Guwen yuan*. Quoted in Wu Yun and Tang Shaozhong. *Wang Can ji zhu* (1984), 50.

2. Suzuki includes Wang Can's "Climbing the Tower," but this was not about the Bronze Magpie Tower.

3. Matsumoto Yukio gives evidence for a group composition. Titles vary.

4. Ding Fubao lists this as a *shi* poem.

5. Mi Heng's famous composition by the same name could not have been written at the Cao court.

Glossary of Select Chinese Terms and Phrases

Ai gong wen zheng. Zi yue, wen wu zhi zheng bu zai fang ce.
哀公問政。子曰，文武之政布在方策

Bai he fu 白鶴賦

Bi Yong 辟雍

biao 表

bu dang 部黨

"bu xue shi, wu yi yan" "不學詩無以言"

bu zheng you you/ bai lü shi qiu 布政優優／百祿是遒

bu zheng 布政

cai 材

ce 策

cheng yijia zhi yan 成一家之言

Chou lin fu 愁霖賦

chou 醻

Chu fu fu 出婦賦

Da shu fu 大暑賦

dan pian 單篇

dang 黨

danggu 黨錮

Danqi fu 彈棋賦

Deng tai fu 登臺賦

Dian lun 典論

"Dong Han de Haozu" 東漢的豪祖

dun tian 屯田

feng li 風力

Fu Huai fu 浮淮賦

fu 賦

gai wen zhang ...

蓋文章經國之大業。
不朽之盛事。 年壽有時而盡。榮樂止乎其身。
二者必至之常期，
未若文章之無窮。
是以古之作者寄身於翰墨，
見意於篇籍。
不假良之辭，
不託飛馳之勢。
而聲名自傳於後。

gong 公

gu 骨

Gua fu fu 寡婦賦

guli 故吏

gushi 古詩

hainei 海內

haozu 豪祖

He fu 鶡賦

hu kou 餬口

Huai fu 槐賦

jiafa 家法

Jiao lei fu 交獵賦

Jiao you lun 交友論

jiao 校

jiao ji 交際

Jie you fu 節游賦

Jiu fu 酒賦

jiu pin zhong zheng 九品中正

juan 卷

Juqumu wan fu 車渠木宛賦

ke 客

kyoodotai 共同體

lei 誄

Liu fu 柳賦

lun 論

Manao le fu 瑪瑙勒賦

meng 盟

mensheng 門生

Midie fu 迷迭賦

ming (fate) 命

ming (reputation) 名

ming (tomb inscriptions) 銘

ming-shi 名實

ningenshugi 人間主義

Pei 沛

pengdang 朋黨

pengyou zhi jiao 朋友之交

pian 篇

qi 氣

Qian Jiao 遣交

qingliu 清流

qingtan 清談

qingyi 清議

ren 仁

rennzhi 仁治

renzhi 人治

ren 仁

rujia 儒家

Rulin zhuan 儒林傳

sangang 三綱

Shan fu 扇賦

Shen nu fu 神女賦

shi (poem) 詩

shi 1 (office holding) 事

shi 2 (office holding) 仕

shi poetry 詩

shi 士

shifa 師法

Shu zheng fu 述征賦

shu 書

si 私

song (to recite) 誦

tai xue 太學

ti 體

tianxia 天下

tixing 體性

tongzhi 同志

Tou hu fu 投壺賦

wen 文

wen/wu 文武

wen/zhi 文質

wenxue 文學

wenyanwen 文言文

wu jing boshi 五經博士

wuchang 五常

wuguan zhonglang jiang 五官中郎將

wulun 五倫

Xi qi fu 喜齊賦

xi 檄

xiangju lixuan 鄉舉里選

xiaolian 孝廉

xiaoxue 小學

xie 寫

xingqing 性情

xiongnu 匈奴

xuanyan 玄言

xue 學

xungu 訓詁

yi (disquisitions) 議

yi (enter into dependence) 依

yi (extraordinariness) 異

Ying fu 鶯賦

Yingwu fu 鸚鵡賦

You lun 友論

you su 油素

yue (bond) 約

yuefu poetry 樂府

yuefu 樂府

zhao 詔

zhengqi fengsu ling 整齊風俗令

zhengtong vs. batong 正通 vs. 霸通

Zhi yu fu 止欲賦

zhi yin 知音

zhu 著

zi yue...子曰：弟子入則孝，出則悌，
謹而信，汎愛眾，
而親仁。行有餘，則以學文。

zou 奏

Bibliography

Primary Sources

Ban Gu (39 C.E.–92 C.E.). *Han shu* (History of the Former Han Dynasty). Reprint, Beijing: Zhonghua shuju.

Chen Shou (233–297). *San guo zhi* (Record of the Three Kingdoms). Reprint, Beijing: Zhonghua shuju, 1959.

Ding Fubao, comp. *Quan Han San guo Jin Nanbei chao shi* (Complete poetry of the Han, Three Kingdoms, Jin, Northern and Southern Dynasties). 2 vols. Reprint, Taibei: Zhongwen chubanshe, 1979.

Ding Yan (1794–1875), ed. *Cao ji quan ping* (Notes and commentary on Cao Zhi's poetry). In *Cao Zijian ji pingzhu er zhong*, edited by Yang Jialuo. Taibei: Shijie shuju, 1973.

Dong Zhongshu (c. 179–c. 104 B.C.E.), attr. *Chunqiu fanlu yi zheng* (Luxuriant dew of the *Spring and Autumn Annals*). Edited by Su Yu. Reprint, Taibei: Heluo, 1973.

Fan Ye (398–445). *Hou Han shu* (History of the Latter Han Dynasty). Reprint, Beijing: Zhonghua shuju, 1963.

Fang Dongshu (1772–1851). *Fang Dongshu ping gu shi xuan* (2 vols.) (Fang Dongshu's writings on ancient poetry). Edited by Wang Zhong. Taibei: Lianjing, 1975.

Fang Xuanling (578–648) et al. *Jin shu* (History of the Jin dynasty). Reprint, Beijing: Zhonghua, 1974.

Gu Yanwu (1613–1682). *Rizhi lu ji shi* (Record of Daily Knowledge). Edited by Huang Rucheng. Reprint, Shanghai: Shanghai guji chubanshe, 1985.

Guo Maoqian (12th century), comp. *Yuefu shi ji* (Collected yuefu poems). Reprint, Beijing: Zhonghua shuju, 1979.

Guo yu jiao zheng (5th–4th c. B.C.E.) (Words of the States). Edited by Zhang Yiren. Reprint, Taibei: Shangwu, 1969.

Han Feizi ji jie (3rd c. B.C.E.). Edited by Wang Xianshen. Reprint, Taibei: Yiwen, 1959.

Hu Yingling (1551–1602). *Shi sou* (Assembly of poems). Reprint, Shanghai: Zhonghua shuju, 1959.

Huainan zi, attr. Liu An (179–122 B.C.E.). Edited by Liu Wendian. Reprint, Beijing: Zhonghua, 1989.

Li ji Zheng zhu (1st c. C.E.) (Book of Rites, with Zheng Xuan annot.). Sibu beiyao ed.

Li Madou (Matteo Ricci 16th c.), comp. Edited by Zhu Tingce and Chen Bangjun. *You lun* (On Friendship). Reprint, Taibei: Yiwen, 1965.

Li Yanshou (7th century). *Nan shi* (Histories of the Southern Dynasties). Reprint, Beijing: Zhonghua, 1974.

Liu chen zhu Wen xuan (Six ministers commentary on the *Selections of Refined Literature*). Reprint, Taibei: Guangwen shuju, 1964.

Liu Shao (fl. 196–248). *Ren wu zhi* (Discourse on human abilities). Edited by Bo Yuan. Reprint, Changsha: Hunan kexue ji shu chubanshe, 1990.

Liu Xiang (77–6 B.C.E.), attr. *Lie nu zhuan bu zhu* (Biographies of eminent women). Edited by Wang Zhaoyuan. Reprint, Taibei: Taiwan shangwu, 1968.

Liu Xie (c. 465–c. 520). *Wenxin diaolong zhu* (The literary mind and the carving of dragons). With annotations by Fan Wenlan. Reprint, Beijing: Renmin wenxue chuban she, 1978.

Liu Yiqing (403–444). *Shi shuo xin yu jiao jian* (New account of tales of the world). Edited by Yang Yong. Reprint, Taibei: Zhengwen shuju, 1976.

Lun yu yi zhu (Confucius's Analects explicated and annotated). Edited by Yang Bojun. Beijing: Zhonghua, 1980.

Lushi chunqiu jiao shi (Master Lu's annals), attr. Lu Buwei (3rd c. B.C.E.). Edited by Chen Qiyou, 2 vols. Reprint, Shanghai: Xuelin, 1984.

Mengzi yi zhu (Mencius). Edited by Lanzhou daxue zhongwen xi. Reprint, Beijing: Zhonghua, 1960.

Shen Yue (441–513). *Song shu* (History of the Liu Song dynasty). Reprint, Beijing: Zhonghua, 1974.

Sima Guang (1019–1086). *Zi zhi tong jian* (Comprehensive mirror for aid in government). Reprint, Beijing: Zhonghua, 1956.

Sima Qian (c. 145–c. 86 B.C.E.). *Shi ji* (Historical Records). Reprint, Beijing: Zhonghua, 1985.

Taiping Yulan (Encyclopedia assembled for imperial inspection during the Taiping era) (978–984). Edited by Li Fang. Reprint, Taibei: Taiwan Shangwu, 1980.

Wang Chong (c. 27–c. 97). *Lun Heng* (Balanced discourses). Reprint, Taibei: Zhonghua, 1981.

Wang Fu (90–165). *Qianfu lun jian* (*Discourses of a hermit*). Edited by Peng Duo with notes by Wang Qipei. Reprint, Beijing: Zhonghua, 1985.

Wang Yi (2nd c.) and Hong Xingzu (1090–1155), eds. *Chu ci bu zhu* (Annotations and revised annotations of the Chu Ci). Taibei: Zhonghua shuju facsimile of Sung ed., 1978.

Wei Zheng (580–643). *Sui shu* (History of the Sui Dynasty). Reprint, Beijing: Zhonghua shuju, 1973.

Xi Jing Zaji (Miscellaneous records of the western capital), Attr. to Liu Xin (d. 23) and Ge Hong (283–363). Edited by Xiang Xinyang and Liu Keren. Reprint, Shanghai: Shanghai guji chubanshe, 1991.

Xiao Tong (501–531). *Wen xuan Li shan zhu* (Li Shan Commentary on the *Selections of Refined Literature*). Taibei: Zhengzhong shuju, 1971 rpt.

Xu Gan (171–218). *Zhong lun* (Discourse on the central). Reprint, Taibei: Shijie shuju, 1958.

Xu Jian (659–729) et al., comps. *Chu xue ji* (Record for elementary study). Reprint, Beijing: Zhonghua shuju, 1962.

Xu Shen (c. 55–c. 149). *Shuowen jiezi* (Explanation of graphs). Annotated by Duan Yucai. Reprint, Taibei: Shijie shuju, 1962.

Xu Tianlin (12th c.), comp. *Donghan huiyao* (Institutes of the Eastern Han). Reprint, Shanghai: Shanghai guji chubanshe, 1978.

Yan Kejun (1762–1843), comp. *Quan Shang gu Sandai Qin Han San guo Liu chao wen* (Complete writings of prehistory, the Three Dynasties, Qin, Han, Three Kingdoms, and the Six Dynasties). Reprint, Taibei: Hongye shuju, 1975.

Yan Zhitui (c. 531–591). *Yanshi jiaxun* (Family instructions for the Yan clan). Reprint, Taibei: Zhonghua, 1974.

Yi li Zheng zhu (Classic of Ceremonies with Zheng Xuan's commentary). Sibu beiyao edition.

Zhang Xuecheng (1738–1801). *Zhangshi yi zhu* (Annotated writings of Zhang Xuecheng). Reprint, Shanghai: Shangwu (1936?).

Zhanguo ce (Intrigues of the warring states) (1st c. B.C.E.), comp. Reprint, Shanghai: Shanghai guji chuban she, 1978.

Zhong Rong (d. 552). *Shi pin zhu* (Ranked Poets). Annotated by Chen Yanjie. Reprint, Beijing: Renmin, 1980.

Zhuangzi ji shi (Zhuangzi). Edited by Guo Qingfan. Beijing: Zhonghua, 1961.

Bibliography of Postimperial Chinese, Japanese, and Western Language Sources

Allen, Joseph R. *In the Voice of Others: Chinese Music Bureau Poetry*. Ann Arbor: Center for Chinese Studies, 1992.

Anderson, Benedict. *Imagined Communities: Reflections on the Origin and Spread of Nationalism*. New York: Verso, 1991.

Anderson, Perry. *Lineages of the Absolutist State*. London: NLB, 1974a.

———. *Passages from Antiquity to Feudalism*. London: NLB, 1974b.

Anhui Hao xian Cao Cao ji yi zhu xiao zu. *Cao Cao ji yi zhu* (Translations and annotations of Cao Cao's collected works). Beijing: Zhonghua shuju, 1979.

Bakhtin, M. M. *The Dialogic Imagination: Four Essays*. Edited and translated by Caryl Emerson and Michael Holquist. Austin: University of Texas Press, 1981.

Balazs, Etienne. *Chinese Civilization and Bureaucracy: Variations on Theme*. Edited by Arthur F. Wright and translated by H. M. Wright. New Haven: Yale University Press, 1964.

Balibar, Etienne, and Immanuel Wallerstein. *Race, Nation, Class: Ambiguous Identities*. Translated by Chris Turner. New York: Verso, 1991.

Bauman, Zygmunt. *Mortality, Immortality, and Other Life Strategies*. Stanford: Stanford University Press, 1992.

Beijing daxue Zhongguo wenxue shi jiaoyuan shi, ed. *Liang Han wenxue shi cankao ziliao* (Reference material on the literary history of the Two Han dynasties). Beijing: Zhonghua shuju, 1962.

———. *Wei Jin Nanbei chao wenxue shi cankao ziliao* (Reference material on the literary history of the Wei Jin, Northern and Southern dynasties). Beijing: Zhonghua shuju, 1962.

Belsey, Catherine. *Critical Practice*. New York: Methuen, 1980.

———. *Milton*. New York: Basil Blackwell, 1988.

Bielenstein, Hans. "Loyang in Later Han Times." *Bulletin of the Museum of Far Eastern Antiquities* 48 (1976): 1–142.

———. *The Bureaucracy of Han Times*. Cambridge: Cambridge University Press, 1980.

Birch, Cyril, comp. and ed. *Anthology of Chinese Literature*. New York: Grove, 1965.

Birch, Cyril, ed. *Studies in Chinese Literary Genres*. Berkeley: University of California, 1974.

Birrell, Anne, trans. *New Songs from a Jade Terrace: An Anthology of Early Chinese Love Poetry*. New York: Penguin, 1986.

Bodman, Richard W. "Poetics and Prosody in Early Medieval China: A Study and Translation of Kūkai's *Bunkyō Hifuron*." Ph.D. diss., Cornell University, 1978.

Boltz, William. *The Origin and Early Development of the Chinese Writing System*. New Haven: American Oriental Society, 1994.

Bourdieu, Pierre. *The Logic of Practice*. Translated by Richard Nice. Stanford: Stanford University Press, 1990.

Brook, Timothy, ed. *The Asiatic Mode of Production in China*. Armonk, N.Y.: M. E. Sharpe, 1989.

Burke, Peter. *Popular Culture in Early Modern Europe*. New York: New York University Press, 1978.

Cai Zongqi. *The Matrix of Lyric Transformation: Poetic Modes and Self-Presentation in Early Chinese Pentasyllabic Poetry*. Ann Arbor: University of Michigan Center for Chinese Studies, 1996.

Ch'en Chi-yun. *Hsün Yüeh (A.D. 148–209): The Life and Reflections of an Early Medieval Confucian*. Cambridge: Cambridge University Press, 1975.

———. *Hsün Yüeh and the Mind of Late Han China: A Translation of the* Shen-chien *with Introduction and Annotations*. Princeton: Princeton University Press, 1980.

Ch'en Shih-hsiang. "The Genesis of Poetic Time: The Greatness of Ch'ü Yüan, Studied with a New Critical Approach." *Tsing Hua Journal of Chinese Studies*, n.s., 10, no. 1 (June 1973): 1–44.

———. "The *Shi-ching*: Its Generic Significance in Chinese Literary History and Poetics." In *Studies in Chinese Literary Genres*, edited by Cyril Birch, 8–41. Berkeley: University of California Press, 1974.

Ch'u T'ung-tsu. *Han Social Structure*. Edited by Jack Dull. Seattle: University of Washington Press, 1972.

Chang, Yvonne Sun-sheng. "Generic Transformation from 'Yuehfu' to 'Gushi': Poetry of Cao Cao, Cao Pi, and Cao Zhi." Ph.D. diss., Stanford University, 1982.

Chartier, Roger. *The Order of Books: Readers, Authors, and Libraries in Europe Between the Fourteenth and Eighteenth Centuries*. Translated by Lydia C. Cochrane. Cambridge: Polity Press, 1994.

Chen Guoqing, ed. *Han shu Yiwen zhi zhushi huibian* (Collected annotations and explications of the Bibliographic Treatise of the Han Shu) Beijing: Zhonghua shuju, 1983.

Chen Yibai. *Cao Zijian shi yenjiu* (Research on the poetry of Cao Zhi). Shanghai: Shangwu yinshu guan, 1928.

Cheng, Anne. *Étude sur le Confucianisme Han: L'élaboration d'une Tradition Exégètique sur les Classiques.* Paris: College de France, Institut des hautes études chinoises: Diffusion de Boccard, 1985.

Cheng, Francois. *Chinese Poetic Writing.* Translated by Donald A. Riggs and Jerome Seaton. Bloomington: Indiana University Press, 1982.

Cherniack, Susan. "Book Culture and Textual Transmission in Sung China." *Harvard Journal of Asian Studies* 54, no. 1 (June 1994): 5–126.

Chow, Kai-wing. *The Rise of Confucian Ritualism in Late Imperial China.* Stanford: Stanford University Press, 1994.

Chow, Rey. *Writing Diaspora.* Bloomington: Indiana University Press, 1993.

Coblin, W. South. "The Initials of Xu Shen's Language as Reflected in the Shuowen duruo Glosses." *Journal of Chinese Linguistics* 6 (1978): 27–65.

———. *A Handbook of Eastern Han Sound Glosses.* Hong Kong: Chinese University Press, 1983.

Connery, Christopher. "In the Voice of Others." *Chinese Literature: Essays, Articles, and Reviews* 15 (1993): 163–73.

———. "Jian'an Poetic Discourse." Ph.D. diss., Princeton University, 1991.

Crowell, William Gordon. "Government Land Policies and Systems in Early Imperial China." Ph.D. diss., University of Washington, 1979.

Cutter, Robert Joe. "Cao Zhi (192–232) and His Poetry." Ph.D. diss., University of Washington, 1983.

———. "The Incident at the Gate: Cao Zhi, the Succession, and Literary Fame." *T'oung Pao* 61 (1985): 228–78.

de Certeau, Michel. *The Practice of Everyday Life.* Translated by Steven F. Rendell. Berkeley: University of California Press, 1984.

de Crespigny, Rafe. "Political Protest in Imperial China: The Great Proscription of the Later Han, 167–184." *Papers in Far Eastern History* 11 (1975).

———. *Portents of Protest in the Later Han Dynasty: The Memorials of Hsiang K'ai to Emperor Huan.* Canberra: Australian National University Press, 1976.

———. The Recruitment System of the Imperial Bureaucracy of the Late Han." *Chung-chi Journal* 6 no. 1 (1966): 67–78.

de Crespigny, Rafe, trans. *The Last of the Han: Being the Chronicle of the Years 181–220 A.D. as Recorded in Chapters 58–68 of the* Tzu chih t'ung chien *of Ssu-ma Kuang.* Canberra: Australian National University Press, 1969.

de Man, Paul. *Blindness and Insight: Essays in the Rhetoric of Contemporary Criticism.* Rev. ed. Minneapolis: University of Minnesota Press, 1983.

Derrida, Jacques. *Margins of Philosophy.* Translated by Alan Bass. Chicago: University of Chicago Press, 1982.

———. *Of Grammatology.* Translated by Gayatri Chakravorty Spivak. Baltimore: Johns Hopkins University Press, 1976.

DeWoskin, Kenneth. *A Song for One or Two: Music and the Concept of Art in*

Early China. Ann Arbor: University of Michigan Center for Chinese Studies, 1982.

Diény, Jean-Pierre. "Les Dix-neuf poemes anciens." *Bulletin de la Maison Franco-Japonaise* n.s. 8, no. 4 (1963).

————. "Les Sept tristesses (Qi ai): A propos des deux versions d'un poème a chanter de Cao Zhi." *T'oung Pao* 65 (1979): 51–65.

Dirlik, Arif. *Revolution and History: The Origins of Marxist Historiography in China, 1919–1937.* Berkeley: University of California Press, 1978.

Dowling, William C. *Jameson, Althusser, Marx: An Introduction to* The Political Unconscious. Ithaca, N.Y.: Cornell University Press, 1984.

Dronke, Peter. *Poetic Individuality in the Middle Ages.* Oxford: Oxford University Press, 1970.

Dubs, Homer. *The History of the Former Han Dynasty.* 3 vols. Baltimore: Waverly, 1938–55.

Dull, Jack. "A Historical Introduction To The Apocryphal (Ch'an-Wei) Texts Of The Han Dynasty." Ph.D. diss., University of California, Berkeley, 1966.

Durot, Oswald, and Tveztan Todorov, eds. *Encyclopedic Dictionary of the Sciences of Language.* Translated by Catherine Porter. Oxford: Basil Blackwell, 1982.

Durrant, Stephen W. *The Cloudy Mirror: Tension and Conflict in the Writings of Sima Qian.* Albany: State University of New York Press, 1995.

Eagleton, Terry. *The Ideology of the Aesthetic.* New York: Basil Blackwell, 1990.

Easthope, Antony. *British Post-Structuralism: Since 1968.* New York: Routledge, 1988.

————. *Poetry and Phantasy.* New York: Cambridge University Press, 1989.

————. *Poetry as Discourse.* New York: Methuen, 1983.

Ebrey, Patricia. *The Aristocratic Families of Early Imperial China: A Case Study of the Po-Ling Ts'ui Family.* Cambridge: Cambridge University Press, 1978.

————. "Patron Client Relations in the Late Han." *Journal of the American Oriental Society* 103, no. 3 (July–September 1983): 533–542.

Fan Ning. "Lun Han Wei Jin shidai zhishifenzi de sixiang fenhua ji qi shehui genyuan" (On the philosophical divisions between intellectuals of the Han Wei and Jin period and the social roots thereof). *Lishi yanjiu* 4 (1955): 113–31.

Fang Zushen. *Han shi yanjiu* (Studies of Han poetry). Reprint, Taibei: Zhengzhong shuju, 1969.

Febvre, Lucien, and Henri-Jean Martin. *The Coming of the Book: The Impact of Printing, 1450–1800.* Translated by David Gerard. Edited by Geoffrey Nowell-Smith and David Wootton. London : N. L. B., 1976.

Finnegan, Ruth. *Oral Poetry.* Cambridge: Cambridge University Press, 1977.

Fischel, Walter, ed. *Semitic and Oriental Studies.* Berkeley: University of California Press, 1951.

Forke, Alfred. *Lun-heng.* Pt. 1, *Philosophical Essays of Wang Ch'ung.* Pt. 2, *Miscellaneous Essays of Wang Ch'ung.* 2 vols. rpt. Reprint, New York: Paragon Book Gallery, 1962.

Foucault, Michel. *The Archeology of Knowledge.* Translated by A. M. Sheridan Smith. New York: Pantheon Books, 1972.

————. "What is an Author?" In *Textual Strategies: Perspectives in Post-Structur-*

alist Criticism, edited by J.V. Harari. Ithaca, N.Y.: Cornell University Press, 1979.

————. *The History of Sexuality.* vol. 1. Translated by R. Hurley. New York: Vintage Books, 1980.

Frankel, Hans. "The Development of Han and Wei Yüeh-fu as a High Literary Genre." In *The Vitality of the Lyric Voice: Shih Poetry from the Late Han to the T'ang,* edited by Shuen-fu Lin and Stephen Owen, 255–286. Princeton: Princeton University Press, 1986.

————. "Fifteen Poems by Ts'ao Chih: An Attempt at a New Approach." *Journal of the American Oriental Society* 84 (January–March 1964): 1–14.

————. *The Flowering Plum and the Palace Lady.* New Haven: Yale University Press, 1976.

————. "T'ang Literati: A Composite Biography." In *Confucian Personalities,* edited by Arthur Wright and Denis Twitchett, 65–83. Stanford: Stanford University Press, 1969.

————. "Yueh-fu Poetry." In *Studies in Chinese Literary Genres,* edited by Cyril Birch, 69–107. Berkeley: University of California Press, 1974.

Freud, Sigmund. *Civilization and Its Discontents.* Edited and translated by J. Strachey. New York: W. W. Norton, 1961.

————. *The Ego and the Id.* Translated by J. Riviere and edited by J. Strachey. New York: W. W. Norton, 1962.

Giroux, Henry. "Reading Texts, Literacy, and Textual Authority." *Journal of Education* 172, no. 1 (1990): 84–103.

————. *Schooling and the Struggle for Public Life.* Minneapolis: University of Minnesota Press, 1988.

Godelier, Maurice. "The Concept of the Asiatic Mode of Production." In *Relations of Production: Marxist Approaches to Economic Anthropology,* edited by David Seddon and translated by Helen Lackner. London: Cass, 1978.

————. "Marxist Models of Social Evolution." In *Relations of Production: Marxist Approaches to Economic Anthropology,* edited by David Seddon and translated by Helen Lackner. London: Cass, 1978.

Goffman, Erving. *Relations in Public: Microstudies of the Public Order.* New York: Harper and Row, 1972.

Graff, Harvey. *The Legacies of Literacy: Continuities and Contradictions in Western Culture and Society.* Bloomington: Indiana University Press, 1987.

Gramsci, Antonio. *The Modern Prince and Other Writings.* Translated by Louis Marks. New York: International Publishers, 1959.

Gu Jiegang. *Gu shi bian* (Collected essays on ancient history). 7 vols. Beijing and Shanghai: Zhicheng yinshuguan, 1926–1941.

Gu Zhi. *Cao Zijian shi jian* (Annotated poems of Cao Zhi). Reprint, Taibei: Guangwen shuju, 1976.

Guillory, John. *Cultural Capital: The Problem of Literary Canon Formation.* Chicago: University of Chicago Press, 1993.

Guo Moruo and Jian Bozan et al., comps. *Cao Cao lun ji* (Collected essays on Cao Cao). Hong Kong: Sanlian shuidan, 1979.

Guo Shaoyu. *Zhongguo wenxue piping shi* (A history of Chinese literary criticism). Taibei: Minglun chubanshe, 1961.

Haidu, Peter. "Modern Reflections on Medieval Aesthetics." *Modern Language Notes* 92 (1977): 875–87.

Halliday, M. A. K. *Language as Social Semiotic: The Social Interpretation of Language and Meaning.* Baltimore: University Park Press, 1978.

Harari, J. V., ed. *Textual Strategies: Perspectives in Post-Structuralist Criticism.* Ithaca, N.Y.: Cornell University Press, 1979.

Harris, William V. *Ancient Literacy.* Cambridge: Harvard University Press, 1989.

Havelock, Eric Alfred. *The Muse Learns to Write: Reflections on Orality and Literacy from Antiquity to the Present.* New Haven: Yale University Press, 1986.

Hawkes, David, trans. *The Songs of the South: An Anthology of Ancient Chinese Poems by Qu Yuan and Other Poets.* London: Penguin Books, 1985.

He Qimin. *Wei Jin sixiang yu tanfeng* (Wei Jin thought and discursive style). Taibei: Taiwan xuesheng shuju, 1976.

Hebei Shifan xueyuan Zhongwen xi gudian wenxue jiaoyuan zu, ed. *San Cao ziliao huibian* (Collected materials on the Three Caos). Beijing: Zhonghua shuju, 1980.

Heller, Agnes. "Review of *Passages from Antiquity to Feudalism* and *Lineages of the Absolutist State.*" *Telos* 33 (1977): 202–9.

Henderson, John B. *Scripture, Canon Commentary: A Comparison of Confucian and Western Exegeses.* Princeton: Princeton University Press, 1991.

Hindess, Barry, and Paul Q. Hirst. *Pre-Capitalist Modes of Production.* Boston: Routledge and Kegan Paul, 1975

Hirst, Paul. "The Uniqueness of the West." *Economy and Society* 4 no. 4 (1975): 447–74.

Holcombe, Charles. *In the Shadow of the Han: Literati Thought and Society at the Beginning of the Southern Dynasties.* Honolulu: University of Hawaii Press, 1994.

Holzman, Donald. "Les débuts du système médiéval de choix et de classement des fonctionnaires: Les neuf catégories et l'Impartiale et Juste." *Mélanges publiés par l'Institut des Hautes Études Chinoises* 11, no. 1 (1957): 387–414.

———. "Literary Criticism in China in the Early Third Century A.D." *Asiatische Studien* 28 (1974): 113–136.

———. *Poetry and Politics: The Life and Works of Juan Chi A.D. 210–263.* Cambridge: Cambridge University Press, 1976.

———. "Les premiers vers pentasyllabique dates dans la poesie chinoise." In *Mélanges de sinologie offets a Monsieur Paul Demiéville.* Paris: Bibliotheque de l'Institut des Hautes Etudes Chinoises, Vol. 20, 2 (1974): 77–105.

Hosek, Chaviva, and Patricia Parker, eds. *Lyric Poetry: Beyond New Criticism.* Ithaca: Cornell University Press, 1985.

Hsiao Kung-chuan. *A History of Chinese Political Thought.* Vol. 1., *From the Beginnings to the Sixth Century A.D.*, Translated by Frederick W. Mote. Princeton: Princeton University Press, 1979.

Hsü, Cho-yun. *Han Agriculture: The Formation of Early Chinese Agrarian Economy (206 B.C.–A.D. 220).* Edited by Jack Dull. Seattle: University of Washington Press, 1980.

———. "The Roles of the Literati and of Regionalism in the Fall of the Han

Dynasty." In *The Collapse of Ancient States and Civilizations*, 176–195, edited by Norman Yoffee and George Cowgill. Tucson: University of Arizona Press, 1988.

Hu Yun, "Dong Han shiqi de wenhua quyu yu wenhua zhongxin." (Cultural regions and cultural centers in the Eastern Han period). *Zhongguo wenhua yanjiu jikan* 4 (January 1987): 155–87.

Huang Jie. *Cao Zijian shi zhu*. (Annotated poems of Cao Zhi). Beijing: Renmin wenxue chuban she, 1957.

———. *Han Wei Yuefu fengjian* (Annotated *yuefu* of the Han Wei period). Hong Kong: Shangwu yinshu guan, 1961.

———. *Wei Wudi Wendi shi zhu* (Annotated poems of Cao Pi). Hong Kong: Shangwu yinshu guan, 1962.

Huang Shengxiong. *Wang Fu sixiang yanjiu* (Studies of the thought of Wang Fu). Taibei: Wen shi zhe chubanshe, 1982.

Hucker, Charles. *A Dictionary of Official Titles in Imperial China*. Stanford: Stanford University Press, 1985.

Hulin, Michel. *Hegel et l'Orient*. Paris: Vrin, 1979.

Ikeda Shūzo. "Xu Gan Zhong lun jiao zhu" (Edited and annotated version of Xu Gan's Discourse on the Central). (Chinese text; Japanese annotations). Published in three parts. *Kyoto daigaku bungakubu kenkyū kiyō* 23 (1984): 8–62; 24 (1985): 73–137, and 25 (1986): 117–200.

Innis, Harold. *Empire and Communications*. Oxford: Clarendon, 1950.

Irvine, Martin. *The Making of Textual Culture: 'Grammatica' and Literary Theory, 350–1100*. New York: Cambridge University Press, 1994.

Ito Masafumi. *Sō Shoku* (Cao Zhi). Tokyo: Iwanami, 1964.

Jakobson, Roman. "Concluding Statement: Linguistics and Poetics." In *Style in Language*, edited by T. A. Sebeok. Cambridge: MIT Press, 1960.

Jameson, Frederic. "Imaginary and Symbolic in Lacan: Marxism, Psychoanalytic Criticism, and the Problem of the Subject." *Yale French Studies* 55/56 (1977): 338–95.

———. *Marxism and Form*. Princeton: Princeton University Press, 1971.

———. "Marx's Purloined Letter." *New Left Review* 209 (January–February 1995): 75–109.

———. *The Political Unconscious*. Ithaca, N.Y.: Cornell University Press, 1981.

Jaspers, Karl. *The Origin and Goal of History*. Translated by Michael Bullock. New Haven: Yale University Press, 1953.

Jiang Zuyi. *Wang Chong de wenxue lilun* (The literary theory of Wang Chong). Shanghai: Shanghai guji chubanshe, 1980.

Jin Fagen. "Dong Han danggu renwu de fenxi" (A biographical analysis of the personnel in the Imperial Proscription of the Eastern Han). *Lishi yuyan yanjiu-suo jikan* 34 no. 2 (1963).

Johnson, David. *The Medieval Chinese Oligarchy*. Boulder: Westview, 1977.

Jügel, Ulrike. *Politische Funktion und Soziale Stellung der Eunuchen zur Späteren Hanzeit (25–220 n. Chr.)*. Wiesbaden: Franz Steiner Verlag, 1976.

Kalinowski, Marc. "Cosmologie et gouvernement naturel dans le *Lüshi chunqiu*," *Bulletin de l'École française d'Extrême Orient* 71 (1982): 187–192.

Kao Yu-kung and Mei Tsu-lin. "Meaning, Metaphor, and Allusion in T'ang Poetry." *Harvard Journal of Asiatic Studies* 38 no. 2 (1978): 281–356.

———. "Syntax, Diction, and Imagery in T'ang Poetry." *Harvard Journal of Asiatic Studies* 31 (1971): 49–136.

Karlgren, Bernard. *Glosses on the Book of Documents.* Stockholm: Museum of Far Eastern Antiquities, 1970.

———. *Glosses on the Book of Odes.* Stockholm: Museum of Far Eastern Antiquities, 1964.

———. *Grammata Serica Recensa.* Stockholm: Museum of Far Eastern Antiquities, 1972.

Karlgren, Bernard, trans. *The Book of Documents.* Stockholm: Museum of Far Eastern Antiquities, 1950.

———. *The Book of Odes.* Stockholm: Museum of Far Eastern Antiquities, 1974.

Kawakatsu Yoshio. *Chugoku no rekishi* vol. 3: *Gi-Shin Nambokuchō* (History of China, vol. 3: The Wei Jin Northern and Southern dynasties). Tokyo: Kodansha, 1974

———. "Gi-Shin Nanchō no monsen kori" (On disciples and formal officials in the Wei Jin period). *Tōhō gakuhō* 28 (1958): 175–218.

———. "Kanmatsu no rejistansu undō" (Resistance movements at the end of the Han). *Tōyōshi kenkyū* 25, no. 4 (1967): 386–413.

Knechtges, David. *The Han Rhapsody: A Study of the Fu of Yang Hsiung (53 B.C.–A.D. 18).* Cambridge: Cambridge University Press, 1976.

Krader, Lawrence. *The Asiatic Mode of Production: Sources, Development and Critique in the Writings of Karl Marx.* Assen: Van Gorcum, 1975.

Kroll, Paul. "Portraits of Ts'ao Ts'ao: Literary Studies on the Man and the Myth." Ph.D. diss., University of Michigan, 1976.

Kuipers, Joel Corneal. *Power in Performance: The Creation of Textual Authority in Weyewa Ritual Speech.* Philadelphia: University of Pennsylvania Press, 1990.

Lacan, Jacques. *The Four Fundamental Concepts of Psycho-Analysis.* Translated by Alan Sheridan. New York: W. W. Norton, 1978.

Lao Gan. *Wei Jin Nanbei chao shi* (History of the Wei Jin Northern and Southern Dynasties). Reprint, Taibei: Hua gang chubanbu, 1971.

Leban, Carl. "Managing Heaven's Mandate: Coded Communication in the Accession of Ts'ao P'ei A.D. 220," in *Ancient China: Studies in Early Civilization*, edited by David T. Roy and Tsuen-hsuin Tsien, 315–342. Hong Kong: Chinese University Press, 1978.

———. "Ts'ao Ts'ao and the Rise of Wei: The Early Years." Ph.D. diss., Columbia University, 1971.

Lefort, Claude. *Éléments d'une critique de la bureaucratie.* Geneve: Droz, 1971.

———. *The Political Forms of Modern Society.* Edited and translated by J. B. Thompson. Cambridge: MIT Press, 1986.

Legge, James, trans. *The Chinese Classics.* 7 vols. Oxford: Clarendon, 1893.

Levi, Jean. *Les fonctionnaires divins.* Paris: Seuil, 1989.

Lévi-Strauss, Claude. *Tristes Tropiques.* Translated by John and Doreen Weightman. New York: Atheneum, 1974.

Levy, Howard. "Yellow Turban Religion and Rebellion at the end of the Han." *Journal of the American Oriental Society* 76 no. 4 (1956): 214–227.

Lewis, Mark Edward. *Sanctioned Violence in Early China*. Albany: State University of New York Press, 1990.

Leys, Simon (pseudonym of Pierre Ryckmans). "One More Art." *The New York Review of Books*, April 18, 1996, 28–32.

Liang, Rongmao. *Xu Gan Zhong lun jiaoshi, fu Xu Gan sixiang yanjiu* (Annotated version of Xu Gan's Discourse on the Central, with an appended study of Xu Gan's thought). Taibei: Mutong, 1979.

Lin Shuen-fu and Stephen Owen, eds. *The Vitality of the Lyric Voice: Shih Poetry from the Late Han to the T'ang*. Princeton: Princeton University Press, 1986.

Liu I-ch'ing. *Shih-shuo Hsin-yü: A New Account of Tales of the World*. Translated by Richard B. Mather. Minneapolis: University of Minnesota Press, 1976.

Liu, James. *The Art of Chinese Poetry*. Chicago: University of Chicago Press. 1962.

———. *The Chinese Knight-Errant*. Chicago: University of Chicago Press, 1967.

Liu Jihua. *Han Wei zhi ji wenxue de xingshi yu neirong* (The form and content of the literature of the Han-Wei transition era). Taibei: Shijie shuju, 1978.

Liu Pak-yuen. *Les Institutions Politiques et la Lutte Pour le Pouvoir au Milieu de la Dynastie des Han Antérieurs*. Paris: Collège de France Institut des Hautes Études Chinoises, 1983.

Liu Rulin. *Han Jin xueshu bian nian* (Annals of Scholarship from the Han-Jin period). 3 vols. Reprint, Taibei: Chang'an chubanshe, 1979 rpt.

Liu Shao (3rd c.). *The Study of Human Abilities: The Jen Wu Chih of Liu Shao*. Translated with an introductory study by J. K. Shryock. New Haven: American Oriental Society, 1937.

Liu Shipei. *Zhongguo zhonggu wenxue shi lunwen za ji* (Miscellaneous collected essays on the medieval Chinese literary history). Edited by Shu Wuxiao. Beijing: Renmin wenxue chubanshe, 1984.

Loewe, Michael. *Chinese Ideas of Life and Death: Faith, Myth, and Reason in the Han Period*. London: George Allen and Unwin, 1982.

———. *Crisis and Conflict in Han China*. London: George Allen and Unwin, 1974.

———. *Everyday Life in Early Imperial China*. London: B. T. Batsford, Ltd., 1968.

———. *Records of Han Administration*. 2 vols. London, Cambridge University Press, 1967.

———. *Ways to Paradise: The Chinese Quest for Immortality*. London: George Allen and Unwin, 1979.

Loewe, Michael, ed. *Early Chinese Texts: A Bibliographical Guide*. Berkeley: The Society for the Study of Early China, 1993.

Lord, Albert Bates. *The Singer of Tales*. Cambridge: Harvard University Press, 1960.

Lu Kanru and Feng Yuanjun. *Zhongguo shi shi* (A history of Chinese poetry). Hong Kong: Guwen, 1961.

Lukács, Georg. *History and Class Consciousness*. Translated by R. Livingstone. Cambridge: MIT Press, 1971.

Luo Genze. *Yuefu wenxue shi* (A history of *yuefu* poetry). Reprint, Taibei: Wen shi zhe chubanshe, 1974.

———. *Zhongguo wenxue piping shi* (A history of Chinese literary criticism). Shanghai: Gudian wenxue chubanshe, 1958.

Luo Jianren. *Xu Gan Zhong lun yanjiu* (Studies of Xu Gan's Discourse on the Central). Taibei: Shangwu, 1973.

Mair, Victor. "Anthologizing and Anthropologizing: The Place of Non-Elite and Non-Standard Culture in the Chinese Literary Tradition." In *Translating Chinese Literature*, edited by Eugene Eoyang and Lin Yao-fu, 231–261. Bloomington: Indiana University Press, 1995.

———. "Buddhism and the Rise of the Written Vernacular in East Asia: The Making of National Languages." *Journal of Asian Studies* 53, no. 3 (August 1994): 707–51.

Mair, Victor, ed. *The Columbia Anthology of Traditional Chinese Literature*. New York: Columbia University Press, 1994.

Makeham, John. *Name and Authenticity in Early Chinese Thought*. Albany: State University of New York Press, 1994.

Mao Hanguang, *Liang Jin Nanbei chao shizu zhengzhi zhi yanjiu* (Studies of elite politics in the two Jin, Northern and Southern dynasties). Taibei: Shangwu, 1966.

———. *Zhongguo zhonggu shehuishi lun* (Essays on the social history of medieval China). Taibei: Lianjing, 1988.

Masubuchi Tatsuo. "Ko-Kan tōko jiken no shihyō ni tsuite" (On the historical evaluation of the Imperial Proscription in the Latter Han). *Hitotsubashi ronsō* 44 no. 6 (December 1960): 53–72.

Matsumoto Yukio, "Sō Hi to Ō Shitsu" (Cao Pi and Wu Zhi). *Ritsumeikan bungaku* 4–5 (1975): 93- 122.

———. "Kenan shidan no keisei katei ni tsuite" (On the formation of Jian'an poetry groups). Ritsumeikan bungaku 184 (1960): 25–43; 186 (1961):23–42; 188 (1961): 60–77; 189 (1961): 24–38.

McCraw, David. "A New Look at the Regulated Verse of Chen Yuyi." *Chinese Literature: Essays, Articles, and Reviews* 9, nos. 1–2 (July 1987).

McDermott, Joseph. "*Friendship and Its Friends in the Late Ming.*" In *Family Process and Political Process in Modern Chinese History*, 67–96. Taibei: Institute of Modern History of the Academia Sinica, 1992.

McKenzie, D. F. *Bibliography and the Sociology of Texts*. London: The British Library, 1985.

Miao, Ronald C. "A Critical Study of the Life and Poetry of Wang Chung-hsuan." Ph.D. diss., University of California, 1969.

Miao Yue et al., eds. *"San guo zhi" xuan zhu* (Selected annotations to the *Chronicles of the Three Kingdoms*). Beijing: Zhonghua shuju, 1984.

Millband, Ralph. "Political Forms and Historical Materialism." *The Socialist Register* (1975): 308–318.

Miller, Roy Andrew. "Problems in the Study of Shuo-wen Chieh-tzu." Ph.D. diss., University of California, 1953.

Morihasa Yokosuka. "Kenan shidan kō" (A study of the Jian'an poetry groups). *Nishō Gakusha Daigaku ronji: Chugoku bungaku hen* (1977): 289–308.

Mungello, David. *Leibniz and Confucianism: The Search for Accord*. Honolulu: University Press of Hawaii, 1977.

Munro, Donald, ed. *Individualism and Holism: Studies in Confucian and Taoist Values.* Ann Arbor: University of Michigan Center for Chinese Studies, 1985.

Ngo Van Xuyet. *Divination, magie, et politique dans la Chine ancienne.* Paris: Presses universitaires de France, 1976.

Nivison, David S. *The Life and Thought of Chang Hsüeh-ch'eng (1738–1801).* Stanford: Stanford University Press, 1966.

Nylan, Michael. "Ying Shao's 'Feng Su T'ung Yi': An Exploration of Problems in Han Dynasty Political, Philosophical, and Social Unity." Ph.D diss., Princeton University, 1982.

Okamura Shigeru. "Go Kan makki no hyōron teki kifū ni tsuite" (On the nature of evaluation in the late years of the Latter Han). *Nagoya daigaku bungaku bu kenkyu ronji (bungaku).* (1976): 66–112.

———. "Sai Yu o meguru go Kan makki no bungaku no susei" (Late Eastern Han literary trends in Cai Yong and his cohort). *Nippon Chugoku gakkai hō* 28 (1976): 61–78.

———. "Sō Hi no Tenron Ronbun ni tsuite" (Cao Pi and the Authoritative Discourses: On Literature). *Shinagaku kenkyū* October, 1960, 24–64.

O'Leary, Brendan. *The Asiatic Mode of Production: Oriental Despotism, Historical Materialism, and Indian History.* Oxford: Basil Blackwell, 1989.

Ong, Walter J. *Orality and Literacy: The Technologizing of the Word.* New York: Methuen, 1982.

Owen, Stephen. *The Great Age of Chinese Poetry: The High T'ang.* New Haven: Yale University Press, 1981.

———. *Traditional Chinese Poetry and Poetics: Omen of the World.* Madison: University of Wisconsin Press, 1985.

Pi Xirui. *Jingxue lishi (A history of classicism).* Edited by Zhou Yutong. Shanghai: Shangwu, 1925.

Pilz, Erich. *Gesellschaftsgeschichte und Theoriebildung in der marxisten chinesischen Historiographie.* Wien: Verlag der Österreichischen Akademie der Wissenschaften, 1991.

Pollard, David. *"Ch'i* in Chinese Literary Theory." In *Chinese Approaches to Literature from Confucius to Liang Ch'i-ch'ao,* edited by Adele Austin Rickett. Princeton: Princeton University Press, 1978.

Poulantzas, Nicos. *Political Power and Social Classes.* Translated by Timothy O'Hagan. London: NLB, 1973.

Powers, Martin. *Art and Political Expression in Early China.* New Haven: Yale University Press, 1991.

Qian Mu. "Du Wen Xuan" (Reading the *Literary Selections*). In *Zhongguo xueshu sixiang shi luncong* 3: 97–133. Taibei: Dongda.

———. *Liang han jingxue jin gu wen pingyi* (An appraisal of the old and new text issue in Han dynasty classicism). Hong Kong: Xinya yanjiusuo, 1958.

———. *Zhongguo xueshu sixiang shi lun cong* (Collected essays on the history of Chinese scholastic thought). Vol. 3. Taibei: Dongda, 1977.

Qian Zhongshu. *Guan Zhui bian* (Pipe awl chapters). Reprint, Hong Kong: Zhonghua shuju, 1980.

Rickett, Adele Austin, ed. *Chinese Approaches to Literature from Confucius to Liang Ch'i-ch'ao.* Princeton: Princeton University Press, 1978.

Ricoeur, Paul. "What is a text?" In *Hermeneutics and the Human Sciences: Essays on language, action, and interpretation*. Edited and translated by John B. Thompson. Cambridge: Cambridge University Press, 1981.

Robb, Kevin. *Literacy and Paideia in Ancient Greece*. New York: Oxford University Press, 1994.

Roberts, Colin H. and T. C. Skeat. *The Birth of the Codex*. London: Oxford University Press, 1983.

Roy, David T. and Tsuen-hsuin Tsien, eds. *Ancient China: Studies in Early Civilization*. Hong Kong: Chinese University Press, 1978.

Said, Edward W. *Orientalism*. New York: Pantheon Books, 1978.

Saussy, Haun. *The Problem of a Chinese Aesthetic*. Stanford: Stanford University Press, 1993.

Schneider, Laurence A. *Ku Chieh-kang and China's New History*. Berkeley: University of California Press, 1971

Sedgwick, Eve. *Between Men: English Literature and Male Homosocial Desire*. New York: Columbia University Press, 1985.

Sohn-Rethel, Alfred. *Intellectual and Manual Labor*. Translated by Martin Sohn-Rethel. London: Macmillan, 1978.

Spiegel, Gabrielle M. *The Past as Text: The Theory and Practice of Medieval Historiography*. Baltimore: Johns Hopkins University Press, 1997.

Stein, R. A. "Remarques sur les mouvements du Taoisme politico-religieux au IIe siècle ap. J.C." *T'oung Pao* 50 (1963): 1–78.

Stock, Brian. *The Implications of Literacy: Written Language and Models of Interpretation in the Eleventh and Twelfth Centuries*. Princeton: Princeton University Press, 1983.

———. *Listening for the Text: On the Uses of the Past*. Baltimore: Johns Hopkins University Press, 1990.

Su Jinren and Xiao Lianzi, eds. *Song shu Yue zhi jiao zhu* (Annotated and edited version of the *Discourse on Music* of the *Song shu*). Jinan: Qi Lu shushe, 1982.

Su Shaoxing. *Liang Jin Nan chao de shizu* (Elite clans of the two Jin and Southern Dynasties). Taibei: Lianjing, 1987.

Sun, E-tu Zen, and John DeFrancis. *Chinese Social History: Translations of Selected Studies*. Washington, D.C.: American Council of Learned Societies, 1956.

Suzuki Shūji. *Kan Gi shi no kenkyū* (Studies of Han-Wei poetry). Tokyo: Taishukan, 1967.

Suzuki Torao. *Fu shi da yao* (A comprehensive history of the *fu*). Translated by Yin Shiqu. Reprint, Taibei: Zhengzhong shuju, 1976 .

Svenbro, Jesper. *Phrasikleia: An Anthropology of Reading in Ancient Greece*. Translated by Janet Lloyd. Ithaca, N.Y.: Cornell University Press: 1993.

Tang Changru. *Wei Jin Nanbei chao shi lun cong* (Collected essays on the history of the Wei Jin Northern and Southern Dynasties). Beijing: San lian shudian, 1955.

———. *Wei Jin Nanbei chao shi lun shi yi* (Previously uncollected essays on the history of the Wei Jin Northern and Southern Dynasties). Beijing: Zhonghua shuju, 1983.

Tang Yongtong, *Wei Jin xuanxue lun gao* (Draft essays on Wei Jin esotericism). Beijing: Renmin, 1957.

Tang Yongtong and Ren Jiyu. *Wei Jin xuanxue zhongde shehui zhengzhi sixiang lue lun* (A concise discussion of the social and political philosophy of Wei Jin dynasty esotericism). Shanghai: Shanghai renmin chubanshe, 1956.

Tanigawa Michio. *Chugoku chūsei no tankyū: rekishi to ningen.* (The search for a Chinese middle ages: history and humanity). Tokyo: Nihon edeitā sukūru shuppanbu, 1987.

Tanigawa Michio, ed. *Chugoku shitaifu kaikyū to chīki shakai to no kankei ni tsuite no sogoteki kenkyū (Synthetic studies of the relationship between the Chinese literati class and local society).* Kyoto: Kyoto Daigaku, 1983.

Tao Xisheng. *Zhongguo shehui zhi shi de fenxi* (An analysis of the literati in Chinese society). Taibei: Quanmin 1954 rpt.

Teng Ssu-yü, ed. and trans. *Family Instructions for the Yen Clan by Yen Chih-t'ui.* Leiden: E. J. Brill: 1968.

Thern, Kenneth L. *Postface of the Shuo-Wen Chieh-Tzu, the First Comprehensive Chinese Dictionary.* Madison: University of Wisconsin Department of East Asian Languages and Literature, 1966.

Thomas, Keith. "Jumbo-History." *New York Review of Books,* April 17, 1975, 26–28.

Thomas, Rosalind. *Literacy and Orality in Ancient Greece.* Cambridge: Cambridge University Press, 1992.

Tjan Tjoe Som. *The Comprehensive Discussions in the White Tiger Hall.* 2 vols. Leiden: E. J. Brill, 1949–1952.

Tökei, Ferenc. *Essays on the Asiatic Mode of Production.* Budapest: Akadémiai Kiadó, 1979.

———. *Genre Theory in China in the Third to Sixth Centuries: Liu Hsieh's Theory on Poetic Genres.* Budapest: Akadémiai Kiadó, 1971.

———. *Naissance De L'élegie Chinoise, K'iu Yuan et Son Epoque.* Translated by the author. Paris: Gallimard, 1967.

Tsien, Tsuen-hsuin. *Written on Bamboo and Silk: The Beginnings of Chinese Books and Inscriptions.* Chicago: University of Chicago Press, 1962.

Tucker, Robert, ed. *The Marx-Engels Reader.* New York: Norton, 1978.

Twitchett, Denis, and Michael Loewe, eds. *The Cambridge History of China.* Vol. 1, *The Ch'in and Han Empires 221 B.C.–A.D. 220.* New York: Cambridge University Press, 1986.

Utsunomiya Kiyoyoshi. *Kandai shakai keizai shi kenkyū* (Studies in the social and economic history of the Han dynasty). Tokyo: Kōbundō, 1954.

Vali, Abbas. *Pre-capitalist Iran: A Theoretical History.* London: I. B. Tauris, 1993.

Van der Loon, Piet. "On the Transmission of Kuan-Tzû," *Toung Pao II,* 41 (1952).

Vandermeersch, Leon. *Wangdao: ou, La voie royale: recherches sur l'esprit des institutions de la Chine archaique.* 2 vols. Paris: École française d'Extrême-Orient, 1977–1980.

Waley, Arthur, trans. *The Book of Songs.* London: George Allen and Unwin, 1937.

Wang Ching-hsien. *The Bell and the Drum.* Berkeley: University of California Press, 1974.

Wang Meng'ou. *Gudian wenxue lun tansuo* (Investigations into classical literary discourse). Taibei: Zhengzhong, 1984.

—. "Shi lun Cao Pi zenyang faxian wen qi" (An essay on Cao Pi's discovery of *qi* in writing). In Wang Meng'ou, *Gudian wenxue lun tansuo.* 69–84. Taibei: Zhengzhong, 1984.

Wang Yao. *Zhonggu wenxue fengmao* (Features of medieval literature). In *Zhongguo xueshu lei bian.* vol. 7., edited by Yang Jialuo. Reprint, Taibei: Tingwen shuju.

Wang Yunxi. *Han Wei Liu chao Tang dai wenxue lun cong* (Collected essays on Han Wei Six dynasties, and Tang dynasty literature). Shanghai: Shanghai gu ji chubanshe, 1981.

Watson, Burton, trans. *Records of the Grand Historian of China.* 2 vols. New York: Columbia University Press, 1961.

Weber, Max. *The Religion of China.* Translated by H. H. Gerth. Glencoe, Ill.: Free Press, 1951.

Wen Yiduo. *Yuefu shi jian* (Annotated *yuefu* poetry). In *Wen Yiduo quan ji*, 4: 95–138. Hong Kong: Nantong, n.d.

Wilhelm, Richard, and Cary F. Baynes, *The I Ching or Book of Changes.* The Richard Wilhelm translation rendered into English by Cary F. Baynes. Foreword by C. G. Jung. Preface by Hellmut Wilhelm. Princeton: Princeton University Press, 1967.

Wong, Siu-kit, ed. and trans. *Early Chinese Literary Criticism.* Hong Kong: Joint Publishing Company, 1983.

Wu Hung. *The Wu Liang Shrine: The Ideology of Early Chinese Pictorial Art.* Stanford: Stanford University Press, 1989.

Wu Yun and Tang Shaozhong, eds. *Wang Can ji zhu* (Annotated poems of Wang Can). Henan: Zhongzhou shuhuashe, 1984.

Xiao Difei. *Han Wei Liu chao yuefu wenxue shi* (A history of *yuefu* poetry in the Han Wei and Six Dynasties). Reprint, Taibei: Chang'an chubanshe, 1976.

Xiao Tong. *Wen Xuan, or Selections of Refined Literature*, vol. 1. Translated by David Knechtges. Princeton: Princeton University Press, 1982.

Xing Yitian. "Dong Han xiaolian de shenfen beijing" (The personal background of the "filial and uncorrupt"in the Eastern Han). In *Di'erqu Zhongguo shehui jingji shi yantaohui lunwenji* (Collected papers from the second conference on Chinese social and economic history), edited by Xu Zhuoyun, Mao Hanguang, and Liu Cuirong, 1–56. Taibei: Hanxue yanjiu ziliao ji fuwu zhongxin.

Xu Fuguan. *Liang han sixiang shi* (Intellectual history of the former and latter Han dynasties). 3 vols. Taibei: Xuesheng shuju, 1977–1979.

———. *Zhongguo meishu jingshen* (The Chinese aesthetic spirit). Taibei: Xuesheng shuju, 1966.

———. *Zhongguo wenxue lun ji* (Collected essays on Chinese literature). Reprint, Taibei: Xuesheng shuju, 1974.

Xu Gongchi. "Cao Zhi shengping ba kao." (Eight questions on Cao Zhi's biography). *Wen shi* 10 (October 1980): 199–219.

———. "Cao Zhi shige de xiezuo niandai wenti" (Questions of dating of the composition of Cao Zhi's poetry). *Wen shi* 6 (June 1979): 147–160.

Xu Shoukai. *"Dian lun: Lun wen zhong de liangge wenti"* (Two questions in the Authoritative Discourse: On literature). In *Jian'an wenxue yanjiu wenji*, edited by Yitan bianjibu. Hefei: Huangshan shushe, 1984

Yang Liansheng. "Dong Han de haozu" (Great families of the Eastern Han). *Qinghua xuebao* 11, no. 4 (1936): 1007–1063.

Yang, Lien-sheng (Yang Liansheng). "Great Families of the Eastern Han." In *Chinese Social History: Translations of Selected Studies*, edited by E-tu Zen and John DeFrancis. (Edited version of Chinese original.) Washington, D.C.: American Council of Learned Societies, 1956.

Yitan bianji bu, ed. *Jianan wenxue yanjiu wenji* (Collected essays on studies of Jian'an literature). Hefei: Huangshan shushe, 1984.

Yoshikawa Tadao, "Gokan matsunen Keishyu no gakufū" (Scholarship in Jingzhou at the end of the Han). *Acta Asiatica* 60 (1991): 1–24.

Yu Guanying. *Cao Cao Cao Pi Cao Zhi shi xuan* (Selected poetry of Cao Cao Cao Pi and Cao Zhi). Beijing: Zuojia chubanshe, 1956.

———. *Han Wei Liu chao shi lun cong* (Collected essays on Han Wei and Six Dynasties poetry). In *Zhongguo xueshu lei bian*, edited by Yang Jialuo, vol. 5. Reprint, Taibei: Tingwen shuju, 1977.

Yu Qiding. *Xian Qin liang han rujia jiaoyu* (Confucian education from pre-Qin through the Han dynasties). Jinan: Qi lu shushe, 1987.

Yu Ying-shih. "Life and Immortality in the Mind of Han China." *Harvard Journal of Asian Studies* 25 (1964–1965): 80–122.

———. *Trade and Expansion in Han China.* Berkeley: University of California Press, 1967

Yu Yingshi (Yu Ying-shih). "Han Jin zhi ji shi zhi xin zijue yu xin sichao" (New currents in thought and new self-consciousness among the literati of the Han Jin transition period). *Xinya xuebao* 4, no. 1 (1959): 24–143.

———. *Lishi yu sixiang* (History and Thought). Taibei: Lianjing chuban shiye, 1976.

———. *Zhongguo zhishi jieceng shi lun (Gu dai pian)* (Collected essays on the history of China's intellectual class: ancient period). Taibei: Lianjing, 1980.

Yu, Pauline. "Poems in Their Place: Collections and Canons in Early Chinese Literature." *Harvard Journal of Asian Studies* 50, no. 1 (1990): 163–97.

———. *The Reading of Imagery in the Chinese Poetic Tradition.* Princeton: Princeton University Press, 1987.

Zhang Dejun. "Guanyu Cao Zhi de pingjia wenti" (Questions of Cao Zhi's evaluation). *Lishi yanjiu* 2 (February 1975): 49–66.

Zhang Peipei. "Dong Han shi feng ji qi zhuanbian" (Literati style in the Eastern Han and its transformation). Master's thesis, National Taiwan University, 1979.

Zhang Shibin. *Zhongguo yinyue shi lun shu gao* (Draft collection of essays on the history of Chinese music). Hong Kong: Youlian, 1974.

Zhong Qi. *Zhongguo shige luncong* (Collected essays on Chinese poetry). Hong Kong: Shanghai shuju, 1977.

Zhongguo lishi ditu ji bianji zu, comp. *Zhongguo lishi ditu ji* (A historical atlas of China). Vols. 1–3. Shanghai: Zhonghua dituxue she, 1975.

Zhu Ziqing. *Zhu Ziqing gudian wenxue lunwen ji* (Collected essays on classical literature). Reprint, Shanghai: Shanghai guji chubanshe, 1981.

Žižek, Slavoj, ed. *Mapping Ideology.* New York: Verso, 1994.

———. *The Sublime Object of Ideology.* London and New York: Verso, 1989.

Zumthor, Paul. *Oral Poetry: An Introduction.* Translated by Kathryn Murphy-Judy. Minneapolis: University of Minnesota Press, 1990.

Index

About the Author

Christopher Leigh Connery is associate professor of literature at the University of California, Santa Cruz, and is the codirector of that university's Center for Cultural Studies. He received his Ph.D. in East Asian Studies from Princeton University and did additional graduate work at National Taiwan University. He previously taught at the University of Puget Sound and Dartmouth College. In addition to his work on early imperial China, he publishes on North American, European, and East Asian conceptions of East Asia and the Pacific. He lives in Santa Cruz, California.